A Literary

168

Internationale Forschungen zur Allgemeinen und Vergleichenden Literaturwissenschaft

herausgegeben von

Norbert Bachleitner
(Universität Wien)

Redaktion: Paul Ferstl und Rudolf Pölzer

Anschrift der Redaktion:
Institut für Vergleichende Literaturwissenschaft, Sensengasse 3A , A-1090 Wien

A Literary Occupation

Responses of German writers in service in occupied Europe

William J. O'Keeffe

Amsterdam - New York, NY 2013

Cover images: The Paris and Ukraine notebooks of Felix Hartlaub and a photo of Hartlaub at his desk in the headquarters war-diary unit, reproduced with kind permission of *Deutsches Literatur Archiv* Marbach.
Photo-editing: Niall O'Keeffe

Le papier sur lequel le présent ouvrage est imprimé remplit les prescriptions de "ISO 9706:1994, Information et documentation - Papier pour documents - Prescriptions pour la permanence".

The paper on which this book is printed meets the requirements of " ISO 9706:1994, Information and documentation - Paper for documents - Requirements for permanence".

Die Reihe "Internationale Forschungen zur Allgemeinen und Vergleichenden Literaturwissenschaft" wird ab dem Jahr 2005 gemeinsam von Editions Rodopi, Amsterdam – New York und dem Weidler Buchverlag, Berlin herausgegeben. Die Veröffentlichungen in deutscher Sprache erscheinen im Weidler Buchverlag, alle anderen bei Editions Rodopi.

From 2005 onward, the series "Internationale Forschungen zur Allgemeinen und Vergleichenden Literaturwissenschaft" will appear as a joint publication by Editions Rodopi, Amsterdam – New York and Weidler Buchverlag, Berlin. The German editions will be published by Weidler Buchverlag, all other publications by Editions Rodopi.

ISBN: 978-90-420-3770-0
E-Book ISBN: 978-94-012-1019-5

Printed in The Netherlands

For Carol

Contents

Acknowledgements

The impetus for the publication of this book comes from the encouragement and advice the author received from Dr. Gert Hofmann and Dr. Manfred Schewe of the National University of Ireland, University College Cork, and Professor Dr. Hans-Walter Schmidt-Hannisa of the National University of Ireland, University College Galway.

1. Introduction

1.1. A civil literature in an uncivil time

Pax in Bello, the superscript Erhart Kästner applied to the unfinished and in his lifetime unpublished third book of his wartime trilogy on Greece and its islands,[1] summed up in epigram the dilemma of the serving soldier of the forces of occupation, seconded from military to literary duties, and attempting to write a civil literature in times and conditions which seemed to prohibit such. Such a civil literature, and one of some objectivity, did emerge in book-length responses in prose from persons in the service of the German occupying forces in the Europe of 1940-1944. The book-length criterion here extends from a two-quire, 32 page booklet (Erhard Göpel's *Die Bretagne*) through essay collections, travelogues, the novella, and the novel. Only the war-diary is not here included, on the grounds of its inherently subjective form, and more so on the grounds that the most revealing of the war diaries are postwar redactions, simply because of the risk to personal safety there had been in writing un-coded text.[2] Although extracts from Horst Lange's 1941 war-diary had already been published, Lange advised his publisher to keep his later diary writings strictly confidential, there being no chance under the then conditions of their being published in their original form.[3] The wartime dairies of of Ernst Jünger are an exceptional case (see here 1.9.)

The claims of the literature of the invaders on the sympathy of non-partisan readers are subject to a moral forfeit, now as then; though it should be noted that a French language translation of Ernst Jünger's *Gärten und Straßen* was a publishing success in 1942. Where the fact of occupation is elided through war-evading, war transfiguring or war-transcending prose, the common charges of 'calligraphy' and of aesthetic escapism must be answered. A countervailing argument is here advanced, that this 'literature of occupation' on account of its contemporary authenticity, its offering of an unsentimental aesthetic within the pervasiveness of war, and on account of innovation in literary form found within it, is the immediate, as distinct from the later, retrospective, literary *Bewältigung* of the wartime experience. The slight in number and among themselves disparate exemplars of this

---

[1] Erhart Kästner, *Griechische Inseln* (Frankfurt am Main: Insel, 1975).

[2] Cf. Marianne Feuersenger, *Mein Kriegstagebuch. Führerhauptquartier und Berliner Wirklichkeit* (Freiburg im Breisgau: Herder, 1982); also *Ursula von Kardorff: Berliner Aufzeichnungen 1942 bis 1945*, ed. by Peter Hartl (Munich: DTV, 1994).
See also Hans Dieter Schäfer, *Das gespaltene Bewußtsein. Deutsche Kultur und Lebenswirklichkeit 1933-1945* (Frankfurt am Main: Ullstein, 1981, 1984), p.45.

[3] Anne M. Wallrath-Janssen, *Der Verlag H. Goverts im Dritten Reich* (Munich: K.G. Saur, 2007), p.367.

contemporary literature stand in quantitative contrast to the surge of German language literary output on the war in the two decades following 1945: according to one determination, over three hundred works to 1960 and, to 1965, apart from works published by pronouncedly militaristic publishers, of some literary worth at least a hundred novels or comprehensive stories.[4] The few contemporary works considered here are therefore by virtue of their relative rarity, published and unpublished, additionally important. The subject works here are also historically important for being records written without the modification of moral, philosophical or factual hindsight, and for their being grounded still, perforce, in political concepts of a Europe deriving from the treaty of Versailles rather than from the treaty of Rome.

The stereotype of an allegorically encoded non National Socialist literature is disputed by Schäfer's *Das gespaltene Bewußtsein* (1981), which title points to the many manifest contradictions between National Socialist ideology and actual praxis in the field of cultural consumption in the broadest sense, from literature to foreign-branded consumer goods.[5] In that context, many of the works studied here would not be remarkable. They were commissioned as *Gebrauchsliteratur*, functional writing, a form which covered also war reportage, travel writing and the diary and the essay, and which was dominant in the 1930s and into the war years.[6] This ascendancy of functional literature, which established itself after 1930 and had its origin in a reaction to the social shocks of the Weimar era, was not supplanted until the advent of the sixties.[7] The functional aim of this literature during the war years was primarily the *Belehrung der Truppe*, the 'improvement' of the troops in terms of their morale and ideological outlook; its public political purpose was the affirmation of an occupation policy of *Korrektheit*. This was self-serving, in France for reasons of promoting efficient economic cooperation, and in Greece, at least initially, for the propaganda value of demonstrating a conscientious cultural custodianship of the antique. In the East, where no armistice was signed, where cities were fought over and the occupation policy was harsh, and where in consequence the social

---

[4] See Jürgen Egyptien and Raffaele Louis, '100 Kriegsromane und Erzählungen des Zeitraums 1945 bis 1965', *Treibhaus. Jahrbuch für die Literatur der fünfziger Jahre*, 3 (2007), 211-237 (p.211), note 1.

[5] See Schäfer, *Das gespaltene Bewußtsein*, pp.7-68,146-208;
p.35: "Es war ein Irrtum, die nichtnationalsozialistische Erzählprosa als Literatur der verdeckten Schreibweise zu interpretieren."
p.146: "Das Dritte Reich ist von einem tiefen Gegensatz zwischen nationalsozialistischer Ideologie und Praxis gekennzeichnet."

[6] Ibid., pp.44,79.

[7] Ibid., pp.41,89.

background was displaced, paradoxically it was there that notable examples of the social genres of the novel and novella were written. As Schäfer has pointed out, the world-shattering chaos of the war surpassed that of the economic crisis of the thirties and left most of the writers remaining in Germany unable any longer to combine empirical and allegorical elements into radical forms of reality interpretation, of *Wirklichheitsdeutung*. The relatively widespread (in Germany) modernism of the thirties had lost its basis.[8] The experimentation with forms by such as Benn, Jünger, Langgässer, Nossack and of the here considered Felix Hartlaub was an undercurrent, not mainstream.[9] The published works examined here were functional in being informative and/or diverting for their temporarily expatriate readers. At the same time, commentary on the unfamiliar could afford an indirect freedom of expression to the authors, and though experimental modernism was out of place, the military imprimatur carried weight with the propaganda ministry when it came to civilian editions and could afford cover for aesthetic allusiveness.

1.2. The propaganda imperative

As an instrument of war policy the value of propaganda had been appreciated too late by the German high command in WWI.[10] The lesson had been learned by the outbreak of WWII. In that conflict, German military propaganda went beyond the 21st century concept of the 'embedded' reporter. The propaganda troops, besides being media professionals, underwent basic military training and, in the case of field-reporter companies, specialist training in addition, to allow these to serve in any arm of the services, by land, sea or air, without encumbering or requiring the protection of combat servicemen.[11] The *Propagandatruppen*, organised in *Propagandakompanien*, were, in fact, a separate service arm. In the occupied countries and in rear areas away from the fronts, propaganda ministry personnel also, organised in *Propaganda-Staffeln*, 'propaganda teams', which included recruited locals, worked side-by-side with the propaganda companies of the military, but were subordinated to and took their operating

---

8 Ibid., p.102.

9 Ibid., p.103.

10 The allies had pursued political propaganda with considerable success, leading to mass desertions in the Austro-Hungarian army, and Bolshevik propaganda directed at German troops on the Eastern front had spread to the civilian population in Germany itself. The German high command reacted too late. Disdain for the use of propaganda persisted in the Reichswehr until the advent of Josef Goebbels as propaganda minister. [Hasso von Wedel, *Die Propagandatruppen der Deutschen Wehrmacht* (Neckärgemund: Vowinckel, 1962), pp.15-19]

11 Ibid., pp.41-42.

directions from the military *Propaganda Abteilung*, the central, coordinating propaganda unit of each army-area high command, responsible for broadcasting, news media, publication, film production, theatre and the arts.[12] Implicit in the apologetics of Hasso von Wedel, the commander of the propaganda troops, is the assumption that such a monopoly of information and disinformation was a legitimate instrument of war policy. Ascribing the blame to the "oberste Führung", von Wedel's claim is that, in the event, sensible and prudent measures were frustrated: "Man wollte die besetzten Gebiete ausnutzen und suchte Arbeitssklaven. Der Erfolg war, daß man Partisanen schuf."[13]

Almost every major occupied city had its own German-published local language newspaper, and in the biggest cities some magazines in colour also.[14] German-language publications included the manifold front newspapers and magazines. Paris had the weekly *Pariser Zeitung* and the bi-weekly *Deutsche Wegleiter*.[15] The readership, comprised overwhelmingly of servicemen, was thus the target of what was understood by Wehrmacht Propaganda, the 'W.Pr.' section of the *OKW*,[16] as 'inner' propaganda, intended for the maintenance of troop morale, for which the term *geistige Betreuung* stood, but which in general service usage was referred to variously as "Betreuung der Truppe", "Truppenbetreuung", or "Wehrbetreuung": terms corresponding to the what was known in the allied forces as 'troop welfare', and which in the allied forces was characterised most publicly by troop entertainments by popular entertainers. In the German forces, where static occupation formations had to be catered for, cultural information and entertainment came together. Publications, some ultimately in book form, were part of a programme which included, besides troop libraries, conducted tours, lectures and brochures, some of these latter being transcripts of radio broadcasts.[17]

The broadly encompassing area of troop welfare was one which, already in the directions issued by the *OKW* in 1938 for the setting up of the

---

[12] Heinz-Werner Eckhardt, *Die Frontzeitungen des deutschen Heeres 1939-1945* (Wien·Stuttgart: Wilhelm Braumüller. Universitäts-Verlagsbuchhandlung GmbH, Schriftenreihe des Instituts für Publizistik der Universität Wien, 1975), pp.23-24.

[13] von Wedel, p.55.

[14] Ibid., p.77.

[15] Cf. Bertram M. Gordon, '*Ist Gott Französisch?* Germans, tourism, and occupied France, 1940-1944', *Modern & Contemporary France*, vol.4, issue 3 (1996), 287-98 (p.289).

[16] *Oberkommando der Wehrmacht*: nominally the co-ordinated command structure of all the German armed forces, but in effect Hitler's personal command staff. Cf. Warlimont, *Im Hauptquartier der deutschen Wehrmacht 1939 bis 1945* (Augsburg: Weltbild, 1990, 2vols).

[17] Cf. Julia Freifrau Hiller von Gaertringen, *„Meine Liebe zu Griechenland stammt aus dem Krieg." Studien zum literarischen Werk Erhart Kästners* (Wiesbaden: Harrassowitz, 1994), p.129.

propaganda companies, was reserved to military alone, and for which the propaganda ministry was to supply material only on request.[18] Although in the latter course of the war, "Betreuung der Truppe" became increasingly influenced by the *Nazionalsozialistische Führungsoffiziere*, the *N.S.F.O.* officers, the counterparts of the Soviet military commissars,[19] the military nonetheless, von Wedel claims, doggedly maintained its independence where possible, and to this end a deliberate cultivation of variety in field press publications was maintained, as a uniform format would have invited the intrusion of Dr. Goebbels.[20] Paramilitary organisations, such as the *Organisation Todt* and the *Reichsarbeitsdienst*, also had their own press and publications.[21] One other agency in particular promoted publications on aspects of culture: the *Kunstschutz* service of the military, responsible for the protection of artworks and cultural monuments in the occupied territories. This was an obligation laid on all occupying military administrations already by the Hague conventions of 1907: it was not observed in the East, but was assiduously upheld in France and Greece. Besides the *Propagandakompanien* and the *Propagandastaffeln*, a *Referat Kunstschutz* section of the military administration, where one functioned, offered an additional publishing platform. In one or other of these structures, journalists, freelance writers, art historians, archaeologists, cartographers, museum curators and other like professionals found themselves active, all subject in the first instance to military and ultimately to political censorship. With effect from 1st April 1940, German publishers were required by personal directive of Goebbels to submit to the literature department of the propaganda ministry their plans for proposed books or brochures, belletristic literature included, which in any way referred to or touched upon the interests of the Wehrmacht, the current war, or political economy. The publishers were required to understand by this the most detailed possible information on the author, the furnishing of the provisional title of the work, a synopsis of work's content and proposed structure, its scope, and the size of the print run – the latter point of information related to wartime paper rationing, a measure which was used thereafter as a form of preventive censorship.[22] These injunctions applied equally to the works of authors serving in the military. A proposed armed forces edition, a *Wehrmachtsausgabe*, was submitted by its author in the

---

[18] von Wedel, p.29.

[19] Ibid., p.60.

[20] Ibid., pp.142-43.

[21] Ibid., p.111; cf. Guido K. Brand's impressions from Russia and France: *Ein Winter ohne Gnade. Osteindrücke eines OT-Kriegsberichters* (Prague: Volk und Reich, 1943), and *Zwischen Domen und Bunkern. Westeindrücke eines OT-Kriegsberichters* (Amsterdam: Volk und Reich, 1944).

[22] Wallrath-Janssen, *Der Verlag H. Goverts im Dritten Reich*, pp.234-45,342.

first instance to the military censor at the area *Wehrmacht-Zensurstelle*. For a civilian edition, the publisher was responsible for submitting the text to the propaganda ministry, though publishers also communicated directly with chief military censor at *OKW* headquarters who, in the person of the erstwhile publishing professional, Jürgen Eggebrecht, proved approachable.[23] It was for the military to sanction the release of a *Wehrmachtsausgabe* in a civilian edition and, if so, to recommend such to the propaganda ministry. Direct intervention with the propaganda ministry by a sympathetic military commander could also help, as in the case of Erhart Kästner's *Kreta*.[24]

1.3. Literary conscripts

A new type of 'self-editor' soldier writers, *Schriftleiter-Soldaten*, had been identified by *Reichspressechef* Otto Dietrich in his foreword to an anthology of war feature-writing published in Berlin in 1941,[25] and also a new type of writing which favoured sensory impressions over reportage of events[26]– this dictated by the sheer scale of the conflict. The press directorate had intuited that sensory impressions could convey more for morale supporting purposes, but also for justification of the victim cost, than the bald 'facts' of the daily *Wehrmachtbericht*.[27] Felix Hartlaub, the soldier on leave of absence, must similarly have intuited that his private impressions from occupied Paris could convey more than reportage, though he himself was unconvinced of this. The short sketches of Hartlaub's nine-month Paris sequence, which for the most part are undated, have a photographic-like time-elapse quality. Erhart Kästner's also wholly time-free impressions from occupied Greece are of a topographical and anthropological warp and weft. Kästner wrote with the express consent of area commanders, but to his own brief, and this unparalleled remit allowed him to use classicism as camouflage in casting the whole tradition of ancient civilisation in opposition to the mechanised era victim-consuming Moloch of contending power ideologies. Other contemporarily publishing writers in military service who distanced themselves in their writings from affirmation of the German war-aims were Erhard Göpel (1906-1966) writing from France, and Martin Raschke (1905-1943) writing from the Eastern Front (Raschke unluckily and fatally posted

[23] On Eggebrecht and the Goverts publishing house and the author Horst Lange, see Wallrath-Janssen, pp.368-69;
on Eggebrecht and Erhard Kästner's *Kreta*, see Hiller von Gaertringen (1994), p.118.

[24] Ibid.

[25] Helmut Peitsch, '„*Am Rande des Krieges*"? Nichtnazistische Schriftsteller im Einsatz der Propagandakompanien gegen die Sowjetunion,' *Kürbiskern*, 3 (1984), 126-149 (p.145).

[26] Ibid., p.146.

[27] Ibid., pp.146-47.

there, mistakenly, for Italy),[28] both prewar associates of Kästner. Others still were Walter Bauer (1904-1976), whose contemporarily published, journal-like accounts span both France and the Eastern front, and Horst Lange (1904-1971) and Hermann Georg Rexroth (1907-1944). These latter, Eastern front, writers were nearest in circumstance to that of literary conscripts, in that the propaganda image of a bestial, inhuman enemy has been read as being unavoidably implicit *by inversion* in their portrayals of human sensitivity.[29]

Schäfer (1981) takes the view that the aesthetic in the writings of the war-diary genre – and all the aforementioned writings have at least surface traits of that genre – appears not as the humane antithesis to war but as a war-accompanying, comforting sound at best[30] (though acknowledging that the diarist Kurt Lothar Tank among others participated in the dissemination of *non* National Socialist literary art).[31] The negative pronouncement on war-diary aesthetic may here be held up to some scrutiny in the example of Bauer's and Tank's writings (the latter a guest writer on a post-victory tour of occupied France in October 1940). In examining the extent to which Kästner's work is *Autonomieästhetik*, at least so in its approach, this study defers to the chronology and commentary on the later revisions in manuscript and published form of Kästner's wartime works provided by Hiller von Gaertringen's literary-biographical study.[32] The output of Kästner's prewar academic colleague, Erhard Göpel, commissioned to write short guides to Brittany and Normandy, but not afforded the war-long dispensation that Kästner enjoyed, is examined for the implicitly embedded plea for a non-supremacist regard for the cultural legacy and way of life of historic European regions which has been claimed for it.[33]

The Hartlaub writings here primarily considered are those known as the 'Kriegsaufzeichnungen aus Paris', and relate to the period when Hartlaub was seconded from uniformed military duty to civilian work for the German foreign ministry, but which assignment was nonetheless in the service of the military occupation of France. The later writings of Hartlaub, those from the period of his service in the war-diary section at the *Führerhauptquartier* (hereinafter, *FHQ*) in the Ukraine and in East Prussia, have already been the subject of a definitive philological study[34] and these therefore are referred to

---

[28] See Hartl, *Ursula von Kardorff: Berliner Aufzeichnungen*, p.137.
[29] Ibid., pp.126-49.
[30] Schäfer, *Das gespaltene Bewußtsein*, p.107.
[31] Ibid., p.83.
[32] Cf. Hiller von Gaertringen (1994), op. cit.
[33] Cf. Eugen Blume, *Erhard Göpel. Rede anläßlich des 100. Geburtstages*, Pinakothek der Moderne, 6 Juni 2006 (Munich: Max Beckmann Gesellschaft, 2006), p.7.
[34] Cf. Christian-Hartwig Wilke, *Die letzten Aufzeichnungen Felix Hartlaubs* (Bad Homburg:

in this study tangentially only. Hartlaub's Paris sketches in their guise as *Großstadtbilder* conceal a subliminal text of, if not resistance, at least rejection of the German pan-European project. His misgivings about that project are explicit in his letters, oblique in his Paris sketches. Hartlaub himself, despite his suppression of the diarist self in the sketches, referred to them as *tagebuchoid* efforts,[35] and the term diary reportage, *Tagebuchreportage*, has been applied to them in attempts at classification.[36] Frederike Müller's dissertation of 1997 noted the styling of Hartlaub in the criticism of the 1950's and 1960's as a diarist and chronicler and, even into the 1990's in particular studies, as a diarist writer of the *Innere Emigration*. In Müller's view this is indicative of the continuing lack of a more general analysis of Hartlaub's complete mature work.[37] This study does not claim to be that general analysis, but does offer a more detailed analysis of and does make wider claims for Hartlaub's Paris sketches than heretofore. In 2002 an annotated edition (revised edition, 2007) of Hartlaub's writings and wartime letters, was published as *Felix Hartlaub. »In den eigenen Umriss gebannt«*.[38] Research conducted by this writer in the Hartlaub archive in the interval bears upon the emendations incorporated into the 2007 edition. The 2007 revised edition supplants the 2002 edition here as referent text, but all citations are referenced to both editions.

Those who could publish while in military service, whether through attachment to the *Propagandakompanien*, or at the express invitation of area commanders as in the case of Kästner, or as contributors to the 1942 compendium, *Frankreich*,[39] were all subject to censorship and to that extent compromised (incautious remarks by one contributor, Gerhard Nebel, led to his banishment to the Channel Islands with the result that his wartime diary

Gehlen, 1967). Wilke, *Literaturwissenschaftliches Jahrbuch der Görres Gesellschaft*, Munich (1966), 263-301 (p.263), refers to this work as an extract from his 1964 dissertation (Würzburg)'*Das Gesamtwerk* und Felix Hartlaub'. In response to enquiry, Würzburg University library could not find a dissertation on record under that title.

35 *Felix Hartlaub »In den eigenen Umriss gebannt«*, ed. by Gabriele Lieselotte Ewenz (Frankfurt amMain: Suhrkamp, 2002, and 2nd edn, rev. by Angrick, Lüst, Strotbek, 2007), pp. 470(2002)/478(2007).

36 See Claus Vogelgesang, 'Das Tagebuch', in *Prosakunst ohne Erzählen*, ed. by Klaus Weissenberger (Tübingen: Niemeyer, 1985), pp.185-202 (p.199), citing Horst (1965).

37 See Frederike Müller, 'Felix Hartlaub – Ein 'poeta minor' der Inneren Emigration. Problematisierung seiner literaturgeschichtlichen Stellung' [dissertation], Saarbrücken: Universität des Saarlandes, 1997, p.17.

38 Ewenz I, II (2002/2007), op. cit.

39 *Frankreich. Ein Erlebnis des deutschen Soldaten* (Paris: Ode, 1942) un-numbered pages; cf. Ludger Tewes, *Frankreich in der Besatzungszeit 1940-1943. Die Sicht deutscher Augenzeugen* (Bonn: Bouvier, 1998), pp.233-35.

written there, *Bei den nördlichen Hesperiden*, could not be published until 1948).[40] Hiller von Gaertringen (1994) in noting that the 1943 civilian edition of his first book, *Griechenland*, was unanimously praised in reviews of the German press for the distance it maintained to immediate contemporary events and its success in directing attention beyond these to the true, original Greece of antiquity,[41] divines a Kästner *Weltanschauung* which coincided with the widespread popular need for diversion from the pressing realities of the war:[42]

> Die Bildungswelt war für Kästner immer ein elitärer Raum gewesen, der abseits der Realität stand, ein Übergriff der einen auf die andere Sphäre war ihm von jeher in beiderlei Richtung suspekt.[43]

The plaudits of a necessarily conformist press would not suffice to support that deduction, were it not that Kästner himself emphatically endorsed it afterwards. What the custodian of antique book treasures at the prewar state library of Saxony in the Japanese Palace at Dresden presented under the guise of a conventional travelogue shot through with passages of high lyricism was, in fact, an idiosyncratic summoning of the *order* of the antique world through the observation of local phenomena as correlatives. That is certainly the intention with *Ölberge, Weinberge*, the revised version of the wartime *Griechenland*:

> So ist das Griechenland dieses Buches nicht das gewohnte: nicht das klassizistische, nicht das archäologische, auch nicht das »ewig glückiche« Land, das nur in den Köpfen der Schwärmer besteht; nichts von der götterfroh-heidnischen Sehnsuchtsgebärde, die der Irrtum eines Jahrhunderts war. [...] Kästner's Liebe gilt Dingen, auf die der Reisende seltener aufmerksam wird:[44]

This is Kästner's own dust-jacket prose, stressing that the view now is not that of a romantic Hellenist yearning for a happy, heathen past where all is dictated by the fates, and not that, implicitly, of his former self of the *Griechenland* view. Yet, the text concludes with an insistence that perception and its explication are still a matter of internalised impressions:

---

[40] See Erik Lehnert, *Gerhard Nebel. Wächter des Normativen* (Schnellroda: Antaios, 2004), p.21; also, Gerhard Heller/Jean Grand, *In einem besetzten Land. Leutnant Heller und die Zensur in Frankreich 1940-1944* (Bergisch Gladbach: Bastei-Lübbe, 1985), p.226.

[41] Hiller von Gaertringen (1994), p.254.

[42] Ibid., pp.248-63.

[43] Ibid., p.257.

[44] Paul Raabe, *Erhart Kästner. Briefe* (Frankfurt am Main: Insel, 1984), p.122.

> Viele Dinge sind von der Feder Kästners ganz durchscheinend gemacht; so verraten sie, was wahrzunehmen eines liebenden Auges und eines treuen Ohres bedarf.[45]

Being free of Kästner's later concern to stress the survival of the antique world in Greek Byzantium and thereafter, through Greek refugees, in the Renaissance,[46] it will be contended here that the earlier book is the superior aesthetic whole.

The philhellenism of the German aesthetic tradition, the traditions of *Bildungsbürgertum*, of a continuing late Wilhemine *Kulturpolitik*, and the survival of the curricular content of Wilhelmine education into the years of the Weimar Republic are inescapable paradigms in the outlook of both writer and readership where the setting is Greece. The aesthetic of the prose therefore, and the claims of that prose *as* aesthetic, is the focus, as also in the case of the other servicemen writers, products of their time and educational background. In the case of Felix Hartlaub, a precocious talent encouraged in the liberal *Odenwaldschule*, a quite literal optic is the means by which, to invert a tenet of Clement Greenberg's, writing suppresses its own denotative medium and attains the effects of painting: "overpower the medium [...] and the adventitious uses of art become more important."[47]

The works of Kästner taken into account here are *Griechenland*,[48] published in Berlin in 1943, *Kreta*,[49] and the last of the wartime trilogy, *Griechische Inseln*, which Kästner never completed as a single volume and which remained unpublished in his lifetime. *Kreta* was first published in 1946. Plans for an earlier publication had been delayed and finally set at nought through the combination of paper rationing, the dispersal of part of the printing run to Danzig, the Russian advance there, and the destruction of the publishing house itself in an air raid on Berlin in February 1945.[50] Kästner was at that point already marooned on Rhodes with the German garrison there. The 1946 edition, from a 1944 typescript, appeared with some omissions, but without any direct revisions by the author, then interned in Egypt.[51] *Griechische Inseln*, notes and trial pieces for which Kästner

---

[45] Ibid.

[46] Cf. Erhart Kästner, *Aufstand der Dinge* (Frankfurt am Main: Insel, 1973), pp.332-33

[47] Clement Greenberg (1940), 'Towards a Newer Laocoon', in Charles Harrison & Paul Wood, *Art in Theory 1900-1990* (Oxford: Blackwell, 1992), p.558.

[48] Erhart Kästner, *Griechenland. Ein Buch aus dem Kriege* (Berlin: Gebr. Mann, 1943).

[49] Erhart Kästner, *Kreta* (Berlin: Gebr. Mann, 1946).

[50] See Hiller von Gaertringen (1994), pp.117-20.

[51] Ibid., pp.183-84. Kästner, writing from British custody, entrusted his sister, Reingart, with the editing of the text, at her discretion. As a typescript from 1944 is extant, but not a typesetting copy of the 1946 edition, the attribution of any other interventions, by the publishers or the Allied censor, cannot be determined.

had already begun in 1943, was worked on through 1944,[52] continued on Rhodes after the 1945 surrender, and later in Egypt in 1946, and was first published in book form in 1975, one year after Kästner's death, from Kästner's typescript of 1947.[53]

Erhard Göpel's two wartime works, *Die Bretagne* and *Die Normandie*, are booklet guides published directly by the military information services and intended for a German soldier readership. *Die Normandie* also appeared in a wartime civilian edition. The diary-styled publications of Walter Bauer and Kurt Lothar Tank from France and the essay contributions of Gerhard Nebel and others in the 1942 collection, *Frankreich*, and of Bauer again and others from the Eastern front, all have in common that they are contemporary accounts, written while their authors were in military service, and published without recourse to postwar editing or revision.

1.4. A Franco-Hellenic axis

The Eastern theatre of operations remained the site of large-scale military engagements, of contesting ideologies, and of an occupation policy which envisaged displacement and colonisation. Territory remained in contention, was culturally a *terra incognita*, and writing necessarily retained the character of the field diary.[54] Armistice had not preceded occupation, hence literary addresses were concerned not, as was the case in France and Greece, with the appearance of a peace, but with the immediate effects, particularly the psychological, of continuing warfare. Above all, the writers' education had contained nothing of the East Slavonic. The German education system had accorded French a position of supremacy as the leading living foreign language taught in German schools, a situation which obtained into the twentieth century, and it was the Third Reich which completed the gradual supplantation of French by English in this position.[55] An inferiority complex, at least at regime level, towards the cultural prestige of France and its language is implied by that change, a complex satirised in Felix Hartlaub's Paris sketch, 'Mitteleuropäische Mondscheinidylle', by a radio voice which boasts that Paris is now sunk to the level of a European provincial city.[56] The fact was, on the contrary, that many ordinary soldiers were enthusiastic for the cultural characteristics of the land they found themselves in,

---

[52] Ibid., pp.184-89.

[53] See Raabe and others, *Erhart Kästner. Werkmanuskripte* (Wolfenbüttel: exhibition catalogue no.43 of the Herzog August Bibliothek, 1984), p.28.

[54] Cf. Helmut Peitsch, '„*Am Rande des Krieges*"?', *Kürbiskern*, 3 (1984), 126-49.

[55] See Manfred Briegel, 'Paris als zweite Heimat? Deutsche Schriftsteller im Exil der 30er Jahre,' in Drost and others, *Paris sous l'occupation. Paris unter deutscher Besatzung*, (Heidelberg: Winter, 1995), pp.523-536 (p.525).

[56] Ibid., p.533.

especially since among the columns in uniform which had been sent into France in 1940 almost every company unit included one or two who because of some artistic talent stood out from among their fellows.[57] *Frontzeitungen*, army-front newspapers and magazines, were quickly established and were, as Eckhardt (1975)[58] has shown, widespread and tenacious in their publication: an unnamed columnist in the *Pariser Zeitung* of 8 August 1944, just two weeks before the German evacuation of the city, was still writing wistfully of his several years of service in Normandy.[59] In Greece, a general programme of introduction to the culture of the Greek antique formed part of troop-welfare measures.[60] Guided tours, lectures, brochures and radio broadcasts were provided. The sites of the classical antique could be visited, but almost all the museums remained closed, a fact which created an intensified demand for information.[61] As with France, a *Kunstschutz* department[62] was set up by the military immediately, and this operated closely with the pre-existing German archaeological institute in Athens. Both operations were led by classical archaeologists.[63] Aligned with the obvious propaganda value of exemplary protection of the antique, education of the troops was a prudent precaution against the negative propaganda that might arise out of thoughtless vandalism. In this, the interests of the regime and those of the scholars and archaeologists happily coincided. In addition, the regime by a backwards projection of its racist ideology presented itself as the blood-heir to the antique.[64] The outstanding role played by German scholars in the rediscovery of Greek antiquity was also advanced in support of this claim.[65] A general impetus was thus lent to the publication of studies on Greece by

---

57 See Tewes, *Frankreich in der Besatzungszeit*:
p.222: "Die deutsche Militärführung schickte 1940 in ihren Marschkolonne eine schier unüberblickbare Flut von Landsleuten. [...] In fast jeder Kompanie gab es ein oder zwei Talente, die durch ihre künstlerische Veranlagung auffielen."
p.235: "Die Deutschen fielen 1940 nicht nur mit dem Maschinengewehr in Frankreich ein, sondern ebenso mit der Schreibmaschine und dem Zeichenstift. Die Begeisterung für die kulturellen Eigenarten des Landes empfanden viele einfache Soldaten, aber nur wenigen gelang es, sie künstlerisch oder literarisch zu verarbeiten."

58 Cf. Eckhardt, *Die Frontzeitungen des deutschen Heeres 1939-1945*.

59 See Gordon, '*Ist Gott Französisch?*', *Modern & Contemporary France*, vol.4, issue 3 (1996), p.296.

60 See Hiller von Gaertringen (1994), p.129.

61 Ibid.

62 Cf. Margot Günther-Hornig, *Kunstschutz in den von Deutschland besetzten Gebieten 1939-1945* (Tübingen: Institut für Besatzungsfragen Tübingen, 1958); also, Walter Bargatzky, *Hotel Majestic. Ein Deutscher im besetzten Frankreich* (Freiburg im Breisgau: Herder, 1987), pp.64-80.

63 See Hiller von Gaertringen (1994), p.32.

64 Ibid., p.156, citing Olszewski, from Hütter (1975).

65 Ibid., p.142, note 100.

scholars and archaeologists, some already working at the Athens institute or attached to the *Kunstschutz* service in Greece.[66] In such a climate Erhart Kästner secured license to roam and write throughout mainland Greece, Crete and the islands, brevetted to do so by local commanding generals, for the duration of the occupation.

France was a political and cultural rival. Greece, the reliquary of antiquity, was not. France, now militarily and politically defeated and its cultural challenge therefore deemed to have been met, might be patronised, even fêted. Greece could be celebrated for its classical past. In these contexts occupier-writers and academics in or out of uniform could write sympathetically on what had been the pre-eminent unified cultural society on mainland Europe in the centuries preceding World War II, and also on the site of antique democracy and of classical thought. In what was written, it is peace, albeit a *Pax Germanica*, and not war which is the theme, a sign, it may be argued, albeit mistaken in its foundation, of the coming abolitionist change which WWII wrought in the European attitude to war as an instrument of policy within Europe.

1.5. The German philhellenic paradigm

That texts from Schiller, Goethe, Jean Paul, Hölderlin and Eduard Mörike should appear in a supplement to the forces newspaper *Wacht im Südosten* already in June of 1941[67] conveys in itself something of the presumption of a German claim on Greece as intellectual property. In the nominally civilian newspaper *Deutsche Nachrichten in Griechenland* in July 1942, the invocation of the poet Hölderlin, the proselytizer Winckelmann, the archaeologist Schliemann and the historian Burckhardt as forming a chain of discoverers leading to a Hellene-derived new spirit of the West is a quite specific declaration of that claim.[68] The common citation of such names points also to a presumption that among the overwhelmingly military readership of these newspapers an educated cadre would recognise the references from their *Gymnasium* schooling. Kästner himself notes, even before the first publication of *Griechenland*, the military edition, that "Natürlich ist es eben kein Buch für den einfachen Soldaten."[69] As reference work for *Griechenland*, Kästner had used a 1941 anthology of antique sources by the same author, Georg von Reutern, whose broadcast series of 'Führungen durch Griechenland' was later issued in book form, in 1943, by the Wehrmacht

---

[66] Ibid., pp.129-37,161.
[67] Ibid., p.142.
[68] Ibid., p.163.
[69] Ibid., p.102.

radio station Athens.[70] *Griechenland*, besides its insistence that all forms of antique Greek public activity not to do with the everyday were religious observances, theatre included, (pp.135,136,232) also stresses that before temples, sacred hillsides were held to be abodes of the divinities and that the external aspect, precincts and surrounding nature of temples were more important than the inner *Cella* (pp.18,87). It is with his second book, *Kreta*, that Kästner's research intensified: on religion in particular, he consulted Erwin Rohde's *Psyche* (1894) and Walter Otto's Dionysian *Die Götter Griechenlands* (1929),[71] though not, it would seem, the *Glaube der Hellenen* (1931-32) of Ulrich von Wilamowitz-Moellendorff, whose scholarship he might earlier have encountered in the *Gymnasium* primer, *Griechisches Lesebuch* (1902).[72] In the opening chapter of *Kreta*, the ascent of Mount Ida, Kästner's enthusiasm for the ancient, anthropomorphic Greek religion is unrestrained; on the summit, it is a veritable confession of faith:

> Im Ereignis des werdenden Tags glaubte ich die Erscheinung des Zeus zu erfahren, [...] Er ist der Junge, der Strahler, der Bringer, der Held; der Stifter der Welt, die wir träumen: der lichten, der klaren, olympischen, griechischen Welt. (p.17)

This is more than the purely figurative and playful insistence in *Griechenland* (p.188) that Pan lived on in the quickening of the spirits that the Grecian mountain landscape imparts, and could find embodiment in a gifted Greek shepherd flute player.

In an explication of his wartime perception of and approach to Greece, Kästner admits that when he first came to Greece he shared the general, Schillerian classicist view, but with time had come to see that that view failed to recognise the role of Byzantium in the transmission of the antique.[73] The Schillerian view, however, explains much of the lyrically sublime that produces the impression of aesthetic escapism, the common charge levelled against Kästner.[74] Indeed, his invocations of a still immanent ancient sanctity about the ceremonial sites of antiquity almost paraphrase the 'Aesthetic Letters' of Schiller:

---

[70] Ibid., p.140.

[71] Ibid., p.181, note 70.

[72] See Susanne L. Marchand, *Down from Olympus. Archaeology and Philhellenism in Germany,1750-1970*, (Princeton: Princeton University Press, 2003), p.138,311.

[73] See Raabe, *Erhart Kästner. Briefe*, pp.193-94.

[74] Cf. Franz Schonauer, *Deutsche Literatur im Dritten Reich. Versuch einer Darstellung in polemisch-didaktischer Absicht* (Olten and Freiburg im Breisgau: Walter, 1961), pp.135-38; also Ralf Schnell, *Literarische innere Emigration 1933-1945* (Stuttgart: J.B. Metzler, 1976), pp.94-98.

> Die Tempel blieben dem Auge heilig, als die Götter längst zum Gelächter dienten [...] Die Menscheit hat ihre Würde verloren, aber die Kunst hat sie gerettet und aufbewahrt in bedeutenden Steinen; [9th letter]

Kästner's seeming preoccupation with the folk religion of ancient Greece was, as is clear from his retort to the correspondent who challenged him on his later apparent 'conversion' to Byzantium,[75] the fundament of his project to honour what survived in man, in folk ways, of the classic Greek ideal. In Schiller's terminology, without the 'play drive' which drew out the beautiful ideal, *Schönheit*, from between the stasis of the striving-for-definition rationality of the 'form-drive' and the flux of the affective sensualness of the 'sense-drive', that is: from between the human inclination to have things remain comfortably unchanging and the human necessity to develop and discard, no ideal polity or any enshrinement of it in stone or word would otherwise have emerged. Schiller's furtherance of the Kantian examination of the possibility of an objective idea of beauty, the universal principle, the possibility of which Kant doubted, leads him to develop the only other conclusion, that aesthetic consensus is a cultural ideal and that an important task of culture is to make man aesthetic, since only out of man's aesthetic appreciation and not out of his physical nature could morality develop (23rd letter). That modern zoology may have determined elements of morality to be present already in animal behaviour need not undermine this view. Thus the *Kallias Fragment* letters lead to the lost 'Augustenburger' letters to his Danish ducal patron, the source of the twenty seven 'Aesthetic' letters. Writing notionally again to this statesman and alluding to the French Revolution as a radical starting point (2nd letter), Schiller stressed the social and ethical implications of aesthetic taste, even if concluding by the 27th and final letter that the ideal was utopian: "Existiert aber auch ein solcher Staat des schönen Scheins, und wo ist er zu finden? [...] in einigen wenigen auserlesenen Zirkeln." In coming to that conclusion Schiller recognises that the human is confronted by three states: 'dynamic' state, of regulations and law; the 'ethical' state, of duties and obligations; and the 'aesthetical' state, the sovereign but insubstantial "Reich der Einbildungskraft" (26th & 27th letters). For Schiller, the aesthetic world or state was quite other than that of even the most complete Platonic republic: function, order, proportion and perfection, "Zweckmäßigkeit, Ordnung, Proportion, Vollkommenheit", are qualities which have nothing to do with the definition of beauty, since these are heteronomous, not free of functional imperatives.[76] Kästner makes no reference to Schiller's aesthetic theory or to its ethical branchings in *Über*

---

[75] Raabe, *Erhart Kästner. Briefe*, pp.193-95.

[76] In the 'Freiheit in der Erscheinung ist eins mit der Schönheit' section of the *Kallias* fragment.

Anmut und Würde – except, perhaps, in an ironic exclamation on the no-holds-barred pancratium: "durchaus nicht mit Anmut und Würde!" (*Griechenland*, p.136) – but does stress in *Griechenland* the significance of proportion, of *Maß*, in the sense of the correct and desirable relationship of the man-made to its natural surroundings. Equally with Schiller, and increasingly so in his postwar writings, Kästner decried the intrusion of science into the realm of the imagination; in that, he ever retained the Schillerian concern:

> Selbst der philosophische Untersuchungsgeist entreißt der Einbildungskraft eine Provinz nach der andern, und die Grenzen der Kunst verengen sich, je mehr die Wissenschaft ihre Schranken erweitert. (2nd letter)

That such an esoteric concept should find its way into a book, *Griechenland*, commissioned in its first edition for a readership of garrison soldiers, accorded with the programme of cultural education whose propaganda sub-text was an implied association with the greatness of ancient Greece, and which paid scant attention to the condition of the contemporary country.[77] Kästner could count on a readership from a country whose philosophical and literary lights had had, in neohumanism, an obsession with Greece.[78] Marchand (2003), citing Fuhrmann, notes that German philhellenism was concerned at first with the comparison between the Greeks and the moderns, and became associatively pro-national only in reaction to Napoleonic occupation and the defeat at Jena.[79] As head of the new *Kultus und Unterricht* section of Prussia's interior ministry, 1809-1810, the Graecophile Wilhelm von Humboldt had introduced the self-cultivation concept of *Bildung*, and with his followers, the *Gymnasium* curriculum. Its programme, though it contained both egalitarian and elitist elements, was non-utilitarian and secular, sharpened intellectual skills rather than imparted content, and its product, the *Bildungsbürger*, was drilled in classical grammar.[80] With state-funded excavation and the expansion of the Royal Museums, archaeology gained academic respectability and social prestige.[81] Later, the *Kulturpolitik* of the Wilhelmine era would conflate archaeology with diplomacy.[82] Yet August Böckh, the champion of *Sachphilologie*, the strict, historicist study of the laws, customs, religion, art and economics, of the whole life of a people, stressed nonetheless that the foundation and source

---

[77] See Hiller von Gaertringen (1994), p.145.

[78] Cf. Marchand, *Down from Olympus*, p.5ff.

[79] Ibid., pp.24-25.

[80] Ibid., pp.26-29.

[81] Ibid., p.49.

[82] Ibid., pp.243,246.

of all, in the case of Greece, lay in Greek religion,[83] and Humboldt regarded the empiricism of the natural sciences studied at university level as prejudicial to the humanities.[84] The *Gymnasium* became, as Marchand notes, "the accepted gateway to university and white-collar careers", though also, after 1870, the preserve not just of the career-oriented, ambitious *Bildungsbürgertum* middle class, but increasingly of the old *Mittelstand* of such as lower officials, teachers and shopkeepers.[85] Collections of classical casts were to be found in every medium-sized German city.[86] The Greek *Bildungsideal* was entrenched, but, characterised by a rigour and discipline-for-discipline's-sake in Latin and Greek studies[87] and a resistance to the encroachment of modern subjects on the part of the classical philologists, it was beleaguered by the movement for school reform.[88] It was Nietzsche's championing of the Dionysian in *The Birth of Tragedy*, and his final aestheticisation of everything: of ontology, cosmology, ethics, anthropology and epistemology, in the *Will to Power* fragments,[89] which pointed to new, non-philological forms of enquiry for an understanding of the Greeks.[90] Students looked elsewhere: to poetry, painting – and to the travel writing of Gerhart Hauptmann.[91] Kästner's *Griechenland* tribute (p.168) could confidently make the claim that Hauptmann was the "Dichter des Griechischen Frühlings, der mir wie tausend anderen schon im Knabenalter das Erlebnis dieses Landes war."

1.6. The literary-critical focus: the aesthetic

Anz (2004) credits von Heydebrand & Winko (1996) with the thorough and synoptic presentation of the empirical-analytical course which literary evaluation research has taken since the 1980's.[92] The varied and complex argumentation of that course has not in the opinion of Anz produced a resolution of its problematic that is satisfactory in theory or in praxis.[93] Anz points to the fundamental cultural relativism of the empirical-analytical approach and to its inconsistent concretisation, interpretation and

---

[83] Ibid., pp.42,43.
[84] Ibid., p.27.
[85] Ibid., pp.125,133.
[86] Ibid., p.125
[87] Ibid., p.134
[88] Ibid., p.117.
[89] See Kai Hammermeister, *The German Aesthetic Tradition* (Cambridge: Cambridge University Press, 2002), pp.138-44,146.
[90] Marchand, *Down from Olypmus*, p.117.
[91] Ibid., p.118.
[92] Anz, in *Literaturkritik*, ed. by Thomas Anz and Rainer Baasner (Munich: Beck, 2004), p.209.
[93] Ibid., p.213.

hierarchical ordering of standards such as 'the good', 'the true', 'the beautiful', 'coherence', 'unity', 'integral wholeness', 'dramatic tension', 'authenticity', 'credibility', 'innovation, 'originality', and 'ambiguity'.[94] Further, the question of whether ethical standards should be superordinate to the aesthetical, is one to which answers are permanently debated within the empirical-analytical approach.[95] Anz's conclusion is that diverging evaluations of a text are by no means necessarily the result of [the application of] differing evaluation standards, but can also be the result of differing descriptions of textual features or of the varying application of abstract terms/concepts themselves deficient in concretisation.[96]

In the von Heydebrand/Winko structural typology of axiological textual values, grouped in a table of "*Ästhetizität / Literarizität*", considerations of self-reference, polyvalence, openness, beauty, coherence, completeness and complexity make up formal aesthetic evaluation. Beside these lie the content-bound axiological considerations of truth, beauty and justice and, detached from both, relational axiological considerations, among which are the deviation-from and the norm-breaking of everyday communication, and originality and innovation in relation to comparable preceding texts.[97] External to formal self-referential, formal content-dependent and to relational axiological values lie the effective, the *wirkungsbezogene*, among which, under the coined sub-heading of *Erkenntnisbedeutsamkeit*, von Heydebrand and Winko list the quality of *Entautomatisierung*, a term from the *Rezeptionsästhetik* of Jauss, which Anz identifies as central to the Jaussian concept of readers' horizon-of-expectation and by which works which stimulate such a de-automatisation of perception distinguish themselves from trivial literature as works of art.[98] Farthest placed from the formal among the axiological values in the Heydebrand/Winko model are affective individual values, hedonistic satisfactions, and the social value of symbolic intellectual capital.[99]

Worthmann (2004) objects to the use by von Heydebrand and Winko of their favoured term *Literarizität* – a coinage translating as 'literaricity' – inasmuch as it is a predicate which dissolves and double-defines 'literature' into the constituents of 'the literary' and 'literaricity'.[100] In determining

---

[94] Ibid., p.214.

[95] Ibid.

[96] Ibid., p.217.

[97] Renate von Heydebrand and Simone Winko, *Einführung in die Wertung von Literatur* (Paderborn: Schöningh, 1996) pp.113-31, and pp.114-15 [diagram].

[98] See Anz, in Anz and Baasner, op. cit., p.213.

[99] See von Heydebrand and Winko, op. cit., p.115.

[100] Friederike Worthmann, *Literarische Wertungen. Vorschläge für ein deskriptives Modell* (Wiesbaden: Deutscher Universitäts-Verlag, 2004), p.40.

Literarizität as a predicate which may be ascribed from either of two reception features: from non-applied fictionality, "Fiktionalität und Zweckfreiheit", or from formal textual features, functional texts which exhibit either are included: diaries, letters, autobiographies, speeches, advertising and entertainment, thus joining the class of autonomous-aesthetical, *autonomieästhetisch*, received literature. From this, Worthmann sees an inconsistency in the continued use by von Heydebrand and Winko of the terms *Sach- und Gebrauchsliteratur*, *Trivialliteratur* and *Unterhaltungsliteratur*.[101] Worthmann proceeds to see in von Heydebrand and Winko's privileging of formal-aesthetic reception (through their focus on 'literaricity') an implicit privileging of formal-aesthetic evaluation,[102] and as a progression from this, a pre-empting of "wer welche Texte wie wertet".[103]

In response, Worthmann proposes a comprehensive model of literary evaluation which, *inter alia*, indicates what a circumscribed place the aesthetic has as a value in the process of assigning values to literary work, as the following paraphrase of some of the prerequisites for this model shows:

- Is adequate in range and terminology.
- Proceeds analytically, avoiding normatives.
- Is strictly systematic in being historically as well as culturally unspecific.
- Takes into account that there are ethical as well as the aesthetical standards of literary evaluation, and clarifies the meanings of norms, conventions and sensibilities [applied in] literary evaluation.
- Recognises that standards of literary worth are socially inherited, and consequently have social, historic, or cultural zones of validity.
- Is multidimensional in its recognition that literary evaluations are mental processes that represent elements of literary reception.[104]

A possible contradiction is here apparent between the non-specificity of the historic and the cultural on the one hand, and the socially, historically and culturally inherited standards of literary worth on the other. A demonstrably consistent application of such a model to subject works of this study, written as they were, perforce, in conditions of historic, cultural and social incongruity, would impose an indeterminable and possibly impractical

---

[101] Ibid., pp.40,41,42.
[102] Ibid., p.46.
[103] Ibid., p.47.
[104] Paraphrased from Worthmann, op. cit., p.18.

explicatory burden. In reference to von Heydebrand and Winko's four arguments for autonomous-aesthetic standards, Worthmann does concede that there may be good grounds for the privileging of autonomous-aesthetic definition and evaluation concepts in literary studies, and that they may represent a significant share of literary evaluation praxis; the objection being only that, as sole basis for an evaluation model, such concepts are restricting.[105] The four arguments of von Heybebrand and Winko are, in précis: 1. only autonomy-aesthetic provides the discipline [of *Literaturwissenschaft*] with its own philosophical object, with *its* own value-criteria; 2. without tradition, condensed in the canon, the new cannot be experienced; 3. autonomy [autonomous] literature in canonical examples is the most complex, and only through engaging with it can the variety of methodical approaches be learned; 4. the subjects range at university facilitates the revelation in theory and in practice of all dimensions of autonomous literature.[106] The autonomous aesthetic is what this study elects to advance as its standard of literary evaluation of its subject texts. Since all expressions of literary opinion, whether value-assertive, expressive or appellative, have the corresponding functional aspects of the referential, the emotive and the conative (conative, in this context, as influence seeking), each of these functional aspects also having aspects of the others,[107] and each of which thereby subverts the autonomy of the others, so it is that objectivity of evaluation is unattainable in the absolute. Pronouncements of literary evaluation differ then, only to the extent that one or other of their three functional aspects, the referential, the emotive, or the conative, is *dominant*.[108] So, forming the *reference* function of an evaluation, an 'autonomous' aesthetic might occupy the position of dominance and therefore superordination to the expressive (of personal taste) and the appellative (to the tastes of others). The autonomy of the aesthetic in that case would still, to satisfy the test of the Worthmann model, have to be supra-cultural, supra-historicist, and at the same time demonstrate a provenance in a preferred prior cultural model or models. This position might be said to be that of Kästner, arguing for attention to the still immanent aura of the homogeneity of belief and cultural expression that was the Greek antique and which had striven at an ideal of human perfection.

Given the axiological objections in truth, justice and humanity which might, however, be raised against the subject texts of this study, the question of literary reception is here first addressed. In the phenomenological approach to texts as expounded by Iser, literary works are bi-polar: the

---

105 Ibid., p.49.

106 See von Heydebrand and Winko, op. cit., p.337.

107 Worthmann, op. cit., pp.241-42.

108 Ibid.

aesthetic is the realisation in the text accomplished by the reader; the author creates the other pole, the artistic.[109] Realisation of an aesthetic is by that explicitly contingent on reader response. Reader response is correspondingly implicit in Iser's statement that the sentence aims at something beyond what it actually says and that this is true of all sentences in literary works.[110] This idea is terminologically defined by Eagleton: "The 'world' of a literary work is not an objective reality, but what in German is called *Lebenswelt*, reality as actually organised and experienced by an individual subject."[111] The works under study in this study, some in the format of travel journal, feuilleton feature or essay and corresponding at least superficially to the category of applied literature, *Gebrauchsliteratur*, as defined by Schäfer, nonetheless construct a literary *Lebenswelt* of the abnormal normality of occupied Europe. That the writers under study wrote in sentences intending beyond what was said will be evident from citations. That an intensified 'aesthetification' could intend beyond itself to underline and undermine an abnormal reality will be argued from the principle of *distance*, a precondition for the creation of an aesthetic view. That principle, as principle, is not found among the aesthetic considerations already mentioned here, unless taken to be subsumed in the concept of the self-referential, in the sense of a literary work referring not to any external reality, but to its own characteristics as a work of art; and the distance principle is also not coterminous with the Jaussian *Entautomatisierung*. The distance principle creates an autonomous space within which an aesthetic view may supplant the normal outlook. Moral responsibility before the referential facts is not thereby escaped. Bullough's (1957) exposition of psychical distance makes the distinction:

> ...psychical distance has a *negative*, inhibitory aspect – the cutting out of the practical sides of things and of our practical attitude to them – and a *positive* side – the elaboration of the experience on the new basis created by the inhibiting action of Distance. [...] this distanced view of things is not, and cannot be, our normal outlook. Distance is a factor in all art [...] it is, for this very reason, also an aesthetic principle.[112]

Psychical distance is therefore a necessary condition of the aesthetic, but is it morally a sufficient one? Bullough goes on to detach, but not entirely to sever, the aesthetic from personal and moral values:

---

[109] See Wolfgang Iser, 'The reading process: a phenomenological approach', *New Literary History*, vol.3 (Winter 1972), 279-99, from Lodge, *Modern Criticism and Theory*, p.212.

[110] Ibid., p.214.

[111] Terry Eagleton, *Literary Theory. An Introduction*, (Oxford: Blackwell, 1996), p.59.

[112] Edward Bullough, *Aesthetics* (London: Bowes & Bowes, 1957), p.95.

> ...it is Distance which supplies one of the special criteria of aesthetic values as distinct from practical (utilitarian), scientific, or social (ethical) values. All these are concrete values, either *directly* personal as utilitarian, or *indirectly* remotely personal, as moral values.[113]

The distinction rests here on a fine point:

> Distance does not imply an impersonal, purely intellectually interested relation of such a kind. On the contrary, it describes a personal relation, often highly emotionally coloured, but of a peculiar character. Its peculiarity lies in that the personal character of the relation has been, so to speak, filtered. It has been cleared of the practical, concrete nature of its appeal, without, however, thereby losing its constitution.[114]

When considering the sustained, heightened aesthetic of Hartlaub's and Kästner's writings in particular, this study relies on that point: personal relations of a practical, concrete nature, when referred to at all, are mentioned merely to carry the narrative. Remotely or indirectly personal values are alluded to only obliquely: of necessity in Kästner's case, as he was writing, at least ostensibly, for the military. In Hartlaub's case the personal and moral are masked by an objective style, analogous to *Neue Sachlichkeit* painting. Monika Marose's dissertation (2000), referring to Schäfer's characterisation of Hartlaub's observation technique as reminiscent of *Neue Sachlichkeit* painting, points out that Hartlaub deliberately distanced himself from the emotional, irrational and reality-hostile tradition of aestheticism.[115] Parker, Davies and Philpotts in their study of the 1930-1960 periodisation posited by Schäfer's *Das gespaltente Bewußtsein*, found that in the case of the periodical *Das innere Reich*, "It is easy to see how in *Das innere Reich* the political solution to crisis offered by National Socialism coalesces with the aesthetic search for stability of meaning which has been the dominant cultural mood since 1930."[116] This study would posit that that the search for stability of meaning through the medium of the aesthetic must have become more acute for those such as Hartlaub and Kästner in particular, who were capable of articulating it, and of doing so from the fortuitously detached vantage points which their exceptional wartime postings afforded. Though it is axiomatic of post-structuralist and postmodernist theory that stability of meaning is a textual illusion, the search for such stability through the production of texts of literariness (leaving aside for the moment the

---

113 Ibid., p.129.

114 Ibid., p.97.

115 Monika Marose, 'Das Eigentliche ist unsichtbar' University of Essen, 2000, p.91.

116 Stephen Parker/Peter Davies/Matthew Philpotts, *The Modern Restoration. Re-thinking German Literary History 1930-1960* (Berlin/New York: Walter de Gruyter, 2004), p.85.

question of literary evaluation of those texts) was a valid one, and the subject texts worthy of study for that. The caveat of a Marxist analysis, where the aesthetic must be viewed, as all else, as a socially produced cultural commodity, would merely confirm that Schiller's presumption of an aesthetically informed and therefore socially complete human was, like German classicism as a whole, a self-evidently abstract project.[117] The texts studied here are, through the constraints of their provenance, similarly also abstract projects.

1.7. A reappraisal of critical reception

Proceeding out of the Worthmann model of literary evaluation, the avoidance of normatives, under the eye of the censor, would require adroit phrasing. To be historically as well as culturally unspecific would in the circumstances have required so much elision as to make another and detached plane of reference a necessity. The recognition of an ethical standard might contravene prevailing occupation policy and pass the censor only if obliquely expressed. Finally, an acknowledgement that standards of literary worth are socially inherited and have social, historic, or cultural zones of validity would simply have made more pointed the non-reciprocal nature of commentary by occupiers.

Horst Denkler's self-avowedly pessimistic conclusion is that, despite many examples of texts effecting applied metamorphosis of the antique to the present, all remained overshadowed by the Third Reich, stuck in the wished-for, the permissible, the tolerated, the evaded; required a backward-looking elucidation, denied themselves an uninhibited reading, and were characterised by a fatalistic resignation.[118] Denkler gives page references to repeated invocations in Kästner's *Griechenland* of the Nordic origin of the ancient Greeks and to the hailing of the ancient Greek virtues of modesty, motivation, liberality, chivalry: "Bescheidenheit, Leistungsbereitschaft, Freisinnigkeit, Ritterlichkeit".[119] Among these references are to be found the 'Persians' passage from Aeschylus (pp.98-103) which renders in Kästner's italics: *beide Schwestern eines Stammes* (p.99), which in context may be read as pointing to the fact that the *current* temporarily defeated enemy – for the Persians, read the British – is of the same stock as the Germans. Kästner's book does close with the 'Flug über Griechenland' chapter and the observation from the air that here is "Nicht Südliches schlechthin, sondern

---

[117] See Rainer Stollmann, *Ästhetisierung der Politik. Literaturstudien zum subjektiven Faschismus* (Stuttgart: Metzler, 1978), p.16.

[118] Horst Denkler, 'Hellas as Spiegel deutscher Gegenwart in der Literatur des „Dritten Reiches",' in *Banalität mit Stil*, ed. by Walter Delabar and others (Bern: Peter Lang, 1999), pp.11-28 (p.27).

[119] Ibid., p.22.

Nördliches im Süden", but also speaks of an "im Süden glücklich gewordenen Volkes", a people from the North, from the age of the *Völkerwanderung*, become *happily* settled in the South (p.269).

From the same colloquium Felix Hartlaub is situated by Andrea Dech both in the Magic Realism movement and also in the left-wing, Verist, branch of the *Neue Sachlichkeit.* His magic-realist traits are the strongly visual, static quality of his *Prosagedicht* pieces: a film-like zoom and wandering-observer technique; propensities to anthropomorphise, to petrify the animate and animate the petrified; a tendency to miniaturisation; pronounced stillnesses contrasting with strong acoustics; backgrounds of decay and stultification, and minimal human communication. Lastly, the withdrawal of the author from the narrative is analogous to the understated surface technique in Magic Realist painting.[120] All Hartlaub's mature work, however (the Berlin sketches and onwards), is situated firmly in the reality of the era as imposed by the regime, whether the oppressive prewar Berlin or the subdued, desolate-seeming Paris: the workless, the poor and the malformed are portrayed unflinchingly. Even the grotesquerie of the *FHQ* sketches is not a gratuitous surrealism, but the stress-induced hallucinations of persons vividly aware that they are living at the well-organised centre of chaos – hence both Magic Realist and Verist.[121] Treatment of the late antique, renaissance, seventeenth century Spain and revolutionary France periods are confined to Hartlaub's juvenilia: there is no recourse to an ideal counter-world in the wartime writings,[122] except an oblique one, not noted by Dech: the repeatedly directed gaze to the *Dächerwelt*, the leaded, tile-armoured mansards of the still-sovereign rooftop world of occupied Paris.

Dech points out that Hartlaub's prose-poetry pieces, his shorter Paris pieces in particular, those most closely resembling Magic Realism, were such as found publication by others in Nazi Germany. However, those sketches with the "Er" figure, whose outlook is less than positive, and Hartlaub's satirical vignettes of German officialdom, would certainly have ruled out any chance of present publication. Even a neutral stance could be construed as a criticism of the circumstances described.[123] Despite humour, the pronounced bleakness of the Paris moods, added to which a usually ironic portrayal of his fellow countrymen going about their duties, was too honest a portrayal to have had hopes of publication before the end of wartime censorship – Dech argues further that the regime's end would have been a

---

120 Andrea Dech, 'Felix Hartlaub. Zwischen Magischem Realismus und Neuer Sachlichkeit,' in Delabar and others, *Banalität mit Stil*, pp.259-83 (p.275).

121 Ibid., pp.277-78, 280-81.

122 Ibid., pp.276-77.

123 Ibid., pp.266, 268, 272.

necessary precondition for publication.[124] Poceeding from C.H. Wilke's philological study, Dech determines that Hartlaub's sketches were intended as trial pieces for a polyperspectival novel which reunited some of the characters at a later point in the war, at the *FHQ*.[125] The novel plan includes in the fantasy of one of the characters a postwar scene so unthinkable inside the prevailing ideology that any thought of its publication had to have been projected beyond the war's end. It is clear that Hartlaub was aware that these later covert writings crossed the line between what was then currently at all permissible and what was illicit. Yet, the persona in Paris sketches is discreet and bites his lip when, in the *Puff*, he almost lets slip that he is a minor official in the diplomatic service. Had the war's outcome been otherwise, the Paris sketches *could* have reached a German reading public.

Schonauer (1961) criticises Third Reich bourgeois literature as harmless, "unverfänglich", and noncommittal, "unverbindlich", and characterised by journalistic feature-writing. The more aspiring of its authors – Schonauer instances here Ernst Jünger's 1934 essay 'Dalmatinischer Aufenhalt' and Friedrich Georg Jünger's 1943 *Wanderungen auf Rhodos* – opted almost exclusively for the landscapes of Western culture: France, Italy and Spain, proceeding in a mistaken notion that aesthetic escapism was an anti-Nazi position. Schonauer dismisses all such attempts as 'calligraphied pastoralism'. Kästner's 'blond Achaeans' passage from *Griechenland* is cited as an instance of ideological calligraphy: "ein Buch [...] in dem das klasssische Bildungsergebnis der attischen Landschaft und das des Krieges mittels der Kalligraphie auf einen ideologischen Nenner gebracht werden."[126] The dismissive charge of 'calligraphy' is repeated in Schnell's (1976) criticism of the literature of the 'inner emigration'. Unlike Friedrich Georg Jünger who in his 1943 published *Griechische Götter* essays had offered the antique as an ideal alternative model to the fascist reality, Kästner, so Schnell makes the distinction, constructs time-transcending (*überzeitlich*) commonalities from the history of ideas (*geistesgeschichtliche Bezüge*) for the political purpose of diverting attention from the actual conditions of occupied Greece.[127] In support of this reading, Schnell quotes selectively from a passage that in whole is, in fact, in praise of the early Byzantine mosaics at the Daphni monastery, and from another passage where Kästner figuratively links the decay of Byzantine masonry at Mistra to the spirit of Oriental fatalism that had infected Greece. While misrepresenting the sense by ignoring Kästner's debunking of the Frankish crusaders and truncating the citation at the point where it proceeds to make clear that such legends

[124] Ibid., p.283.

[125] Ibid., p.264.

[126] Schonauer, *Deutsche Literatur im Dritten Reich*, pp.134-35 and [notes] pp.194-95.

[127] Schnell, *Literarische innere Emigration 1933-1945*, pp.94-97.

stirred the fantasy of ardent Graecophile Germans (and by inference, only such), Schnell attributes 'Nordic' race triumphalism to Kästner. More sustainably questionable, perhaps, is the conclusion of this passage, where Kästner quotes a Goethe *Faust* stanza to suggest that the 'hammer of fate' had struck again in the spring of 1941 on the names of Thermopylae, Olympia, and Corinth. Schnell's interpretation of the 'Persians' passage: "...schafft er suggestiv eine überzeitliche Gemeinsamkeit, deren politische Funktion in der Ablenkung von der geschichtlich-gesellschaftlichen Bedingungen der Besetzung Griechenlands besteht", is perplexing, given that Kästner's essay is wholly about the matter of the message of Aeschylus' play: that it behoves victors to have a sympathetic understanding of the plight of a temporarily defeated enemy lest the daemonic forces visit the same fate on them in turn.

Schnell construes the 'blond Achaeans' episode also as an escape from the wartime reality of Greece at the expense of a mythical simultaneity (*Gleichzeitigkeit*). The 'Fahrt nach Griechenland' chapter was written in the course of July 1941,[128] and the Homeric bathing scene is found already recounted in a private letter to Gerhard Hauptmann dated 3rd July, with the concluding phrase: *es ergab sich unversehens ein völlig arkadisches Bild.*[129] In *Griechenland*, the phrase reappears as: *unversehens ergab sich ein völlig klassisches Bild* (p.10). The spontaneity of the classical imagery is evident from the Hauptmann letter, making Hiller von Gaertringen's explication the more plausible: that Kästner's retention of the episode in the postwar *Ölberge, Weinberge* indicates that that book is less an account of his wartime fate than a rendering of account, a *Rechenschaftsbericht*, on his unfolding love story with Greece.[130] The other critics seem not to have noted Kästner's own justification, in the text, for the text: "Wer auf Erden hätte jemals mehr Recht gehabt, sich mit jenen zu vergleichen als die hier – *die nicht daran dachten?*" (italics added). Those young men had no notion of themselves as being in the mould of classical Greek heroes; that image springs spontaneously, *unversehens*, from Kästner's own mind. Kästner adds that not one of them but had left a fallen comrade or friend behind in Crete: *Sie kamen vom schwersten Siege.* No equivalence, however, is established between the four-and-a-half thousand German war graves at Chania and the three-and-a-half thousand Cretans who lost their lives and the sixty villages destroyed or seriously damaged through the German/Italian occupation.[131]

---

128 Hiller von Gaertringen (1994), p.171.

129 Hiller von Gaertringen, *Perseus-Auge Hellblau. Erhart Kästner und Gerhart Hauptmann: Briefe, Texte, Notizen* (Bielefeld: Aisthesis, 2004), pp.273-74.

130 Hiller von Gaertringen (1994), p.334.

131 Marlen von Xylander, *Die deutsche Besatzungsherrschaft auf Kreta 1941-1945* (Freiburg: Rombach, 1989), p.139

Kästner was not aware of the extent of British presence on the island in the direction of partisan activity or of the acute threat to his own life while on the Omalos plateau in November 1943, but did know at the time of previous reprisal actions by German forces on the island.[132] Criticism to date has not proposed an approach within which such happenings, even if they had been fully known, could have been acknowledged without negating the literary project that was *Kreta.*

1.8. Prevailing literary form

The writers wrote in multiple guises: art-historical guide (Göpel, Kästner); art historian (Göpel); cultural cartographer (Kästner); *flâneur* (Hartlaub); Walter Bauer in the pose of simple, serving soldier; Kurt Lothar Tank as military-tour guest (for the 1940 section of his 'Paris' diaries), Horst Lange and H.G. Rexroth on the Eastern Front in purely fictional characters or narrating personae. The writers varied also in their discourse: in the case of Göpel, regional landscape as determinant of character and culture; in the case of Kästner, the classical sites of Greece as architectural and landscape studies and as stage for sometimes metaphysical reflections on the culture of the antique; in the case of Hartlaub, the occupied city from the viewpoint of the anonymous, mildly sardonic *flâneur.* The writing, in so far as it was a form of extended travel impressions, might be seen superficially as continuation of the travel writing vogue carrying over from 1930s Germany.[133] Schäfer has pointed out that the thirties enthusiasm for travel had led to a revival of travel literature, above all in diary forms, and that the high point of the popularity of this form was reached during the war, when the diary and war reporting genres mixed and press war-reporters liked to dress their reportage as sketches and mood pictures.[134] Schäfer adds that so pervasive and influential was the diary culture of the thirties and forties that all literary currents, albeit in very different ways, participated in it.[135] Schäfer's periodisation survey orders Kästner's "Griechenlandtagebuch" into the war-and-travel journal genre,[136] even though from the geographically site-specific structure of Kästner's *Griechenland* of early 1943 and of his later *Kreta* it is clear that these books are intended not as diary accounts or travel journals, but rather, overtly, as guides to the sites and culture of the antique and to the inherited and determining influence on Western culture. It should be noted also that Kästner is scathingly critical of the passivity of mere tourism and, implicitly, of travel journal literature

132 See Hiller von Gaertringen (1994), pp.411-12.

133 Cf. Schäfer, *Das gespaltene Bewußtsein*, pp.44,107.

134 Ibid.

135 Ibid., p.105.

136 Ibid., p.106.

springing only from that: "hat man vergessen, daß Reisen eine Kunst ist, die ebensoviel an Sammlung, an Frommheit und Bildung voraussetzt, als sie sodann gewährt, und daß es ohne Bemühung zur Antwort nicht geht?".[137] It should be noted also that Hartlaub similarly disdained the *Reisegesellschaft*, 'coach party', mentality of his colleagues in Paris: "Wohl oder übel hat man sich da-mit [sic] abgefunden, ganz in der Reisegesellschaft zu existieren, was sehr anstrengend und unfruchtbar ist."[138] In emphasising the popularity of the diary genre Schäfer instances the provision of a 'diary pack' with specimen entries which appeared in 1941.[139] Diary keeping, like the *Feldpost*, was seen as good for the morale of the troops, and for propaganda.[140] The publishers of Jünger's *Gärten und Straßen* brought four conquest-celebrating diary accounts of the Polish and French campaigns onto the market in 1940-1941.[141] As closely related with such propagandist accounts Schäfer sees, among others, the diary accounts of Walter Bauer and Kurt Lothar Tank, and groups these into the category of the existential-philosophical and confessional which seeks to aestheticise the war out of the actuality of life, "aus der Zone des Lebens"[142] – a view and categorisation which it is here proposed to re-examine.

With the exception of Lange's novella, *Die Leuchtkugeln*, and Rexroth's novel, *Der Wermutstrauch*, the writings here examined are all variants, when categorised broadly by genre, of the prevailing diary and travel-journal mode, but to regard them as merely period pieces in a given mode would be to disregard their worth as tests of the *application* of literary form. Hartlaub's diaries – designated such in the editions of his sister, Geno Hartlaub – in Schäfer's opinion elevate the diary genre into a high sphere of literary art: "rücken die Gattung in einen hohen Kunstbezirk."[143] Similarly, Kästner and Göpel intended, in Iserian terms, beyond the direct subject matter of their writing assignments.

Brenner (1997) styles the rise of travel literature in the Weimar Republic as *der Kult der Zerstreuung*:[144] "der moderne Tourist schreibt nicht, er liest

---

137 Erhart Kästner, *Kreta* (1946), p.65.

138 Ewenz I (2000/2007), pp.462/470.

139 Schäfer, *Das gespaltene Bewußtsein*, p.107.

140 See Martin Humburg, *Das Gesicht des Krieges. Feldpostbriefe von Wehrmachtsoldaten aus der Sowjetunion 1941-1944* (Opladen-Wiesbaden: Westdeutscher Verlag, 1998), p.269.

141 Schäfer, *Das gespaltene Bewußtsein*, pp.106-7.

142 Ibid., p.107.

143 Ibid., p.45.

144 Brenner, 'Schwierige Reisen. Wandlungen des Reiseberichts in Deutschland 1918-1945, III: Reiseliteratur im »Dritten Reich«,' in *Reisekultur in Deutschland: von der Weimarer Republik zum »Dritten Reich«*, ed. by Peter J. Brenner (Tübingen: Max Niemeyer, 1997), pp.127-176 (p.139, citing Kracauer).

bestenfalls."[145] The modern tourist therefore, in contrast to the journal-writing traveller of the nineteenth century, had to be written *for*. The indulgence in diversion, *Zerstreuung*, from modern life afforded by improved motor transport, by the development of cruise voyaging and, for the adventurous, long-distance air travel, led already in the Weimar Republic to new forms of describing experience, these most commonly reportage, in which the exotic was functionalised for diversion, and formally and stylistically so in the feature-writing style of the feuilleton.[146] That continued to be the case throughout the Nazi regime, even after the point when leisure travel was out of the question.[147] *Zerstreuung* was still a useful palliative. The popularity of mass travel had been exploited by the regime through the *Kraft durch Freude* programme and even a fictional account of such travels could still find a readership in 1942.[148] Brenner's study, in posing the question as to how far and to what extent *NSDAP* domination had, if at all, led to an epochal change in literary and cultural development points to indications from other studies (Barbian, Eichberg, Ketelsen, Strothmann) that the pre-existing, proto-fascist trends towards uniformity of political and everyday life, particularly in literature, had merely been accelerated by the element of compulsion accompanying the new regime.[149] That the effects of the old (and freely chosen) forms of travel and the new (and officially organised) on German travel literature had not been (as of 1997) researched, as Brenner notes,[150] does not detract from the fact relevant to this study that there was, in any case, continuity and undiminished popularity in travel literature continuing into the war years themselves. Moreover, as Brenner citing Strothmann points out, a whole series of German writers participated in *NSDAP*-organised war tourism to Spain, Poland, France and Russia or Norway.[151] Brenner notes that the war-reporting of the military propaganda companies soon evolved into a genre of its own.[152] The 1940 section of Kurt Lothar Tank's *Pariser Tagebuchblätter 1938-1939-1940* was the result of a *Wehrmacht* organised field visit, and Walter Bauer wrote his *Tagebuchblätter aus Frankreich* as a serving soldier in a transport company. The publishing success of the latter, six printings, is an example of the popularity that travel literature from the theatres of war could enjoy when civil leisure travel was

[145] Ibid.

[146] Ibid., 139-41.

[147] Ibid., pp.155 (note 97), 163 (note 132, citing A.E. Johann (1943), *Das Land ohne Herz* and Elizabeth Schucht (1942), *Eine Frau fliegt nach Fernost*).

[148] Ibid., p.153, citing Hans Biallas (1940), *Der Sonne entgegen.*

[149] Ibid., pp.142-43.

[150] Ibid., p.145.

[151] Ibid.

[152] Ibid., p.147.

out of the question and in its stead the war could, for a time, still be presented as adventure. Though rendered difficult through currency exchange controls introduced even before the war, foreign travel for leisure had continued to enjoy a growing popularity.[153] The popularity of the derivative literary form which offered escape from the anxiety of tense times is understandable, but it was a form capable, as Brenner points out, of being exploited for propaganda purposes: a Baedeker guide to the 'Generalgouvernement' slave state of southern and eastern Poland, from 1943, now seems grotesque.[154] Works whose provenance is traced ultimately to some variant of 'war tourism' surmount that categorical relegation only through what intrinsic literary merit they may claim.

All but one of Hartlaub's fragments from France are set in Paris and constitute an attempt to write *flâneur* literature, as defined by Walter Benjamin and Franz Hessel,[155] from the point of view of an observer whose necessarily detached viewpoint was further distanced by his status as occupying alien, and in Hartlaub's case, additionally by a discomfiture among his own countrymen caused by his aquiline profile. Kästner's literary output by contrast was narrator-centred, with the narrator sometimes conjoined with a single other travel companion as 'we' (as in *Griechenland*, with his illustrator, Helmut Kaulbach). Kästner's working format, though not the *object* of his writing, is that of the travel-journal account; the journeys are to specific points of interest, those encountered interact with the narrator. The detachment and anonymity of the *flâneur* do not come into play.

In Erhard Göpel's Brittany and Normandy guide books the personae of traveller-raconteur or detached *flâneur* are both equally absent. There is no record of one-to-one personal encounters; instead, the reader is presented with set-piece descriptive encounters: with Mont St. Michel in *Die Bretagne*, with mounted horsemen emerging out of a morning mist in *Die Normandie*. The latter encounter, in the opening chapter, is collective, as is the only other, with a Flemish settler, in the final chapter. Göpel's use of "wir" in these instances suggests that he is most probably travelling in attachment to a *Propagandakompanie* unit. The writer's viewpoint is elsewhere in these two booklets to be discerned only indirectly, from the general tenor of the writing.

---

153 Ibid., p.151; also Schäfer, *Das gespaltene Bewußtsein*, p.155, citing Grundberger (1972).
154 Brenner, *Reisekultur in Deutschland*, p.148.
155 Cf. *Walter Benjamin*, *Gesammelte Schriften*, 7 vols, vol.5.2 (Frankfurt/Main: Suhrkamp, 1982), ed. by Rolf Tiedemann; also, *Franz Hessel. Sämtliche Werke in fünf Bänden*, vol.2 (Oldenburg: Igel, 1999), ed. by Hartmut Vollmer and Bernd Witte.

The exploitative harshness of German-enforced administration regimes in the captured cities of the East may be read from the example of Kiev.[156] Demolitions by the departing Soviet forces, as at Kiev and Rostov, added to the hardships suffered by the citizens. A lack of chateaux or of Hellenic ruins and growing attacks in the countryside by Soviet partisans deterred military 'tourism'. The book-length works which seek to present a detached, literary view of that land and its peoples present rather the abandoned and the displaced than the settled population, in so far as that was left undisturbed. The theatre visit in Taganrog in H.G. [Hermann Georg] Rexroth's novel, *Der Wermutstrauch*, is hurriedly concluded to the sounds of uncomfortably close shellfire. Martin Raschke's longing for the stone culture of the classical South as refreshment from the wooden and earthy East[157] represents the unsatisfied thirst of the post-expressionist, technical-metropolitan modernist for reference points amid an estranging natural vastness. Not just the war, but the lack of a Western European urban density disoriented the cultural compass of the venturing soldier-writers. The best of what they produced was in consequence an adaptation of the bourgeois-cultivated forms of novel and novella.

1.9. The *Kriegstagebuch*: mastery and criticism

The literary success of Ernst Jünger's wartime diaries began with the 1942 publication of *Gärten und Straßen*. When discovered by the censor, the art of camouflaged speech which Jünger deployed in *Gärten und Straßen* prevented the appearance of a second edition.[158] Consequently, the continuation volumes, *Das erste Pariser Tagebuch* and *Das zweite Pariser Tagebuch*, remained with the rest of his wartime and immediate postwar diaries unpublished until they appeared under the titles *Strahlungen I* and *II* in 1949. Marose (2000), citing a passage from *Das erste Pariser Tagebuch*, goes so far as to say that Jünger embodied the very type of occupier "den Hartlaubs gesamte Ablehnung und Verachtung trafen."[159] Jünger may appear morbid in experiencing a thrill from being alone in uniform among a French crowd at Vincennes on the feast day of Joan of Arc in May 1941: "ähnlich wie man

---

156 Cf. V. Danilenko, 'German Occupation of Kiev in 1941-1943: Documents of the Nazi-controlled City Administration,' at: http://www.eastview.com/docs/CM807408_rev.pdf [accessed 1 February 2012].

157 Raschke, 'Im Schatten der Front. Aufzeichnungen', in *Hinweis auf Martin Raschke*, ed. by Dieter Hoffmann (Heidelberg&Darmstadt: Lambert Schneider, 1963), p.121.

158 See *Das 20 Jahrhundert. Von Nietsche bis zur Gruppe 47*, catalogue of permanent exhibition at the Schiller National Museum and German Literature Archive at Marbach am Neckar, ed. by Bernhard Zeller (Munich: Kösel, 1980), p.276.

159 See Marose, 'Das Eigentliche ist unsichtbar', p.104.

mit brennender Kerze träumend durch ein Pulvermagazin spaziert",[160] but in doing so unashamedly portrays the occupier's state of heightened sensation. It is a similar "höhere Neugier", an elevated curiosity, which fascinates him two weeks later when ordered to oversee the execution of a deserter: "Ich sah schon viele sterben, doch keinen im bestimmten Augenblick."[161] The account is as compassionate as it is unsparingly detailed, and can be read as a covert plea for a humane understanding of the human condition. In relation to diary keeping and letter writing then, the remark of Marianne Feuersenger, secretary in the war-diary section of the *FHQ*, "es war damals unmöglich 'Klartext' niederzuschreiben", applied to the very keeping of a diary, let alone one for publication.[162] Afforded a certain licence by virtue of his standing as celebrated author and war hero holder of the *Pour le Mérite*, Jünger, though viewed with suspicion (his Paris protector, chief of staff West, Hans Speidel, had been warned by Keitel against him),[163] had entrée at the highest levels in France, and his *Pariser Tagebuch* volumes I and II, published later in *Strahlungen*, present a rarefied view of the occupation. These are postwar publications, however, and *Gärten und Straßen* ends with an entry of 24 July 1940, just four weeks after the armistice (it should be noted here that *Gärten und Straßen* was later attacked, in a 1943 review, for being overly sympathetic to the French).[164] These publications of Jünger therefore lie outside the criterion of contemporary literature-of-occupation defined for this thesis, one publication essentially predating the occupation and the others published later, in peacetime, and so subject to possible postwar redaction. Both *Gärten und Straßen* and its *Strahlungen* successor texts are nonetheless cited here variously as relevant and illuminating sources.

In acknowledging Jünger as master of the *Kriegstagebuch* form, Kästner elucidates his own reservations about the form's merits. He lauds Gerhard Nebel as an accomplished student of the master, who writes according to the master's prescription: "ein Drittel Schlangen, Krabben und Quallen, ein Drittel Lesefrüchte, [...] ein Drittel Ereignisse des Tages und des Kriegs."[165] This artful mixture of the grotesque (see Jünger's diary digression on edible snakes, 12 July 1942), of literary elitism and of actual day-to-day experience is not, Kästner is quite clear, the genuine diary: that has documentary worth and only incidentally literary worth, if any (Kästner cites here the Anne

---

160 See Jünger, 'Das erste Pariser Tagebuch', in Jünger, *Strahlungen I* (Munich: Klett-Cotta, 2003), p.237.

161 Ibid., p.242.

162 Marianne Feuersenger, *Mein Kriegstagebuch*, p.13.

163 See Jünger, *Strahlungen II* (Munich: DTV/Klett-Cotta, 1988), p.109.

164 Ibid., p.120.

165 Erhart Kästner, 'Der intellektuelle Gefreite', *Allgemeine Zeitung* (Mainz), 16 April 1949.

Frank diary as being such). The literary, cultivated, *Zuchtform* of the diary heightens and literarily stylises experience: "Nun wird der Tagebuchstoff literarisiert, überhöht, auf Hochform gebracht."[166] Such literary 'diaries' are then no more real diaries than epistolary novels are transcripts of real letters. The impromptu nature of the form, its "Abgerissenheit", is turned to advantage, for it is among all literary forms the least binding; it is the adolescent stage of selective ecstatics: "...es ist unter allen literarischen Formen die am wenigsten verpflichtende Form. Es ist die Entwicklungstufe der punktuellen Ekstasen, ...".[167] Nebel, in Kästner's opinion, has so mastered this form as to succeed in concealing the feature of it that is contrary to the very nature of diary itself: *composition*.[168] This 1949 essay on the diary form, contained in a books review, is illuminating of what Kästner himself was *not* engaged upon in his wartime Grecian trilogy: personal experience belonged either in a diary or travel journal, as a document of record, else it was material for free literary composition.

1.10. Editions and source texts: methodology

The 1967 philological study by Christian-Hartwig Wilke[169] established that the Hartlaub editions published to that time by Geno Hartlaub, sister of Felix Hartlaub, titled *Von unten gesehen* (1950), *Im Sperrkreis* (1955) and *Das Gesamtwerk* (1956) had omitted much from the original texts, presenting arbitrarily abridged versions of the sketches. A later and enlarged edition of *Im Sperrkreis* released by Geno Hartlaub in 1980 acknowledged and purported to make good the omissions of the earlier editions. A reader in making a comparison with the Ewenz (2002/2007) Suhrkamp editions of Hartlaub's mature writings and 1939-1945 letters will see that while missing passages had been restored in *Im Sperrkreis*, sentence truncations and word omissions remained. The Ewenz editions in contrast retain and elucidate the abbreviations and acronyms appearing in the originals, and provide commentary also from, among other sources, the unpublished 10-volume journal of the Hartlaub family. However, an examination conducted by Wilke of 250 pages of the Ewenz text, not including the Hartlaub letters reproduced in that edition, listed over 600 mis-transcriptions or misreadings, and that error rate was extrapolated by Seibt (2003)[170] to a possible one to two thousand errors in the whole edition.[171] This author, undertaking an

[166] Ibid.

[167] Ibid.

[168] Ibid.

[169] See Wilke, *Die letzten Aufzeichnungen Felix Hartlaubs*, pp.33,75.

[170] See Gustav Seibt, 'Im Sperrkreis des Dilettantismus', *Süddeutsche Zeitung*, 6 February 2003, p.16.

[171] Ibid.

examination of typescripts and original manuscripts in the papers of Felix Hartlaub at the *Deutsches Literatur Archiv* (hereinafter *DLA*) at Marbach, encountered a similar incidence of error or omission, but did find the 2002 edition text to be faithful and accurate where the MS was of reasonable legibility and free of deletions and insertions: e.g., some omissions, particularly from the longer, later sketches, corresponded to detached passages of miniscule and hurried script occurring in the MS. The often anacoluthic syntax and the hasty script in which the originals are written pose a difficulty in faithfully divining the sense intended by the hand of the author, and can result in unfixed subtleties of meaning – these latter in themselves one of the pleasures to be had from their author. The emendations of the re-edited Suhrkamp edition of 2007, not evident to the reader except by close comparison of the two editions, afford philological confirmation of a graphologically difficult MS and, happily, restore Hartlaub's sharp *apercu.*

Recognising, belatedly, what Wilke (1967) had achieved with limited access to the original Hartlaub papers, Geno Hartlaub in her afterword to *Im Sperrkreis*, the 1984 edition of her brother's work,[172] acknowledged the need for a full philological edition. Such a full edition, reproducing all Hartlaub's archived correspondence, has yet to appear. Marko (1987) regretted that for lack of funding *and for lack of political-intellectual interest*, no philologically reliable, historical-critical edition had to that point been published.[173] Marko's comment, coming just two years before the end of the cold war, is pertinent. Müller (1997)[174] noted in a postscript to her dissertation that an academically funded edition of Hartlaub was then in planning: this was the Suhrkamp edition of 2002. The redactors[175] of the revised edition which issued in September 2007 provided an extended introduction and revised and enlarged historical notes, the notes on the Paris sketches alone being extended from four-and-a-half to thirteen-and-a-half pages.[176]

A graphical curiosity of the Hartlaub notebooks is that only the two Paris notebooks contain illustrations, these on the left-hand pages which Hartlaub reserved for insertions and revisions. Neither the notebook from his doctoral study time in Berlin, 1938-1939, nor the notebook containing the sketches from his 1939-1940 military service in the Wilhelmshaven area, nor

---

172 See Geno Hartlaub, afterword to *Im Sperrkreis* (Frankfurt am Main: Fischer, 1984), p.213.

173 See Kurt Marko, 'Felix Hartlaubs Zeugenschaft wider den Missbrauch der Vergangenheit. Mehr als 40 Jahre danach,' *Zeitschrift für Politik. Organ der Hochschule für Politik. München*, issue 34, year 3 (1987), 280-291 (p.288).

174 Frederike Müller, 'Felix Hartlaub – Ein 'poeta minor' der Inneren Emigration', p.62.

175 Andrej Angrick, Hajo Lust, Regine Strotbeck.

176 *Felix Hartlaub »In den eigenen Umriss gebannt«* (Frankfurt am Main: Suhrkamp, 2007).

the single notebook from the Ukraine contain any such marginal sketches. Graphologically, it is also noteworthy that alone the handwriting of the Wilhelmshaven notebook is consistently legible throughout, with regularly formed characters. The other notebooks, particularly the succeeding Paris and Ukraine notebooks, display an increasingly hurried script with diminished and in places, were it not for the syntactical context, wholly indistinguishable character formation.

All the manuscript notebooks, however, do share a common feature: a page or pages, with headings, marked with an x where the heading has been used as the title of a completed sketch. There are two such pages in the black-covered Paris notebook [*DLA* 93.17.38] and one in the spiral-bound, buff-covered one [*DLA* 93.17.26]. The headings, ninety-five in all in manuscript on the three lists here mentioned and now transcribed in the notes to the 2007 edition, vol. II, pp.64,68,72-3,73-74 together with two other, shorter listings also transcribed in the 2007 edition notes, vol. II, pp.69,71, indicate a surplus of unworked mental material. Some of the headings are recognisable as sections incorporated in completed sketches: "Das nette Klofräulein" and "Wachlokal" for example, are developed sections within, respectively, 'Die Hochburg' and 'Das eroberte Ministerium'; and "Le Pornographe" is recognisable in the figure of the 'professor' in 'Die Hochburg'. Other headings are intriguingly suggestive of actual encounters and observations: "General im Theater", "Tafelrunde", "Beim Tailleur", "Rodin Mus.", "Les Clochards", "Der deutsche Picasso". Had more time been granted to him in Paris, more would certainly have come from his pen then. Afterwards, had he not needed to be concerned for his ability to make a postwar living, or been urged towards further scholarship by his father (and by his war-diary superior, P.E. Schramm), had not concern for their safekeeping put his Paris notebooks out of his reach in the intervening years, more must certainly have come out of these evocative promptings.

This author takes issue only with the conclusion in the introductions to the Suhrkamp editions that the torsi which make up Hartlaub's *Gesamtwerk* (and not merely the 1955 edition of that title) are such by reason of being involuntarily incomplete.[177] Wilke (1967), noting that the fragmentary, taken for granted in the diary entry, is the exception in a work of literary art, proceeds to argue that a fragmentary literary work is an art work in its potential rather than in its realisation.[178] Wilke's observation pertains to Hartlaub's early literary development. The singling out of chance experiences, "das Herausgreifen irgendeines zufälligen Lebensfragmentes",

---

[177] See Ewenz II (2002/2007), p.38.

[178] See Wilke, *Die letzten Aufzeichnungen Felix Hartlaubs*, pp.141-42.

avoiding sympathy or advocacy, "unter Verzicht auf Mitleid, Anwaltschaft", was what Hartlaub had intuited as the alternative to formally aesthetic renderings, this already as a twenty year old in 1933.[179] Wilke cites the now much-quoted passage from Hartlaub's letter draft of February 1941 to his literary confidant Professor Gustav Radbruch: "Am besten erzähle ich Ihnen einfach, was sich alltäglich in dem Stadtgebiet, durch das meine täglichen Wege führen, sichtbar zeigt; vielleicht kommt man gerade damit dem Unsichtbaren, das natürlich das Entscheidende ist, am nächsten.",[180] and divines that Hartlaub pursued that conviction gradually, from sketch to sketch, in the course of his time in Paris.[181] The extract of that letter draft to Radbruch as reprinted in Geno Hartlaub's *Das Gesamtwerk* includes a passage which does not appear in the Suhrkamp editions:

> …Die Trostlosigkeit, Leere, détresse der Stadt ist noch ärger als erwartet… Das charakteristische Klima ist arktisch, ich sehe so viel Beispiele von fortschreitender Verunmenschlichung, haarsträubendem Egoismus, kaltschnäuziger Blasiertheit, muß mich selber dauernd gegen Einbrüche aus diesen Regionen wehren... Man muß hoffen, doch noch Zeiten zu erleben, in denen das ganze unermeßliche Leid einmal irgendwie zum Bewußtsein, zur Sprache und Gestaltung ... kommt."[182]

An illuminating declaration, the lack of a confirmed dating for which again points to the need, still not met, for a complete critical edition of the Hartlaub letters. Of his later experiences Hartlaub would declare, also to Radbruch:

> Jetzt wird mir aber immer klarer, dass es für meine Generation […] eigentlich garkeine andere Aufgabe geben kann. Die Frage nach der Genese, nach dem wie war es möglich wird wohl die einzige sein, die noch an uns gerichtet werden wird, zu der vielleicht noch etwas zu sagen sein wird."[183]

Clear and penetrating reportage is to be found in Hartlaub's letters, and a literary and still more penetrating treatment of how it was psychologically possible, of the question, *wie war es möglich*, is to be found in his wartime sketches, among which, it is argued here, the Paris sketches constitute not torsi, but a successful literary whole.

---

179 See *Felix Hartlaub: in seinen Briefen*, ed. by Erna Krauss and G.F. Hartlaub (Tübingen: Wunderlich, 1958), p.113.

180 See Wilke, *Die letzten Aufzeichnungen Felix Hartlaubs*, p.159; Ewenz I (2002/2007), pp.467/475, dates this letter to 1 March 1941.

181 Wilke, *Die letzten Aufzeichnungen*, p.162.

182 See Geno Hartlaub (ed.), *Das Gesamtwerk* (Frankfurt am Main: Fischer, 1955), p.458.

183 See Ewenz I (2002/2007), pp.706/715.

Erhart Kästner, a librarian at the state library of Saxony at Dresden before the war, had authored catalogue publications in 1934 and 1936,[184] but had not published creatively before the war. His postwar writings in book form were concerned still predominantly with Greece and in his lifetime included a revised edition of his 1943 *Griechenland*. Kästner's interest later widened from the classical Greek to the succeeding Byzantine. This study concentrates on textual analysis of the two works published without postwar revision, *Griechenland* and *Kreta*. Kästner's papers are archived at the *Herzog August Bibliothek* at Wolfenbüttel and are extensively referenced in Julia Freifrau Hiller von Gaertringen's literary biography. Further appreciations of Kästner by von Gaertringen are available online from the Detmold municipal library. Selections of Kästner's correspondence have been published by his successor at Wolfenbüttel, Paul Raabe (1984), by Petzet (1986), and by von Gaertringen (2004). Of these two writers considered at length in this thesis, Kästner's survival and continued engagement with the topic of Greece afforded much later insight on his authorial intentions, about which in Hartlaub's case only the bare texts and some sparse comments filled with self-doubt are left to guide the scholar.

Erhard Göpel, friend of Kästner, who had a special interest in bookbinding, and had published a monograph on that topic in 1938,[185] published as an art historian after the war, but wrote nothing more for publication on the subject of the war period. The bulk of Erhard Göpel's papers are archived at the Bavarian state library in Munich. The Walter Bauer archive is housed at the Merseburg municipal library, with some information from this also available online. Bauer, but not Göpel, has been the subject of a published literary biography.[186] Critical appreciations of Martin Raschke, whose papers are in the state library of Saxony at Dresden, appeared in 1963 (Hoffmann) and 2002 (Haefs, Schmitz). Helmut Peitsch's 1984 monograph[187] critically appraises the works of those writers assigned to the Eastern front, among them Raschke, and its conclusions are here engaged with.

This study foregrounds those occupied territories whose pre-eminent rank in the canon of Western European cultural tradition elicited a cognizant response. Metaphysical conjurings of the antique and variations on a metropolitan *flâneur* literature both related to a civil order, present or past. In the continuous land warfare of the Eastern front, servicemen writings were penned in the literary deficit of an *absent* civil and social order.

---

184 See Hiller von Gaertringen (1994), p.505.

185 Cf. Erhard Göpel, *Der Buchbinder Ignatz Wiemeler* (Leipzig, Vienna: Brünn, 1938).

186 *Walter Bauer – ein Lebensweg von Merseburg nach Toronto* (Halle: Projekte, 2004).

187 Peitsch, '„Am Rande des Krieges"?', loc. cit.

2. *Kulturpolitik*: courtship, custodianship

2.1. Myth and realities

The topic of the occupation experience resurged in France after the period of Gaullist orthodoxy.[1] The Gaullist myth of a divided France defeated by superior weaponry and recovering its freedom and honour through heroic resistance was critically examined in a huge range of post-1968 histories.[2] A parallel surge of self-analysis occurred in Germany following reunification and the end of the Cold War. A prior parallel, between French and German contemporary writing on the subject of the occupation, cannot be drawn. Hartlaub's covert writings from Paris, no more than Jünger's, do not deal narratively with the conditions of occupation, although Hartlaub's sketch, 'Impression', is a vividly coded critique (see 5.9.). On the French side, clandestine novels, written and published during the occupation, treated the dilemma of collaboration with some discretion.[3]

The simple temptation of a human relationship could lead to a form of collaboration on a personal level. This in its literary treatment did not preclude the occupier from a sympathetic role. The plot of Vercors's (Jean Bruller) clandestinely published 1942 novel, *Le Silence de la Mer*, is that of the resolute self-imposed silence of a father and daughter towards a sympathetic German officer billeted on them.[4] Walter Bargatzky's own real-life love affair proceeded to a formal engagement, supported by the girl's parents, and a relationship of mutual esteem was formed between Bargatzky and the girl's demobilised French officer father – a Giraudist. The affair ended within a year. The girl consorted with other German officers. With Bargatzky's help she fled to Germany. Bargatzky, perplexed, continued to receive letters and greetings by post from the now three times married lady every year without fail, for forty years afterwards.[5] Real life relationships were here more complex, random, and less plot-driven than their fictional treatments, pointing to the lack of a German equivalent to the clandestine novel of the occupation period.

---

[1] Colin Nettlebeck, 'Getting the Story Right: Narratives of the Second World War in Post-1968 France', in Gerhard Hirschfeld and Patrick Marsh, *Collaboration in France. Politics and culture during the Nazi Occupation, 1940-1944* (Oxford/New York/Munich: Berg, 1989), pp.252-293 (pp.254-56).

[2] Ibid., pp.271-72.

[3] Cf. Michael Kelly, 'The View of Collaboration during the 'Après-Guerre'', in Hirschfeld and Marsh, op. cit., pp.239-51 (pp.244-45).

[4] Ibid., p.244.

[5] See Walter Bargatzky, *Hotel Majestic*, pp.113-18.

The Bargatzky romance, although it had French parental consent, had become dangerous to pursue by the Autumn of 1943.[6] That was fully two years after the incidence of sabotage and random assassination of German soldiers and officials in France had intensified after the June 1941 invasion of Russia, an intensification fomented, according to German intelligence, in communist circles.[7] Bargatzky's account of the auction of terror that followed through the execution of hostages is, on his own admission, macabre.[8] For this official of the justice ministry, whose office had to legally rubber-stamp execution orders, though it did not issue them,[9] life in occupied France was "ein ständiger Wechsel von Freude und Schrecken."[10] Tact was called for in verbal communication between acquainted occupiers and occupied, lest either be compromised, and avoidance of direct reference was tacit, as in this extreme example: while he was temporarily hospitalised, a cleaning lady, whose husband was a POW in Germany, of her own volition changed the flowers by Bargatzky's bedside every day. One morning, for the fourth or fifth time that week, they heard the execution salvos from the nearby Mont-Valérien fortress. The woman looked directly at Bargatzky, remarking only: "Ils sont beaux, les cyclamens, n'est-ce-pas?"[11] On hearing the same sound, a character in Claude Morgan's clandestinely published *La marque de l'homme* is swayed from collaboration to resistance.[12]

Bargatzky saw four succeeding states of attitude and perception: at first the mass, "korrekt, zugeknöpft, abwartend", much as Hartlaub had noted; then others ready for collaboration and eager for alliance in politics, culture, propaganda, and the black market; then a third group in the background, hostile, resistant; and then, towards the end, a fourth, delirious with thoughts of a liberating army at the gates.[13] The first days, however, once the panic had subsided and the population began to return to Paris, produced the uneasy quasi-normality which Hartlaub distilled in his sketches and eventually used to satirise its impossibility as a basis for a new order in Europe. In Bargatzky's words, it was "Der Gipfel des Absurden, daß alles ans Normale grenzt. Die Kulisse ist unversehrt, nur das Leben fehlt."[14]

Gerhard Hirschfeld observes that a history of the collaboration of the people of an occupied country is always a history of the occupying power as

---

[6] Ibid., pp.116-17.
[7] Ibid., p.83.
[8] Ibid., pp.89-90.
[9] Ibid., p.89.
[10] Ibid., p.112.
[11] Ibid., p.91.
[12] See Michael Kelly, in Hirschfeld and Marsh, *Collaboration in France*, p.244.
[13] Bargatzky, *Hotel Majestic*, p. 57.
[14] Ibid., p.59.

well.[15] Michels (1993), notes the irony of the first German cultural institute on French soil being established at a time when the two nations were still formally at war with one another.[16] Singularly, for the first time the middle of a war also, a network of German cultural institutions modelled on the *Paris Institut* was extended throughout German-allied and occupied Europe.[17] Michels concludes that these, though presenting their activities as a refined form of cultural politics, were a reflection of the high value attached by the German regime to psychological influence over populations, and that this view was reinforced by the perception that France had in the past gained more international influence by the same cultural means than her military strength should have warranted.[18] Centrally sponsored cultural activities concealed a second, more immediate purpose of the regime, that of diverting attention from the otherwise unwelcome presence of occupation forces.[19] The activities sponsored by the Paris Institute attracted an initial and enduring interest on the part of some in the French population. In explanation, Michels suggests that the shock of the sudden defeat, the relatively mild-seeming[20] terms of the armistice and the unexpectedly disciplined behaviour of the occupation troops may have led temporarily to a genuine interest by some French people in the neighbouring land and its culture.[21] A concern for their careers on the part of people on the public payroll such as teachers or administrators may have led these to deem it prudent to be seen to continue to occasionally appear at Institute-directed lectures and cultural presentations.[22] The initiative for the founding of the German Institute, Michels concludes, sprang from those German functionaries who saw in the sudden collapse of France and the ensuing lack of structured directives for the future *Frankreichpolitik* a career opportunity to direct German-French cultural relations themselves, along lines of their own determination.[23]

An affirmation of the duty of cultural protection, recognised also in WWI,[24] came from the regular army itself through its setting up in July 1940

---

[15] Hirschfeld and Marsh, *Collaboration in France*, p.7.

[16] See Eckard Michels, *Das Deutsche Institut in Paris 1940-1944* (Stuttgart: Steiner, 1993), p.63.

[17] Ibid., p.265.

[18] Ibid., p.266.

[19] Ibid., pp.60,64.

[20] For French disillusionment on this point, cf. Eberhard Jäckel, *Frankreich in Hitlers Europa. Die deutsche Frankreich Politik im Zweiten Weltkrieg* (Stuttgart: Deutsche Verlags-Anstalt, 1966).

[21] Michels, *Das Deutsche Institut in Paris*, p.263.

[22] Ibid., p.254.

[23] Ibid., p.64.

[24] See Wilhelm Treue, 'Zum nationalsozialistischen Kunstraub in Frankreich. Der

of the *Gruppe Kunstschutz*, the architectural and fine-arts protection service (hereinafter *KS*), to which were added divisions for the protection of libraries, archives and sites of antiquity. One of these sub-divisions of the *KS*, the *Referat* "*Vorgeschichte und Archäologie*",[25] undertook the card-indexing of museum and private collections of antiquities, the existence of some of which had hitherto been unknown to the French cultural authorities.[26] In addition, director of the *KS*, Prof. Dr. Franz Graf Wolff-Metternich, set up a fine-arts staff for the making of a photographic record of mediaeval French artworks, under the supervision of Professor Hamann of the University of Marburg. The photographic campaign was conducted from the beginning of October 1940 through the end of September 1941, when continuation of the work was entrusted to the Paris *Institut*.[27] A research project of the *KS* pre-history *Referat*, on the Germanic folklore of Wallonia, northern France and the German/French language-border regions, the so-called "Frankenunternehmen", was carried out with particular emphasis.[28] A scholarly undertaking, unobjectionable in itself, it begged the question of whether or not it was initiated ultimately from above, in connection with the 'Nordostline'/'Schwarze Linie'/'Führerlinie' notion of a Germanised region extending to French Flanders, Ardenne, Alsace-Lorraine and Burgundy.[29] Günther-Hornig's (1958) study which extends to the other occupied territories also, notes that the *KS* in its culture and monuments activities in Greece, realising that its assurance of freedom of activity (and, implicitly, of freedom from political interference) came from the military itself, applied itself intensively, acting through the commander-in-chief Greece, to providing reading material, lectures and guided tours for the troops, the conducted tours and winter lectures proving extremely popular: "daher widmete sich der KS beim Militärbefehlshaber in Griechenland intensiv der Belehrung der Truppe."[30] Kästner's commission from General Mayer to write *Griechenland* was granted for the same purpose of *Belehrung der Truppe*. Similarly, the *KS* service in France, coming directly under military command, would have had a guiding role in such publishing ventures as Erhard Göpel's *Die Bretagne* and *Die Normandie* (Göpel thanks specifically Count

---

„Bargatzky Bericht",' *Viertelsjahrshefte für Zeitgeschichte* no.13, vol.3 (Munich: Oldenburg, 1965), 285-337 (p.285), also Margot Günther-Hornig, *Kunstschutz in den von Deutschland besetzten Gebieten 1939-1945* (Tübingen: Institut für Besatzungsfragen Tübigen, 1958, also Bargatzky, *Hotel Majestic*, pp.64-65.

25 Günther-Hornig, op. cit., p.42.

26 Ibid., pp.43-44.

27 Ibid., p.45.

28 Ibid., p.46.

29 See Jäckel, *Frankreich in Hitlers Europa*, pp.89-90.

30 Günther-Hornig, op. cit., pp.66,67.

Metternich for the provision of some of the photographic plates reproduced in *Die Normandie*).

In the attempts by the German embassy in Paris under ambassador Abetz to remove to the embassy artworks from the Louvre and Rotschild collections, and the confiscations of the *Einsatzstab Reichsleiter Rosenberg*, both used the spurious claim of 'securing' dispersed or (where the departed owners were Jewish) 'abandoned' art collections. These activities and the personal plunderings of Göring were all resisted by the military administration in a losing rearguard action.[31] Though the *Kunstschutz* service in France had by 1942 received an enlarged remit and was henceforth known as the *Gruppe Kunst- und Kulturverwaltung*, [32] Count Metternich, who had championed the military's defence against the plunder,[33] was relieved of his post by direct order of Hitler in June 1942.[34] The motives of the military were practical, in seeking to prevent actions which would further damage French-German relations and in consequence make the task of the military administration more difficult. The military, since it formally held ultimate responsibility for all matters within the occupied zone, did not want its reputation undeservedly sullied by the actions of others.[35] The 'Bargatzky report', drafted in January 1945 with reference to the Paris *Kunstschutz* files, documents how the military, fearing an outright political fiat from Berlin, had relied on objections based on grounds of competence and procedural authority when resisting the intrusions of other agencies.[36] Bargatzky claims for the military that though appropriated French artworks were to be seen furnishing German offices in Paris and even in the embassy itself, not a single such painting or piece of sculpture was be found at the military administration headquarters in the Hotel Majestic.[37] Though the Rosenberg *Einsatzstab* arrived in Greece also, directly after the German invasion, and undertook archaeological excavations of its own without reference to the military's *Kunstschutz* service, only a single large-scale Greek artwork in the care of the *KS* was expropriated to Germany, whereupon the head of the service in Greece asked to be relieved of his duties.[38] Within the military administrations, whether as exemplary of good discipline or for the instruction of garrison soldiers where conspicuous *Korrektheit* was the public

---

[31] Cf. Treue, 'Der Bargatzky Bericht', loc. cit.

[32] Günther-Hornig, op. cit., p.37.

[33] See Hildegard Brenner, *Die Kunstpolitik des Nationalsozialismus* (Reinbeck bei Hamburg: Rowohlt, 1963), pp.146,150.

[34] Günther-Hornig, op. cit., p.34.

[35] See Treue, 'Bargatzy Bericht', loc. cit., pp.298-99.

[36] Ibid., p.298.

[37] Ibid., p.299.

[38] Günther-Hornig, op. cit., pp.73-74.

political policy (in grotesque contrast to the policy of national dissolution pursued in Slavic Poland)[39] or whether out of concern for military's own self image and international reputation (reports of art plundering had appeared in the American press already in 1940),[40] there was therefore a corresponding readiness to promote cultural appreciation in the form of literary output by and for German servicemen.

2.2. France: the centrality of Paris

The image of occupation soldiers in uniform, at their easels, capturing Paris on canvas, is well-known. Two major art exhibitions of such art were mounted (one by the *Luftwaffe*) and reproductions of the exhibited works, some in colour, appeared in *Frankreich, ein Erlebnis des deutschen Soldaten*, a limited-edition collection of essays by German servicemen writers which appeared with a foreword by *Generalleutnant* Schaumburg, commandant of the *Gross-Paris* military region, in May 1942.[41] The publication contained also, besides extracts from Ernst Jünger's *Gärten und Straßen* which was published in French translation in the same year, as *Jardins et routes*, essays on the regions of France, from Flanders to the Pyrénées, and two essays celebrating Paris in particular. The collection, conceived as a literary follow-up to one of the exhibitions, '*Kunst der deutschen Wehrmacht in Paris*', of early Autumn 1941, offers exemplars of the contemporary perceptual framework of educated German witnesses within a *Weltanschauung* that might still, to that point, before hindsight had made the determining consequences of the reversal before Moscow in the winter of 1941 apparent to all, admit of the plausibility of a new civil order in a unified Europe. Laval and Darlan, after all, had bid for a place in this new order with their *Plan d'un ordre nouveau en France* of April 1941 (only to have it impressed on them afterwards, in the light of the paramountcy of the needs of *Barbarossa*, that France's role was to be that of a supplier).[42] The editor and, as the frontispiece calligraphy says, instigator of *Frankreich* was a *Hauptmann* Heinz Lorenz, the same who in the following year edited *Soldaten fotografieren Frankreich: ein Bilderbuch mit Erzählungen*, also the product of an exhibition, 'Soldaten fotografieren und filmen', staged in Paris in the Spring of 1942. Lorenz was later press secretary under *Reichspressechef* Otto Dietrich. With a print run of just two thousand, *Frankreich* is not conceived as propaganda for wide dissemination,

---

39 Cf. Hildegard Brenner, *Die Kunstpolitik des Nationalsozialismus*, pp.131-41.

40 See Treue, 'Bargatzky Bericht', loc. cit., p.299.

41 *Frankeich*, ed. by Heinz Lorenz (Paris: Ode, 1942); cf. Tewes, *Frankreich in der Besatzungszeit*, pp.233-35.

42 See Jäckel, *Frankreich in Hitlers Europa*, p.160ff.

even within the military, but propaganda it is, of a culturally self-persuasive kind.

The contributors are, so the frontispiece-text on the book's provenance, serving in France *um die Freiheit Deutschlands und die Neugestaltung Europas*. Lt. General Schaumburg's introduction begins: "Der Waffenstillstand im Walde von Compiègne war geschlossen." An *armistice* had been signed. The military reality is tactfully elided. Affectionate words follow: the German soldier had in the meantime come to know "die lieblichen Gefilde der Île de France [...] die Herbheit des normannisch-bretonischen Küstengebietes, den üppigen Garten der Touraine, die grünen Rebenhänge Burgunds und die weite Landschaft der nordöstlichen Provinzen." The same soldier is portrayed as a cultural tourist who has sought contact with the French people and language, visited the cathedrals and châteaux, "bestaunte die in den Städten aufgehäuften Kunst- und Kulturschätze" (here General Schaumburg grants more to the French provinces than one contributor allows: Gert Buchheit's essay, 'Erlebnis einer Hauptstadt', considers the unchallenged cultural pre-eminence of Paris among French cities and contrarily concludes that Germany's history of fragmented states had bestowed on it the compensation of provincial cities that were the cultural equals of *its* capital, Berlin). Editor Lorenz in his piece, 'Der Rhythmus von Paris', regards the cosmopolitan aspect of Paris as a distortion of the true nature of the native Parisians, a "Zerrbild" that smacks of the socialist ferment in Berlin after the end of the First World War, "Kaffeehausparlamentarismus", and condescendingly wishes in conclusion that Paris, "*im Gefüge eines neuen europäischen Staatenbundes*" (italics added), will remain as ever, 'Paris'.

Günther Rehbein's essay, 'Schlösser der Île France', remarks *inter alia* that the more formally orthodox style of palatial building known as French classicism, being more modest and restrained, "keuscher, verhaltener", was therefore "uns Deutschen vielleicht näher." The theory of French centralisation was familiar, "der uns geläufigen These von der französischen Zentralisierung", and had prepared the visitors, falsely, it is pointed out, for a picture of monotonous uniformity: "so fanden wir vieles daran zu berichtigen." It is noted that Marie Antoinette forsook palaces for a make-believe pastoral parkland idyll and that Napoleon, "der grosse Organisator", built nothing new in that regard and contented himself with the renovating Malmaison. The Sun king had found the cold resplendence of Versailles too much in the end and had the *Grand Trianon* built as his retreat, his successor in turn disdaining that and erecting the *Petit Trianon*. In the history of such great building works is "die Geschichte menschlicher Grösse, Sehnsucht und Schwäche" to be found. *Overreaching* is hinted at, with unwitting irony, though the significance of the buildings, their history and that of their builder-occupants is conveyed in economic, vivid sketches with scholarly assurance.

An *Oberstleutnant* Walter Chompton elects to make an examination of Touraine, particularly of the power-plays of its history, in an attempt to define the patriotic expression "La douce France". The French have not burdened the Loire with busy steamers and rattling dredgers as the Germans would have done, "*weil wir so müssen nach unserem Gesetz*" (italics added). The struggles of the nobles had not altered the land; its people loved still the land above (implicitly) *any* rulers, "*weil sie müssen nach mütterlichem Gesetz*" (italics added). The contrast implied between the two governing forms of *Gesetz* is nonetheless a patronising one. The author earlier refers to the original "dreigeteilte Wurzel des keltisch-römisch-germanischen Erbguts" forming in later history one *Stamme*, this now consigned (so his conclusion would make it appear) to bucolic relegation.

The contribution of poet and serving *Propagandakompanie* reporter, Kurt Kölsch, 'Traumland Burgund', refers at the outset to the migration of the Germanic Burgundians (though not to their successors, the Germanic Franks). The cleanliness of his lodgings, on the outskirts of Beaune in sight of its famous vineyards, impressed: "glänzte von Sauberkeit wie nie zuvor oder nachher in Frankreich, eine Beobachtung, die man übrigens oft in Burgund und insbesondere in den bäuerlich besiedelten Gegenden, "*wo sich vielleicht mehr von dem germanischen Element erhalten hat*, machen kann." (italics added). This last observation may be prompted by the author's earlier expressed surprise at "die Ähnlichkeit dieser Landschaft mit meiner pfälzischen und westmärkischen Heimat" – or not. On the rise and fall of the independent Duchy of Burgundy, the Burgundian Netherlands and Luxembourg: "Geschichte und Kunst in diesem Land floss mir zusammen zu einem Bild stolzen und aufrechten Menschentums, das sich erhöht hatte über die Flachheit westlerischen Denkens und das darum in dem Frankreich der vergangenen Zeit zugrunde gehen musste!" The use of the anti-democratic term *westlerisch*, a borrowing from the revolutionary theorist Ernst Niekisch, begs the question of what model of thinking is here applauded.

'Wiedersehen mit Flandern', the contribution of Jürgen Hahn-Butry, author, propagandist and founder of the association of First World War soldier-authors, *Die Mannschaft*, recalls an experience of that war. The flat and empty cornfields of the Ukraine had seemed surprisingly alien to the author, himself a native of the flat North Sea landscape of *Niederdeutschland*, and now like Kölsch also a *Kriegsberichter*. A recollection of the shell-flattened levels of French Flanders and of a youthful, 17 year-old infatuation with a farmer's daughter and of a recent journey to re-locate the site and the burial place of farmer and daughter, both later unfortunate victims of British shelling, awakens a longing. A sentimental tale, but with a political sub-text: the old French-Flemish farmer of those years had been aware that "sein Land einst zum »dütschen Riek« gehört habe!" His younger successor of 1941 speaks French only and is embarrassed to admit that as a child he, too, spoke Flemish, but makes the conciliatory concession that "er müsse es nun wohl erst wieder lernen, meinte er schliesslich *versöhnlich*" (italics added). Evidently, the plans for a greater German *Reich* encompassing all the Germanic lands, including French Flanders, are known to or intuited by the young landowner.

The traces of propagandistic preconditioning evident in the above mentioned contributions are absent in the contribution of Aachen museums director Felix Kuetgens,[43] who writes of an at times precarious and giddying climb into the heights of Rheims cathedral. Encountering the handiwork of the mediaeval master stone-carvers literally face-to-face, as his title, 'Gotiker sehen dich an', suggests, Dr. Kuetgens acknowledges that he is there in fulfilment of the obligations of the "Kunstschutz in Frankreich" service. No comparisons are made or invited with German gothic: the "Gotiker" are pre-existent to the modern nation states. A *Major* Hugo Cadenbach, most probably the same distinguished postwar banker and leading figure in business and cultural life of that name, of Aachen also, writes a charming account of a voyage by punt through the dune-locked lagoons, *étangs*, of the Côte d'Argent in the Pyrenean south west corner of France. The wartime background is echoed only in casual metaphor: occasional lone pines which "gleichsam als Wächter seewärts die Ausschau halten", and the Courant d'Huchet, the outflow channel of the Étang de Léon, which breaches to the sea "in erneutem Ansturm, an einer schwachen Dünenstelle."

The diary extracts of Ernst Jünger date from late June to early July of 1940, the weeks immediately after the armistice, and deal, in Jünger's inimitable botanical style of studying the human species, with life on the march. Gerhardt Nebel's essay is one of the longer among the ten in the book and postulates a figuratively feminine nature for France: "Dass der Franzose *ganz anders als wir* ein Wesen der Gesellschaft ist, wurde von der weiblichen Gottheit bewirkt, die über die französische Erde herrscht." (italics added). National stereotyping sits uneasily amid the romantic hyperbole. Nebel, (1903-1974), an admirer of Jünger and a writer on classical philosophy, argues that Germany and France are opposite and complementary: the one young, undaunted and masculine in nature, the other essentially feminine and with the acquired scepticism of maturity. If the register is that of romantic fantasy, the tone is inescapably patronising.

---

[43] Dr. Kuetgens continued as director of the Aachen museums service after the war: cf. Tewes, op. cit., p.231.

Germany and France are inextricably bound together, by their wars, mutual occupations and ceding of provinces, as "Träger der beiden letzten grossen Kulturen des Abendlandes" – Anglo-Saxon culture forms a conspicuously absent third. The French have an entirely different relationship to order, organisation and bureaucracy: "Eine totale fehlerlose Organisation ist ihnen unheimlich und wohl auch unerträglich, und etwas Anarchie nicht nur liebenswert, sondern geradezu notwendig." They value being, out of which achievement comes, more than the achievement itself: "Auch schätzen sie die Leistung nicht so hoch ein; höher steht ihnen das Sein, aus dem die Leistung quillt", but they are "zu skeptisch und zu realistisch, um gute Bürokraten zu sein." This is not the implicit claim to superiority it might be, for Nebel concludes the passage with a stinging condemnation of the passion for order: "erst wo die Seele ein Chaos geworden ist, werden Aktenschränke und Karteien zu metaphysischen Bedürfnissen." Nebel was already somewhat of an intellectual dissident, in that his essay of the previous year, 1941, 'Auf dem Fliegerhorst',[44] had likened Luftwaffe aircraft to scaly flying insects and had further developed the analogy to compare the modern mechanised state to an organised colony, such as that of termites or of jellyfish, in which all individuality is subordinated. Indeed, Nebel's *Frankreich* essay bears the revolutionary title "Marianne", with quotation marks, and the sub-title 'über einen Zug des französischen Wesens.' Besides familiarity with the subject, he writes, a certain distance is needed; the everyday is not perceptible, and one comes to knowledge of one's own people only by the study of another:

> Wer über eine nationale Eigentümlichkeit urteilen will [...] muss [...] über einen gewissen Abstand von ihr verfügen. [...] so weiss ich über mein eigenes Volk nichts, wenn ich nicht Erfahrungen mit anderen Nationen machen, also vergleichen konnte, und für die Besonderheit des andern Volkes bleibe ich blind, solange ich mich im Gestrüpp des Allzumenschlichen herumschlage.

A distance from the *Gestrüpp des Allzumenschlichen*, the undergrowth of the human hurly-burly, was also a distinguishing feature of Felix Hartlaub's writings: the 22 year old Hartlaub admits in a letter from 1935[45] to an ever-lively sociological and anthropogeographic interest. Nebel purports to see the effects of the differing national history-lines in physiognomy:

> ...wenn man deutsche und französische Gesichter vergleicht, [...] die einen: breitflächig, mit entweder verschwimmenden oder harten Kontouren, bei weitem noch nicht zu Ende gearbeitet, Rohmaterial, an dem noch Jahrhunderte und

---

[44] See Nebel, 'Auf dem Fliegerhorst,' in *Von den Elementen* (Wuppertal: Im Marées Verlag, 1947), pp.120-25; first published in *Neue Rundschau* 52 (1941) pp.606-08.

[45] See Krauss, *Felix Hartlaub: in seinen Briefen*, p.149.

> mannigfache Schicksale tätig sein können, unempfindlich, schwerfällig; die andern: jede Fläche gleichsam bis zur Linie verfeinert und aufgebraucht, beweglich, witternd, weich, luftig.

In support of his premise that the defining difference between France and Germany is that between the feminine and masculine natures, the following:

> Wer mit offenen Sinnen Räume betritt, in denen das Französische herrscht, wird sich niemals der starken Beimischung von Weiblichkeit entziehen können, die hier zu finden ist.

Nebel adds that the French are the only European people to have placed a woman, Jeanne d'Arc, at the centre of their national myth – Delacroix's *Liberté* is not mentioned.

In another essay, also published in Paris in 1942, 'Paris und das Wasser'[46], Nebel, pointing out that the ancient name of the settlement, Lutetia, refers to water and marsh and that the name of the old aristocratic centre, the Marais, does the same, stresses the fluvial character of the city that owed its foundation to the crossing of the Seine waterway with the Roman road from Orléans to Rheims. Felix Hartlaub, too, refers affectionately to the Parisians as the *Lutetier*. Nebel, in his 1940 essay on the elements, 'Von Inseln, Flüssen und Bergen',[47] writes of the Rhine that it mediates between East and West in that it unites the German concept of the forest with French notion of the garden. More contentiously, in the same passage: "Hier begegnen die beiden letzten Kulturen Europas, die französische und die deutsche, einander."[48] This notable second omission of Anglo-Saxon culture would be valid in the context of a continental Europe, but coincides unfortunately with the propaganda view of Britain as a rival, colonial, overseas power. It is the elemental, however, which is of paramount interest to Nebel; hence, in 'Paris und das Wasser':

> ...die Seine [...] bringt in das Starre und Zerrissene der Häusermassen eine glatte, schmelzende und elementare Fläche hinein. [...] so verwundert es nicht, daß Brücken und Quais zu den wesentlichen Schönheiten der Stadt gerechnet werden.[49]

The description of the elemental is here very similar to those of Hartlaub's Paris sketches with the riverside titles 'Hochwasser', 'Quai', 'Lustbarke' and 'Ufer, draussen.' These, in their still, detail-saturated prose style are among Hartlaub's most lyrical and, because of their deliberate quietude, the most

---

[46] See Nebel, *Von den Elementen*, pp.32-34 and p.32 (note).
[47] Originally published in *Monatschrift* 42 (1940); see contents index, *Von den Elementen*.
[48] Nebel, *Von den Elementen*, p.27.
[49] Ibid., p.33.

poignantly anti-war in sentiment. Only in 'Ufer, draussen' is the war as menace alluded to, and then only as a distant irritant: "Und das ewige Flugzeug, das unsichtbar in den Wolken sucht und bohrt, wie eine zornige, flachköpfige Wespe."[50]

It is the eclectic biographer (Rilke, von Papen, Mussolini) and historian, then *Oberleutnant*, Gert Buchheit,[51] who seeks to come to grips architectonically with that which had evoked from Hartlaub a succession of of sharply detailed and subtly hued impressions of strongly individual facades optically cohering into a fluid yet distinctive overall Lutetian style. Buchheit, in his contribution 'Erlebnis einer Hauptstadt', sees even the high-mansarded, shoulder-to-shoulder standing housing blocks of the Paris *banlieu* as seeming to orient themselves under the power of an unseen magnetic needle towards the centre and to order themselves so that they appear to be of an "aus unbestreitbarem formalen Instinkt geborenen Bautypus." The orderly accentuation of the horizontal is balanced by an anarchic struggle in the vertical: fields of masonry uprights, an accumulation of windows and a host of chimneys create an infectious upward movement of gripping monotony, "eine mitreissende Aufwärtsbewegung von packender Monotonie." Where Hartlaub saw a metaphorically unconquerable alternative earthscape in "Dächermeer", "Kaminwald" and "Schiefergebirge",[52] Buchheit's surreal simile and personification convey simply a roof-top disorder straining away from the centralising order of the streetplan:

> Wie eine aberwitzige Vegetation aus vierkantigen und runden Schäften, aus blechernen und tönernen Röhren, so stechen diese Kamine von Paris in die Luft, und auch die blaugrauen Dächer selbst wirken irgendwie fremdartig, denn meist sind sie kniestockmässig umbrochen, gleichsam angewölbt, als wollten sie Kuppeln werden.

Hartlaub, whose early drawings are marked by the grotesque, could see something reptilian in the roof of the Hotel Sully, "das Dach mit seinen tausend Schieferschuppen",[53] and in fusing the blue-grey of the zinc and lead Paris roofs with atmospheric hues from the Paris sky coined many compounds which form in his work a mood theme that is examined later in

---

[50] Ewenz I (2002/2007), p.98.

[51] Cf. Buchheit, *Rainer Maria Rilke, Stimmen der Freunde* (Freiburg im Breisgau: Urban, 1931); *Franz von Papen, eine politische Biographie* (Freiburg im Breisgau: Bergstadt, 1933); *Mussolini und das neue Italien* (Berlin: Büchergilde Gutenberg, 1938).

[52] Ewenz I (2002/2007), pp.120/121,72-73/72,98.

[53] Ibid. (2002/2007), p.100.

this study. Buchheit, too, is alert to colour, seeing it as distinctively apparent in the awnings and sun-blinds of Paris:

> die Markise, man kann sie nicht wegdenken von dieser Stadt. Weissgrau, lawendelblau [sic], auch mit Weiss und Rot gestreift, hin und wieder auch ockergelb wie die Segel der Adria- Fischerboote

While sharing Hartlaub's appreciation of the visual, Buchheit sees also in the geometric ordering of the Paris street layout an aspect of French centralisation under the revolutionary diktats of equality and fraternity – an enforced equality and fraternity of building style:

> Die Beschränkung des Baustils auf ein sehr einfaches geometrisches System offenbart ein Dienstbewusstsein [...] ein Dienstbewusstsein weniger gegenüber der inneren Struktur des Hauses, wie es z.B. in den italienischen Renaissancepalästen so klar vor Augen tritt, als vielmehr dem Stadtbild, dem Stadtganzen selbst gegenüber. [...] diese Unterordnung unter ein höheres Gesetz der »égalité et fraternité« ist schliesslich so stark, dass sie alle Stile als ein Verwandtes miteinander verbindet und dadurch dem Stadtbild von Paris seine einzigartige Einheit verleiht.

The ordering of both the inner and outer city is geometrically functional, but bestows on Paris a communal *Grundakkord.* Buchheit adds that the monumental of no particular era dominates the city, other than is the case in Augustan in Rome or the Munich of Ludwig I; rather, a multi-epochal style with here and there a distinctive domestic monument as in the red-bricked, stone-framed *Henri IV* Place des Vosges with its steep-slated roofs. In conclusion, Buchheit sees in this subsumption of styles a concentration of all intellectual life in one city, something which its fragmented history had prevented in Germany: "Wer würde in Deutschland Wien oder Hamburg, Dresden oder Köln als Provinz bezeichnen? Oder wer würde umgekehrt behaupten wollen, dass Berlin als Kulturstätte die Gesamtheit der deutschen Kultur umfasse?" The contrast is at least even-handed, even if the inclusion of Vienna as a city in *Deutschland* speaks to the times. Paris fares very well in the benign commentaries of the *Frankreich* contributors, and nowhere is so crass a judgement made as the following:

> So wurde Paris wieder zur großen Mitte, zur denkerisichen Zentrale, die das Ausmaß des Krieges durch einen unaufhörlichen Prozeß fluktuierender Arbeit *vor der Stagnation des Bürokratismus bewahrt.* (italics added)

So the pronouncement of Guido K. Brand, whose 1942 tour of *Organisation Todt* undertakings in France prompted the unflattering claim.[54] In contrast,

---

[54] Guido K. Brand, *Zwischen Domen und Bunkern. Westeindrücke eines OT-Kriegsberichters*

Buchheit's essay establishes that for German intellectuals, Paris, as the single cultural metropolis of France, held a special rank and commanded an intellectual rigour when addressed in print.

As Tewes (1998) has observed, *Frankreich* is the work of experts who present themselves as admirers of France and who give witness for the most part through romantic transfiguration.[55] For the greater part the book is such a work, and is marred only incidentally by lapses which betray an absorption, in cases perhaps unconscious, of the propaganda of expansion and hegemony. *Frankreich* is thus a benchmark of conventional liberalism against which the egregious originality of Kästner and Hartlaub may be measured.

A moral objector may with justice point out that it was the same General Schaumburg who (deputising in the absence of his superior, Otto von Stülpnagel, who would later resign on the same issue) on 22 August 1941 proclaimed in reaction to the assassination of a German naval official that all French detainees held for whatever reason would henceforth be considered hostages liable to execution in the event of any such future attacks.[56] The moral objection is not diminished by the fact that the hostage shootings which followed, particularly in the period from September 1941 to May 1942, thereafter moderated in number,[57] and though as occurrences shocking to the French public and worsening of popular mood, had little overall effect on the totality of Franco-German relations.[58] In the German military administration conservative elderly officers and officials, framed by the values of the pre 1914 era, gave the tone. In the embassy there was a younger generation, shaped by the less rigid Weimar era, and almost all of whom were well acquainted with French matters and honestly well disposed towards German-French understanding, but at the same time nationalist in outlook and convinced of a German culture superior to the Western liberal model.[59] The contradiction between the absolutist hegemonic nature of the ultimate political intentions towards France of the regime in Germany and the sentiments of individual members of the German military and civil administration and legation service in France (Abetz was not formally accredited to Vichy) was succinctly expressed in Abetz's formulation: "Man müsse nicht erst den Krieg gewinnen wollen, um dann Europa zu schaffen; man müsse im Gegenteil Europa schaffen, um den Krieg zu gewinnen."[60]

(Amsterdam: Volk und Reich, 1944), p.74.

[55] Tewes, *Frankreich in der Besatzungszeit*, p.233.

[56] See Jäckel, *Frankreich in Hitlers Europa*, pp.186-87,194.

[57] Ibid., pp.197-98.

[58] Ibid., p.198.

[59] Ibid., p.70.

[60] Ibid., p.218.

The ambassador's conviction that co-operation was more fruitful than coercion did not imply partnership for France; rather, as he had earlier envisaged it, the role of honoured subordinate retaining an undiminished agro-economy, viniculture, and fashion and leisure industries, but with its heavy industry deliberately weakened.[61] Friedrich Sieburg, attached to the Abetz embassy, and whose 1929 *Gott in Frankreich?* had popularised in Germany just such a patronising view of a nation deemed humanist to a fault, in a March 1941 lecture reminded intellectuals of the *Groupe Collaboration* that in his, Sieburg's, previous lectures of 1936 and 1937 he had sought to impress on his French audiences that the emerging world transformation was no diabolic invention of the Nazi regime, but an 'almost cosmic' (read: preordained) world development. *Gott in Frankreich?* had been, so Sieburg, a book *about Germany*.[62] Sieburg's intellectual canvassing of 1941 might cast the suspicion on the Francophile essay contributors to *Frankreich* that they too are writing through didactic inversion about Germany, not France. Such a reading would be profound to the point of cynicism if applied to the *Frankreich* contributors on whom, it may be suggested, a process of occupation-normalisation may already have been at work.

Sartre remarks that the artificial social and cultural existence which the Germans upheld in Paris: the theatrical seasons, the horse racing, the macabre-seeming fine art and literary festivals, all had the simple purpose of showing to the world that France was in good health, that Paris still lived. A curious consequence, Sartre observes wryly, of the French policy of centralisation.[63] The occupation was, Sartre insists, an enormous social phenomenon that affected 53 million human beings.[64] Although the vast majority of the population held back from any contact with the German army there yet developed a kind of bashful and indefinable solidarity among the Parisians with the German *Landsers*, whom they found to be basically so alike their French army counterparts, but it was a solidarity unaccompanied by liking or sympathy; rather a solidarity based on the sheer biological habituation of rubbing shoulders with them in the daily round of necessities.[65] Even towards the German military administration and uniformed-official class, some of which the rational mind knew with certainty to be responsible for the night-time raids and arrests – Sartre adds that there was no one in Paris of whom a friend or relative had not been

---

[61] Ibid., p.70.

[62] Ibid.., p.69, and Schonauer, *Deutsche Literatur im Dritten Reich*, pp.172-73.

[63] *Jean-Paul Sartre. Paris unter der Besatzung. Artikel, Reportagen, Aufsätze 1944-1945*, ed. By Hanns Grössel (Reinbek bei Hamburg: Rowohlt, 1980) [from the French original, 'Paris sous l'occupation', *La France libre* (London) no. 49 (15 November 1944)], p.46.

[64] Ibid., p.40.

[65] Ibid., pp.41-42.

arrested, abducted, or shot – it was impossible, as they appeared in their daytime briefcase-carrying guise hurrying like so many lawyers to their offices, to sustain the night-time feelings of wild hate.[66] The German uniforms in their faded, pale and unassuming green became an almost expected spot of colour amid the dark civilian clothing, which as a mass simply opened and closed about them.[67] An inevitable process of normalisation had begun, even though, as Sartre points out, the familiar occupiers would have been mercilessly cut down had the order to do so been issued (and the means provided).[68] The normalisation process in Sartre's view has nothing to do with the phenomenon of collaboration, which he believes to be universal and deriving from pre-existing defects in social integration.[69] While discounting some literary hyperbole in Sartre's account – Bargatzky's four-level analysis is more discriminating – the assumption of a corresponding process of normalisation in the perceptions of the individual German occupier is plausible. The authorial intentions of the contributors to *Frankreich*, with the possible exception of the Jünger diary excerpts, may equally plausibly be assumed to have been in the process of forming within that paradigmatic paradox of human solidarity.

2.3. Greece: apprehending the antique

While *Frankreich* reads in parts, ironically, as the projections of German Romanticists, the occupation of Greece summoned up in the main the efforts of German classicists. Besides a series of leaflets of the *Kunstschutz* service whose cumulative print runs totalled almost half a million,[70] official guides to Greece and to the settings of the antique were also published in book format: *Hellas*,[71] a collection of academic articles, in 1943, and *Der Peloponnes* in 1944.[72] The introduction to *Hellas* by Walther Wrede, the first director of the Athens branch of the German archaeological institute, with whom and with whose writings Kästner was acquainted,[73] was not found in

---

66 Ibid., p.43-44.

67 Ibid., p.41.

68 Ibid.

69 Sartre, 'Was ist ein Kollaborateur,' in Grössel, op. cit., p.61 [from the French original, 'Qu'est-ce qu'un collaborateur?' in *La Republique française* (New York) year 2, no. 8, August 1945].

70 See Hiller von Gaertringen (1994), pp.136-37.

71 *Hellas. Bilder zur Kultur des Griechentums*, ed. by Hans von Schoenebeck and Wilhelm Kraiker (Burg bei Magdeburg: August Hopfer, 1943); see Hiller von Gaertringen (1994), pp.137,139.

72 *Der Peloponnes. Landschaft, Geschichte, Kunststätten* (Athens: LXVIII Army Corps, 1944); see Hiller von Gaertringen (1994), pp.153-55.

73 See Hiller von Gaertringen (1994), pp.106,175,526.

otherwise securely re-bound university library copies consulted by this author:

> Was der Deutsche hier sucht, was ihn immer wieder bannt [...] die Spuren [...] eines Erbes, von dem er etwas in sich trägt; das Vermächtnis eines Volkes, das verwandtem Blut entstammte und sein Dasein zur höchsten dem Menschen erreichbaren Veredelung steigerte.[74]

The ideological claim is further amplified: "uns Heutigen, die wir unser Dasein auf seinen *natürlichen* Grundgesetzen neu aufbauen wollen"[75] (italics added). The overtly ideological introduction – Wrede may elsewhere be seen in full party uniform, replete with jackboots, conducting a group of German staff officers about the Acropolis of Athens[76] – belies the scholarly quality of the contributions of German archaeologists and German Graecophile academics. The articles, diagrams and illustrations for this souvenir volume[77] were virtually all ready by December 1941,[78] but sanctioning of scarce paper supplies was delayed until 1943.[79] The general tenor of the work is evident from the titles of the exclusively doctoral contributions: 'Die Göttergestalten', 'Das Heldentum in Homers Ilias', 'Aus Griechenlands Geschichte', 'Das Heiligtum', 'Der Tempel', 'Das Theater', 'Olympia', 'Die Akropolis von Athen', 'Zur griechischen Plastik', 'Attische Gefässmalerei', 'Das byzantinische Griechentum', 'Die Rede des Perikles für die Gefallenen.'[80] The contribution of Andreas Rumpf on Greek theatre points out that the Greek theatres in stone of the fourth century BC as at Epidauros and Priene appeared generations after the lives of Aeschylus, Sophocles, Euripides, and Aristophanes, and that drama itself emerged first in 534 BC, in Athens, when Thespis introduced respondents, the first 'actors', to the what had until then been a sacred chorus.[81] Ernst Buschor's contribution on Greek sculpture, 'Zur griechischen Plastik', sees in the grace of the balanced, single-axis marble figures of the early style a connection with the especially profound life-stratum, "Lebensschicht", portrayed.[82] Co-editor Wilhem Kraiker's contribution on Greek vase painting, 'Attische Gefässmalerei', illustrates how the portrayal of nobility in human emotion came to displace mythic-heroic content, and progressed to the portrayal of

---

[74] Schoenebeck & Kraiker, *Hellas*, p.3.
[75] Ibid.
[76] See Marchand, *Down from Olympus*, p.346.
[77] See Hiller von Gaertringen (1994), p.137.
[78] Ibid.
[79] Ibid.
[80] Schoenebeck & Kraiker, *Hellas*, index.
[81] Ibid., pp.55-61.
[82] Ibid., p.85

reflection and inner preoccupation, before the art fell victim to its own success through mass production.[83] The thrust of these contributions is to evidence the Greek foundation of humanist, Western civilisation. A rhetoric of repossession and custodianship as though by right of succession to other Danubians: the Achaean, Ionian and Dorian – or by right of German scholarship – cannot be read as implicit in the individual texts.

Hiller von Gaertringen, however, (1994, p.161) singles out the contribution of Ernst Kirsten on the history of Greece (*Hellas*, pp.19-26) as explicitly racial-biological and anti-democratic. The Greeks as such, in contradistinction to the pre-existing populations, had migrated southwards from the Danube basin "als indogermanisches, im wesentlichen nordisch bestimmtes Volk" (*Hellas*, p.19). Kirsten stresses that new perspectives on the phylogeny of the Greek people had emerged: "neue Wege zum Verständnis" (p.20). Kirsten's exposition actually offers, rather, a *socio*-biological rationale for the evolution of Greek history. His argument is that creative power and the will to rule, "Schöpfungskraft und Herrscherwillen", resided always in the governing elites, from the Mycenaeans onwards, while cultural values (in the sense of tradition) and civil values were preserved through the perseverance of the passive elements in the native populations (p.22). The intensification of trading activity, originally introduced by the "Semitic" Phoenicians (p.22), led to the granting of equal citizenship – to those who through trading wealth could aspire to it: Kirsten draws a comparison to the rise of the guilds in the middle ages. This Grecian democracy was "nur eine erweiterte Oligarchie" (p.25). The latest of the invaders, the Dorians, now Spartans in their warrior-state mode, won the Peloponnesian war, but lost the future to the economically more progressive 'democratic' states (p.23). Yet, while exemplifying the socio-cultural development of the 6th century Ionian *colonial* cities where "in der Begründung aller Wissenschaften auf ionischem Boden ihre Krönung fand", Kirsten asserts that it was the rapid interpenetration of races there which denied duration to this flowering of creativity: "Doch die rasche Mischung mit allen fremden, *ja fremdrassischen Elementen* in der Demokratie versagte dieser Schöpferkraft die Dauer" (p.24, [italics added]). The analysis is nonetheless, up to its conclusion, consequential and unsentimental: the Greeks were themselves by the coming of Philip of Macedon "durch ihre Herkunft reif" to become a subject people (p.25). The successors of Philip bowed to the Franks, and theirs to the Turks (p.26). The irony is not lost on Kirsten that the Greek language survived only through the existence of an unchanging (in political status) underclass, but this underclass "hat Geschichte nur erfahren und erlitten, nicht gelebt" and was the antithesis of

[83] Ibid., pp.88-96.

cultural achievement: "Ihre weltgeschichtliche Rolle ist die des Gegenbildes einer Kulturleistung, die in Sternenstunden der Menscheit gerade dieser gestaltlosen Masse gegenüber die reinste Form menschlicher Wertentfaltung gefunden hat." In all Greek ages, so Kirsten, only an aristocracy and a ruling class had been creative; their freedom to be so, he stresses, always resting on hegemony over a Helot class: "Schöpferisch war auf griechischem Boden allzeit nur eine Aristokratie, eine Erobererschicht, die Unfreien, Heloten oder Sklaven, gegenübertrat." (p.26), thus "ein nordisches Herrenvolk" had built on southern soil models of perfect attainment. So the buildings of the Acropolis speak "zu den vom Nordland Kommenden" with the same youthful clarity and freshness of the time of their creation (p.26). The attainment of the classical ideal was unique, as were the socio-political conditions that allowed of it (Kirsten does not stress the religious imperatives). Admiration for the ideal is justified through an evolutionary, as though it were a matter of evidential fact, line of argument – a not illegitimate premise, but it is the concluding presumption of association and, more sinisterly, an implicit suggestion of socio-political emulation which are objectionable. The Athenian ideals celebrated in Thucydides' account of the speech of Perikles for the fallen of Athens are summarised by Kirsten as "die Gesetze des natürlichen politischen Zusammenlebens in edler Menschlichkeit, der Abgestimmtheit des einen auf den anderen im Staate, der Harmonie" (p.24). That the same Athenian citizen-democracy rested on a slave economy is expressly acknowledged, "Ohne die Sklaverei ist das aristokratisch-vornehme Leben der Bürger der attischen Demokratie nicht denkbar" (p.25). Kirsten's concluding evaluation of the Greek achievement is sociologically stark; his insistence on the determining force of a "nordisches Herrenvolk" (p.26) addresses the antique historical context, but uttered within the covers of a publication such as *Hellas*, invokes at the very least a mode of thinking formed in nineteenth century concepts of colonial expansion, concepts not yet abandoned by the early 1940's, even among the Western democracies.

A matter-of-fact, erudite style is what most distinguishes the scholarly contributions of *Hellas* from the ephemeral, straining-at-the-metaphysical impressions which characterise Erhart Kästner's *Griechenland*. More than a matter of writing style is in question. Carl Weickert's contribution on the Greek temple is a case in point: illustrated with architectural diagrams and referencing photographic plates in the appendix, Weickert starts from a different premise. Whereas Kästner emphasises that the natural sites of the temples and their surrounding aura were sacred long before temples were erected,[84] Weickert sees in the temple the expression of the idea that what

[84] See Kästner, *Griechenland* (1943), p.18.

attained perfection, be that something that was perfectly *made*, was sacred: "denn jeder Körper ist dem Griechen heilig, wenn er Vollkommenheit erlangt. So baut er seinen Tempel" (*Hellas*, p.36). The only reference to Northern influence is to the rectangular pattern of the temple plan, deriving from the wooden structures of the original Northern homeland (p.36). Perfection, to be appreciated, must be demonstrable, and in the Doric order the necessary precision of balance between support and burden, between vertical and horizontal, the fundamental motif of all architecture, was most evident and least obscured by ornamentation (p.39). In the Doric temple was pure architecture which contained within it the laws of eternal validity; it was the gift of humankind to the divinity (p.44). In the Parthenon, stereometric correction was built into the structure so that it would appear perfect from the viewing angle, and even appear to have life: the columns lean inwards, resting on pediments hewn with lightly inclined surfaces, the corner columns in like manner diagonally inclined; the base of the whole structure is lightly bowed as though it were a sail pinned down at the four corners and lightly inflated by the wind (p.50, 53). There took shape and ruled in the Greek temple architectonic form; this form is strict and unyielding, "streng und unerbittlich", and equates to the laws governing nature; its creator and (genetic) carrier is the people in the line of their genetic succession: "Ihr Schöpfer und Träger ist das Volk in der Abfolge seiner Geschlechter." (p. 54). Oligarchy and helotry are not mentioned, and only in the softening influence of the oriental peoples with whom the Ionians had greater contact is change in form attributed to racial influence (p.47).

The densely written sections of *Der Peloponnes*, on the geology, geography, history, antique sites and ecclesiastical architecture of the Peloponnese and its regions from earliest times to the modern, belie the modest declaration of the book's title page that it is published by an army corps command "von Soldaten für Soldaten". Moreover, the many plans of antique and ecclesiastical sites, and an appendix of diagrammatic maps of the communication routes, geology, horticulture, hegemonies and demographic shifts of the Peloponnese testify to a considerable effort of research on the part of the contributors and the cartographical staff. The two hundred and seventy pages of text and illustrations are ordered over five thematic chapters, each dealing with the entire land mass of the Peloponnese. The account given of the succeeding migrations and intrusions after 2000 BC, of pre-Dorians, Dorians, Goths, West-Goths, Macedonians, Romans, Slavs, Arab Corsairs, Franks, Venetians, Albanians and Turks, is referenced to the capacity of Greekdom to survive, accommodate, absorb and ultimately to re-establish itself. No special *nordische* attributes are credited in this. The book's late appearance – the foreword by air force general Felmy is dated 8.

December 1943 – suggests that it was some time in gestation, and its spare and dense style throughout makes it improbable as a hurriedly prepared propaganda piece trumpeting conspicuous care for the antiquities. The language is politically neutral: the plural term *Gaue* is used, but in a topographical context and by extension into *Kantone* (pp.50-51). The hortatory foreword makes reference to the decay of nations and their cultures and insists that only the willpower and courage of a whole people can save it "vor dem Untergang". The general's concluding remark: "Wer erblickt in diesem Spiegel der Geschichte nicht das Schicksal der eigenen Nation?"[85], if not intentionally ambiguous, is at least unintentionally ironic when read in the context of the historical analysis which the book offers, particularly that on Sparta. The history chapter (pp.42-158) is the longest in the book, and the chapter sections which trace the long-term, self-erosive effects of the racially exclusive, economically self-contained and excessively militarily-reliant polity operated by Sparta (pp.51-83) project dryly onto the structure of the contemporary German regime. In the hegemony of the Dorian Spartans was also a more immediate parallel to the German expansion: it rested on a tripartite alliance of Spartans, of wholly subjugated indigenous peoples as Helots, and of strategically dominated but domestically autonomous peripheral peoples as *Perioikoi*. There was a parallel too, with France, in the cultural eminence later accorded by Rome to Sparta: the risk of Sparta's re-emergence as a power was pre-empted by a calculated promotion of Sparta's Peloponnesian rivals (p.83). To the genuine cultural reverence evidenced for the heritage of Greece in the publications *Hellas* and *Der Peloponnes* might be added, in so far as it spoke for the soldiers among the writers, the admiration expressed by the *Führer* himself for the heroism of the Greek defenders of 1941,[86] but complete political compliance had been an implicit condition of *that*.

The classicist, scholarly tone of *Hellas* and *Der Peloponnes* stands in stark contrast to the barbarous ferocity of the insurgency and counter-insurgency hostilities during the occupation of Greece. These writings stand in equally stark contrast to the ephemeral impressions of Erhart Kästner's peregrinations through Greece, Crete, and the islands. Kästner evinces a (Gerard Manley) Hopkins-like striving to convey heightened sensations in new word-compounds, and his historical and antique references are slight to the point of dilettantism. Being neither journal nor travelogue nor guide book, *Griechenland* and its companion volumes make up a *Unikat*.

Kästner had visited Kalavryta in 1942, but the ten days of burnings and civilian massacre conducted in that area in December 1943 took place after

---

[85] *Der Peloponnes*, p.5.

[86] See Hiller von Gaertringen (1994), p.162.

the publication of *Griechenland*.[87] However, Hiller von Gaertringen points to Kästner's failure to mention in his then work-in-progress, *Griechische Inseln*, the deportation in 1944 of the Jewish population of Rhodes, which he witnessed; also to his description of the onslaught on the Dodecanese after the Italian capitulation in 1943 as a *Heldenkampf*.[88] In mitigation, Hiller von Gaertringen notes that Kästner then, consistent with the realisation that his project to continue writing about a Greece seemingly at peace was no longer tenable, ceased writing[89] (in the sense of ceasing to write with an intention to complete his Greek trilogy for contemporary publication). Of what he had written, Hiller von Gaertringen supplies the corrective that the books as commissioned were intended primarily not for a far-removed reading public, but for a readership of soldiers who *knew* what was taking place in Greece. Von Gaertringen also speculates that Kästner may have felt that a certain contribution to propaganda was expected of him.[90] On the charge of escapism, Kästner's literary biographer notes that the strong demand for copies of *Griechenland* among *Wehrmacht* units showed that with his concept of an ideal counter-world Kästner had answered a general need. [91] Von Gaertringen concedes that he did indulge in escapism – in the tradition of Romantic seekers after Greece – and in that tradition and in pursuit of a higher reality, banished the banal and the everyday.[92] His biographer's assessment of Kästner's achievement in Greece runs as follows:

> Kästner verstand seinen literarischen Aufruf zur Humanität als einen Akt des passiven Widerstands. Die Bücher erwuchsen seinem Bestreben, die eigene Integrität zu bewahren; sie waren zugleich der Versuch, in der Leserschaft zur Aufrechterhaltung der persönlichen Humanität des einzelnen beizutragen und seine Widerstandshaltung gegen den Zerfall aller Werte im nationalsozialistischen Krieg zu bestärken.[93]

Further exposition will be here advanced to evidence that a preoccupation with the canonical aesthetic of the antique, with form and proportion – proportion in the allusive sense of proportionality also – and with physical grace, was a prudently effective way of conveying ethical distance.

---

[87] Ibid., p.336.
[88] Ibid., p.207.
[89] Ibid., p.208.
[90] Ibid., pp.252,199.
[91] Ibid., p.254.
[92] Ibid., p.249.
[93] Ibid., p.250.

3. Literature on two fronts

3.1. Involuntary tourism

In his essay, 'Einer wie Felix Hartlaub',[1] Durs Grünbein maintains that in reading Felix Hartlaub one understands the Second World War as "das größte Reiseunternehmen der Deutschen in diesem Jahrhundert." Grünbein coins the expression "Europatourismus für die *Habenichtse*". This, he suggests, was part of the war's appeal to the 'have-nots' the underclass on whose instincts Hitler had knowingly played from the outset. Neither Göpel, Hartlaub, nor Kästner belonged to an underclass; all three had been intent on academic careers, and now found themselves involuntary 'tourists'.[2] The commissions awarded to the former art historian Göpel and former Saxony state-library librarian Kästner to write officially approved cultural guides resulted in works of quite different approach from two men who had worked together in 1938-1939 on the *Gutenberg-Reichsausstellung* Leipzig exhibition project.[3] Göpel's book on Normandy is a densely written potted history which reveals the architectural and bibliophile enthusiasms of its author. Kästner's books on mainland Greece and on Crete are equally full of enthusiasm, for landscape and for classical architecture, but are of a contrastingly exuberant and unrestrainedly lyrical expression. Hartlaub in his Paris peregrinations is unencumbered by official commissions to write and records his impressions *as might a tourist.* Unlike Jünger, who dined at the *Ritz and George V* hotels as one of an elite circle of regime-critical figures named for the latter, the '*Georgsrunde*', and even when on a tour of the Caucasus was a guest at high tables: "nachmittags Generaloberst von Kleist zu Tisch"; "mittags beim Oberbefehlshaber, Generaloberst Ruoff,"[4] Hartlaub, struggling in his inadequate civilian wardrobe to maintain appearances at table and touring Paris on foot and on the métro (on which Germans had free travel)[5] was much more the *Habenichts.* Hartlaub remarked from his visits to Berlin in 1944 that "dieser Stoff ist eigentlich ja viel gewaltiger noch als das Frontgeschehen, ausserdem wirklich neu, was man von dem Schlachten der Uniformierten ja weniger sagen kann."[6] What was new about this war was the experience of the *civilians*, particularly the city dwellers.

[1] Durs Grünbein, 'Einer wie Felix Hartlaub', in *Galilei vermißt Dantes Hölle und bleibt an den Maßen hängen. Aufsätze 1989-1995* (Frankfurt am Main: Suhrkamp, 1996), pp.190-95.

[2] Cf. Gordon (1996), '*Ist Gott Französisch?*', loc. cit.

[3] Cf. Hiller von Gaertringen (1994), pp.59-60.

[4] Cf. Jünger, 'Kaukasische Aufzeichnungen', in *Strahlungen I* , pp.426,440.

[5] See Gordon (1996), '*Ist Gott Französisch?*', loc. cit., p.290.

[6] Ewenz I (2002/2007), pp.671/680: letter to parents, 6 January 1944.

Hartlaub seems to have intuited this about the civilian experience in occupied Paris also. To render this experience, he essayed something new in the genre of the metropolis, *flâneur* literature.

Seibert's (1995) discussion of contemporarily published eyewitness accounts from German participants instances Walter Bauer's publishing success,[7] *Tagebuchblätter aus Frankreich* (1941), as celebrating the victor perspective, and the effort at interpretation in Kurt Lothar Tank's *Pariser Tagebuch* (1941) as unwittingly revealing of the insecurity anxiety of the occupiers.[8] Bauer, a qualified teacher unsuccessful in establishing himself in that career, had first published in 1927 and, though politically out of favour from 1933 until 1940,[9] published again and had popular success once more with his *Tagebuchblätter aus dem Osten* (1944). Seibert's summation of Bauer's account from the France of 1940, "der deutsche Angriffskrieg wurde hier gefeiert als große Fahrt, als erlebnisgesättigte Bildungsreise eines lyrisch gestimmten Dichtersoldaten",[10] omits note of Bauer's insistent distancing of himself, the writer, from the role of wartime observer which had fallen to him. Bauer's interchangeable refrain: "ich bin Soldat",[11] "ich kam als Soldat",[12] "jetzt, da ich Soldat bin",[13] "hier liege ich, ein Soldat",[14] and "ein anderer, als ich vor Monaten war: ein Soldat",[15] would be excessive, were it intended only as self-exculpation, but his resentment of the uniform stresses disjuncture: "diese Uniform und das Leben das sie bewirkte, dieses Leben, das uns von allem einst Gelebten fortriß."[16] In the enforced detachment from self Bauer does recognise the advantage of heightened perception which the estranged circumstances of wartime bring:

> Ich glaube, in dieser Zeit tiefsten Getrenntseins von den Dingen meines alten Lebens sind meine Augen wacher, meine Sinne empfindsamer geworden, es ist mir manchmal, als wüchse ich in eine neue Schau der Dinge hinein.[17]

---

7 See Schäfer, *Das gespaltene Bewußtsein*, p.44.

8 See Peter Seibert, 'Deutsche Ansichten der besetzten Stadt,' in Drost and others, *Paris sous l'occupation*, pp.58-73 (pp.60-61).

9 Walter Bauer archive, Stadtbibliothek Merseburg: 'Walter Bauer – Zeittafel seines Lebens,'at: http://www.fh-merseburg.de/index.php?id=1353 [accessed 31 January 2012].

10 See Seibert, loc. cit, p.60.

11 Walter Bauer, *Tagebuchblätter aus Frankreich* (Dessau: Karl Rauch Verlag, 1941), pp.12,97.

12 Ibid., pp.27,28,45.

13 Ibid., p.94.

14 Ibid., p.56.

15 Ibid., p.6.

16 Ibid., p.32.

17 Ibid., p.45.

Bauer's *Tagebuchblätter*, 'diary pages', from France do bring the reader on a *Bildungsreise* through the grand sites of Amboise, Chartres, Mont Saint-Michel and Verdun, but on one devoid of conscious triumphalism. It is rather peace which is stressed: at Amboise his reflections are on a famous resident, Leonardo da Vinci; at Chartres, he equates the stillness of the cathedral interior with mankind's longing for peace; quartered by Mont Saint-Michel, news reaches him that a friend, the poet Otto Gmelin, has fallen; at Verdun he recalls the hesitation of his brother before ringing the doorbell, home on leave from that front, uncertain of crossing the boundary to the normal world again. The soldier-writer now finds himself in the middle of what seems like an epoch changing war, "in diesem, alles verwandelnden Krieg."[18] He watches the strain of concentration and the faraway absorption on the face of a colleague truck driver as he writes a letter home. Such a simple one he regards above many others who are too quick and ready to record their feelings: "viele, die so schnell mit der Feder sind, schnell mit ihren Empfindungen; mit allem, auch mit dem Verrat ihrer selbst."[19] Effusive reports to the home front, Bauer appears to imply, say too little in saying too much, and are a betrayal of their writers' integrity. Like the Heinrich Böll of the *Briefe aus dem Krieg*,[20] Bauer is lyrical about the sea, the "Wogenfelde des Meeres", which seem to transmit a light up to the clouds, "die leuchtenden Schaumländer",[21] but unlike Böll, remarks little about the French citizenry he meets: an angler, an innkeeper and a schoolboy guide are the only figures,[22] fleetingly encountered. The legitimacy or otherwise of the occupation is ignored as not being the concern of the *Soldat*.

Kurt Lothar Tank's literary credits begin in 1935 with the text supplied to Otto Schönstein's self-published collection of stereoscopic photographs of Venice[23] and include another collaboration with the photographer Schönstein, in 1942, *Deutsche Plastik unserer Zeit*, [24] which featured an introduction by Albert Speer. Tank later collaborated, postwar, with Paul Raabe, Kästner's colleague and successor at the Wolfenbüttel library, on an illustrated biography of Gerhard Hauptmann.[25] Like Hartlaub, Tank finds

---

[18] Ibid., p.65.

[19] Ibid., p.39.

[20] *Heinrich Böll. Briefe aus dem Krieg 1939-1945*, ed. by Jochen Schubert (Cologne: Kiepenheuer & Witsch, 2001, 2 vols).

[21] Ibid., p.46.

[22] Ibid., pp.49-50,77-78,85-86.

[23] Cf. *Venedig. Ein Raumerlebnis* (Diessen am Ammersee: Raumbild-Verlag Otto Schönstein, 1935).

[24] (Munich: Schönstein, 1942).

[25] Cf. Tank, *Gerhart Hauptmann in Selbstzeugnissen und Bilddokumenten* (Rowohlt,1959).

himself lodged in a requisitioned hotel in Paris, also in 1940. As with Hartlaub, the omnipresence of the German military vehicles projects itself as alien and intrusive: "Die Wagen der deutschen Wehrmacht beherrschen das Straßenbild, zumal in der Mitte von Paris, in der Nähe der Oper, wo wir Zimmer im Grand Hôtel angewiesen erhalten."[26] Hartlaub renders a similar scene as "Avenue de l'Opéra. Das graue Feld der parkenden Wehrmachtsautos."[27] The diarist narrator in Tank's diary is struck by the completely normal-seeming demeanour of the Parisians, and asks himself if this is equanimity, indifference, or simply sheer vitality: "Ist dies nun Gleichmut, Gleichgültigkeit, oder ist es Lebenskraft?"[28] Hartlaub, writing privately from Paris in January 1941, had detected a deliberate air of arch indifference, manifested among the Parisians by an untypically reserved silence: "Am Auffallendsten ist das absolute Schweigen, zu dem sich die Lutetier, so schwer es ihnen fallen muss, entschlossen haben."[29]

Tank pens notably lyrical descriptions of the cathedrals of Laon and Rheims,[30] and is impressed, as was Bauer, at Chartres. Only the latter part of Tank's diary, just over twenty seven pages, relates to the occupation period, and deals with an army-organised tour in which he participated in October of 1940.[31] The diary sections dating from the autumn of 1938 and the Spring of 1939 contain much digression on the subject of Clemenceau, of whom Tank was then researching a biography; Tank had already in 1937 published a work on the Napoleon III period, specifically on Gambetta.[32] There is polemic against the 'hate treaty', "Haßvertrag", of Versailles, the effective sole authorship of which Tank ascribes to Clemenceau.[33] There is in his 1941 foreword a blatantly patronising endorsement of the subordination of France into the 'new European order':

> Und doch gibt es eine andere, gesunde Tradition in Frankreich, die seines Bauerntums. Frankreich wird diesen Weg gehen müssen, um zur Einordnung in die neue europäische Gemeinschaft zu gelangen.[34]

There is also an erudite study of Notre Dame as anthropology.[35] There is a study of the mausolea of Père Lachaise as a city of the dead within the living

---

[26] Kurt Lothar Tank, *Pariser Tagebuch 1938-1939-1940* (Berlin: S. Fischer, 1941), p.107.
[27] Ewenz I (2002/2007), p.79.
[28] Tank, *Pariser Tagebuch*, p.107.
[29] Ewenz I (2002/2007), pp.459/467: letter to parents, 15 January 1941.
[30] Cf. Tank, *Pariser Tagebuch*, pp.109,126-27.
[31] Ibid., p.102.
[32] Cf. Kurt Lothar Tank, *Gambetta. Ein politischer Kampf gegen Despotismus und Anarchie* (Essen/Berlin: Essener Verlagsanstalt, 1937).
[33] See Tank, *Pariser Tagebuch*, pp.34-35,91.
[34] Ibid., p.12.

city of Paris, playing on the tenet of the *Code Civil* which states "La vie privée doit être murée", and contrasting the French predilection for walled-in privacy, which Böll in the *Briefe* remarked on,[36] with the German preference for the sylvan *Waldfriedhof*.[37] This dates from 1939, as does his affectionate study of the Parisian cafés which leaves him with the fanciful impression that most of French literature is actually written in cafés, or at least as if the writers imagined themselves seated in cafés.[38] The 1940 section of the diary, entitled "Fahrt durch das besetzte Frankreich. Oktober/November 1940" contains no more historical or political speculation. The largest sub-section amounts to what is a short story of ten pages, not out of place in the context of a battlefield tour, about a selfless fallen comrade, obviously a personal memoir, pointedly non-Christian in moral, but at the same time carefully distanced from the regime-promoted virtue of sacrifice for victory.[39] The 1940 journey spanned just seven days, too short a time for anything like a civil literature to gestate, but, though prefacing a description of enthusiastically co-operative rebuilding under military direction, the following sentiment seems to express something personally felt, not just a formulation of the aims of psychological warfare:

> In Rethel wurde mir klar, daß nach einer Schlacht immer noch eine zweite und wahrscheinlich entscheidendere zu gewinnen ist, nach der Schlacht der Waffen die der Herzen und des Geistes.[40]

In his 1941 foreword Tank claims to have striven in his diary account to avoid the impressionistic as well as the simplistically dogmatic.[41] He was at least aware of these two poles in directly addressing French social, economic and political life as he did. Where Bauer's diary avoids engagement with the relationships of occupation by use of the caveat *ich kam als Soldat*, Tank's forthright observations reveal in their honesty the split consciousness, Schäfer's *gespaltenes Bewußtsein*,[42] in which opposing principles could be accommodated.

Citing Schäfer's discussion of the non-fascist literature of the younger generation which concludes that almost all the war diaries of literary worth

---

[35] Ibid., pp.43-45.

[36] Cf. Böll, *Briefe* I, pp.504,675.

[37] Tank, *Pariser Tagebuch*, pp.57-58.

[38] Ibid., p.54.

[39] Ibid., pp.113-23.

[40] Ibid., pp.104-5.

[41] Ibid.; cf. pp.12-13.

[42] See Schäfer, *Das gespaltene Bewußtsein*, pp.146-208.

of those years were not intended for immediate publication,[43] Seibert agrees that the most interesting and the most productive were those pursued in private.[44] Even Hartlaub's fragmentary output from his nine-month period in Paris, however, though private, must have been written with some at least subliminal aspiration to later publication – and he could not have presumed a return of liberal publishing conditions. Despite Hartlaub's own low opinion of them, "meine an sich so kümmerlichen Aufzeichnungen aus Paris",[45] the safekeeping of the Paris notebooks mattered to him most, "Von meinen Sachen liegt mir am meisten an den beiden Schnellheftern aus P[aris]."[46] Had he lived, they were not intended to remain *Schubladenliteratur*. Indeed if, as Schäfer argues, genres and their popularity endured past the social and political turning points of 1933 and 1945 and through the interval between, it is not beyond reasonable supposition that Hartlaub's Paris sketches, had hostilities been otherwise decided, might have looked forward to an acceptance as postwar, and not necessarily post-*regime* satires.

Contributions on French life also appeared in the weekly German language *Pariser Zeitung* and particularly in the bi-weekly guide, *Der deutsche Wegleiter*. The view of Byron (1996) on these is that "In reinforcing the Nazi view, publications such as *Der deutsche Wegleiter* and the *Pariser Zeitung* are reminiscent of literature from many other cultures which stereoptypes or essentialises other cultures."[47] An examination of that view lies outside the scope of this work and would properly be an aspect of the study of the German front newspapers and magazines (see 1.2).[48]

3.2. The Francophile's dilemma

> Die Deutschen in Frankreich wählten unterschiedliche Wege, um ihre Erlebnisse zu verarbeiten. Zu den aufwendigen Methoden zählte die Führung eines Tagebuches oder die Unterhaltung eines regelmäßigen Briefverkehrs. Mancher suchte hier eine Art von schriftlichem Gedächtnis aufzubauen.

This comment from the Tewes study of the experiences of former service people who had been stationed in occupied France[49] is taken from the chapter entitled 'Der Einzug des Alltags', the 're-entry of the everyday': the

---

43 Ibid., pp.7-68: 'Die nichtnazionalsozialistische Literatur der jungen Generation im Dritten Reich', (p.45).

44 See Seibert, in Drost and others, *Paris sous l'occupation*, p.61.

45 See Ewenz (2002/2007), pp.637/646: letter of 13 September 1943.

46 Ibid., pp.731/741: letter of 30 November 1944.

47 Gordon, '*Ist Gott Französisch?*' loc. cit., p. 289.

48 Cf. Eckhardt, *Die Frontzeitungen des deutschen Heeres 1939-1945*.

49 Tewes, *Frankreich in der Besatzungszeit*, p.151.

necessity of humans to establish a daily norm, however abnormal that norm might be. The commonest methods of ordering the experience in memory were the maintenance of a diary or the cultivation of regular correspondence. Correspondence as a way of building a written memory, *eine Art von schriftlichem Gedächtnis*, was a confessional and self-representational mode and even at that, because of wartime censorship, necessarily guarded and oblique in expression. For one such as Hartlaub, reading and acquiring books according to a planned reading programme and already making literary experiments, correspondence was often about the circumstance of writing, with his father, G.F. Hartlaub, seeking to play the role of academic mentor. Hartlaub, a Francophone since his early schooldays visit to Brittany and a Francophile since a later student-exchange stay in Strasbourg, and intent on writing a post-doctoral work on 19th century French literature, could take little comfort from the fact that he was a *civil* servant of the occupation, as the unease of his "Er" focal character shows. Another administration official of the occupation, one of the senior military administration, temporary-officer officials viewed by the regular military as simply uniformed party-members and thus attracting the common nickname *Goldfasanen*,[50] 'golden pheasants', was Walter Bargatzky, who wrote this of the dilemma of the Francophile:

> Es gibt einen militärischen und politischen Waffenstillstand, keinen kulturellen. Bleiben wir bei unserer Sympathie für französische Lebensart, so kehren wir, wenn sich die Dinge in Deutschland nicht ändern, bis zu gewissem Grad als Fremde zurück. Fremde, die sich untereinander am besten verstehen.[51]

Hartlaub's recognition that he was already such a *Fremder* among his own people was heightened by the alienation he felt in Paris from the metropolis he so admired. It is this alienation which adds an extra detachment to the *flâneur* stance of his prose. He expressed the obverse of Bargatzky's dilemma: the other penalty for complicity in the occupation was a compromised claim to be a Francophile at all, "Wir sind uns alle darüber klar, dass wir hier im Frieden und als Einzelne nie mehr hinkönnen."[52] *Hinkönnen*, a coining, with the sense of an unregainable destination; this was especially painful to Hartlaub, who did not fail to appreciate the heightened assertiveness in French culture in response to the military collapse: "Der Krieg und der Zusammenbruch müssen in eine ganz einzigartige Blüte des

---

[50] See Walter Bargatzky, *Hotel Majestic*, p.49; see also Hartlaub's use of the term in 'Im Dickicht des Südostens', Ewenz I (2002/2007), pp.179/181.

[51] Bargatzky, *Hotel Majestic*, p.52.

[52] Ewenz I (2002/2007), pp.454/462.

Schauspiels hineingewettert sein; dasselbe gilt von Film und Literatur."[53] The calculated cultivation of support for the Third Reich that lay behind Hitler's benign policy towards French cultural life permitted, but did not *cause* this efflorescence.[54]

It is Hartlaub whose early drawings contain so much of the Rhine port architecture of his native Mannheim who is in his Paris Sketches the architectural successor of Franz Hessel. Hessel, whose *Spazieren in Berlin* (1929) was hailed by Walter Benjamin as the return of the *flâneur*, "die Wiederkehr des Flaneurs",[55] is the *flâneur* of the architectural. In a chapter entitled 'Etwas von der Arbeit' he speaks of "Tempel der Maschine" and "Kirchen der Präzision"[56]. Late in his Paris exile Hessel lamented the clearances for the new Speer Berlin to which much ornate domestic architecture of the Karl Friedrich Schinkel school was sacrificed.[57] Hessel had written of Berlin, "In der Bauhütte des Neuen lebt noch eine Zeitlang das Alte weiter."[58] Hartlaub is not overtly nostalgic, and his one nostalgic remark in the sketches is vague as to recollection and ironic in tone, "In einem Studentencafé am Boul[evard Saint] Mich[el]. Er war hier schon mal, vor fünf Jahren, 8 Jahren, im Zuge der Völkerverständigung."[59] Hessel is nostalgic for the classically built Berlin of the Schinkel school, now in its state of demolition appearing actually antique, with its classical interiors appearing Pompeiian in ruin. This temporary gift of a visible past, a "sichtbare Vergangenheit", is owed, ironically, to the clearances of the Speer school.[60] Nostalgia, also Hessel's here, by definition recognises the inexorable and the irreversible. Hartlaub's many *Purpurblaus* and *Atlasblaus* of the Paris sky, fickle light-play on house facades and palette of pastel hues, avoiding the starkly lit and the sharply defined, suggest more a state of subdued hibernation. At other times the summer sun blurs, petrifies and makes arid.[61] Encoded is a sadness at the city's *temporary* loss of vitality, and a frustration with the unfixed picture of the present.

---

53 Ibid. See also Michels, *Das Deutsche Institut in Paris 1940-1944*, pp.69-70.

54 Ibid.; for background to the German control of French cultural production see Hanns Grössel's introduction to Gerhard Heller/Jean Grand, *In einem besetzten Land. Leutnant Heller und die Zensur in Frankreich 1940-1944* (Bergisch Gladbach: Bastei-Lübbe, 1985), pp.11-27.

55 See Hessel, new edition, published as *Ein Flaneur in Berlin* (Berlin: Arsenal, 1984), pp.277-81.

56 Ibid., p.21.

57 See *Letzte Heimkehr nach Paris. Franz Hessel und die Seinen im Exil*, ed. by Manfred Flügge (Berlin: Arsenal, 1989), p. 25.

58 Ibid.

59 See Ewenz I (2002/2007), p.53, "Place Pigalle".

60 See Flügge, *Lezte Heimkehr nach Paris*, p.25.

61 See Ewenz I (2002/2007), 'Das eroberte Ministerium', pp.120/121; also, 'Paar auf

There was an urge to write home from occupied France, weekly among some, as Tewes' study has found.[62] J.H. Reid's claim that Heinrich Böll in his daily letters from France is "Walter Benjamins Flaneur, der Intellektuelle, der kritische, doch voyeuristische Beobachter, der von der Gesellschaft, die er beobachtet, sowohl abgestoßen wie fasziniert ist"[63] raises a question on the selective process by which experience is transformed into literary creation. No substantial work of fiction emerged from Böll's two years as unit messenger, food-forager and interpreter, and the felicitous lyricism of the *Briefe* from France is not recovered in the three short stories[64] and one novella which make up the sum of Böll's postwar fiction set specifically in wartime France (his wartime literary efforts from 1939 onwards amounted to just two short trial-pieces).[65] He had been happiest when stationed on directly the sea coast, where merely scanning the empty sea was a form of escape: "Glaubst du, daß es ein Vergnügen ist, mit dem Glas weit aufs Meer hinauszuschauen, obwohl man dort »nur Wasser« sieht?"[66] In *Das Vermächtnis*, the novella, the swamp and salt marsh landscape of the Somme and Seine/Eure estuaries which also he had found "berauschend schön"[67] is cast as a negative mood-backdrop to an anti-war melodrama:

> Dort, in der nordwestlichen Ecke der Normandie, zieht sich parallel zur Meeresküste ein Streifen Landes, der die schwermütige Verlorenheit von Heide und Sumpf zugleich atmet; man sieht wenige sehr kleine Siedlungen, verlassene und verfallene Gehöfte, seichte Bäche, die träge den versumpften Sommearmen zufließen oder unterirdisch versacken.[68]

This is, and is not, the same "sonderbar reizvolle sumpfige Departement Somme" which Böll viewed on a train journey from Calais to Amiens.[69] The dried up watercourses are the same he crawled through on exercises, but which, contrary to the desolation stressed in the fiction, in the original experience offered exhilaration and escape:

Montmartre', pp.136-37/138-140.

[62] Tewes, *Frankreich in der Besatzungszeit*, p.151.

[63] Böll, *Briefe* II, afterword, p. 1605.

[64] See *Heinrich Böll. Werke. Kölner Ausgabe*, 27 vols. (Cologne: Kiepenheuer & Witsch), vol.2 (2002), pp.121-37, 'Gefangen in Paris'; vol.3 (2003), pp.115-29, 'Vive la France!'; pp.459-66, 'Unsere gute, alte Renée'.

[65] See Böll, *Kölner Ausgabe*, vol.I, pp.461-64.

[66] Böll, *Briefe* II, p.915.

[67] Böll, *Briefe* II, pp.905-6.

[68] Böll, *Das Vermächtnis* (Bornheim: Lamuv, 1982), p.15.

[69] Böll, *Briefe* I, p.491.

> Heute morgen sind wir fast vier Stunden im Gelände herumgekrochen, durch Stoppelfelder, halbverblühte Büsche, durch ausgetrocknete Bachläufe, die mit den tollsten, wildesten Blumen und Sträuchern fast zugewachsen waren; ach, alle tollen, wilden und süßen Gerüche des Herbstes haben mich sehr beglückt...[70]

The first postwar efforts at fiction described in the correspondence with E.A. Kunz suggest a mismatch between Böll's self-estimation and his actual mastery of the material: "Sie spielt in Frankreich, in einer Landschaft und einem Milieu, das ich vollkommen beherrsche";[71] this on *Das Vermächtnis*, on 24 May 1948. In financial desperation, the first fifty pages had been typed in just two days.[72] The 88-page draft strained Böll's ability: "Vermächtnis beendet. Deo gratias" was the notebook entry of 28 June 1948.[73] Despite revision with the help of his wife, Annemarie, the work was rejected.[74] In the spring of 1949, the work was taken up again, but with reluctance: "Das »Vermächtnis« liegt hier und harrt der gründlichen Ueberarbeitung, aber ich habe keine Lust mehr."[75] The work remained unpublished until 1982. The deliberately negative representation of the landscape of the wartime French Channel coast had served to convey an anti-war message, but the fuller, sympathetic if sometimes exasperated account of real-life encounters with the French people is found in Böll's *Briefe*, not in his fiction.

3.3. Culture shock: the East

The shock to the German sensibility presented by the Soviet east is well conveyed in Guido Karl Brand's account of a six-week tour made in the midwinter of 1941/42, *Ein Winter ohne Gnade* (1943).[76] As on his tour of occupied France later in 1942, the writer and literary historian Brand was attached as a war reporter to the military construction and logistics *Organisation Todt.* The widespread destitution, the primitive living conditions even in the environs of the Soviet show city of Novo Saporoshje, the countless displaced persons wandering the roads "von Leningrad bis an die Krim" (p.219), the absence of a market economy to supply and give employment to the people, the statistically damned unproductiveness of collectivised soviet agriculture (p.154) – these social shocks are registered in passages which, though framed with anti-Soviet and anti-Semitic polemic

---

[70] Böll, *Briefe* I, p.464.

[71] *Heinrich Böll. Die Hoffnung ist wie ein wildes Tier*, ed. by Herbert Hoven (Munich: DTV, 1997), p.74.

[72] Ibid.

[73] Ibid., p.455.

[74] Ibid., p.101.

[75] Ibid., p.194.

[76] Guido K. Brand, *Ein Winter ohne Gnade. Osteindrücke eines OT-Kriegsberichters* (Prague: Volk und Reich, 1943).

(p.41, "die Gehirne der jüdischen Machthaber"; p.168, "die jüdisch-bolschewistische Propaganda") read, the German hegemonist presumption notwithstanding (p.109, "Menschen, den das Schicksal dazu ausersehen hatte, Europa in seine macht zu nehmen"), as a genuine humane concern.

Brand had read the canonical writers of the Tsarist and of the Soviet era (pp.25, 167-8). In the hope of finding the time to read in them something to to arm himself against the idea thus gained of the Soviet colossus, "mich zu wappnen gegen einen Koloß, den ich aus vielen Büchern kannte", he carried in his suitcase two volumes of Nietzsche (pp.69-70). Awed by the scale of the Soviet arms factories uncovered in the course of the German advance (p.43), Brand, citing Moltke, sounds a note of caution that the military outcome may not be assured (p.27); the campaigns in the West were, in comparision to the undertaking in the East, no more than large-scale commando operations, "Stoßtruppunternehmen" (p.42). A Nietzschian belief in the will to power was for him therefore a recourse of *doubt*.

Brand's account, relieved though it is by engagingly told anecdotes of hardships encountered in the Russian winter, is reportage: impressions relate to the contemporarily immediate, and are coloured by propagandist prejudice. The scorched earth destruction of the retreating Russian military is attributed only to the senseless rage and hate of a *bestialised* soldiery: "...sinnlosen Wut und des Hasses vertierer Soldateska" (p.131). In contrast, literary accounts from servicemen writers as littératurs consider impressions beyond the short-term contemporary, as when Martin Raschke in his 'Im Schatten der Front' sketches perceives in the East a survival of a pre-mechanised, age-old *wood* culture, still providing solutions of crafted beauty for all activities and purposes:

> Das Leben hier schien mir älter als bei uns. Die Menschen bedienten sich der Ergebnisse einer jahrtausendalten Holzkultur, die schöne Formeln für alle Tätigkeiten ausprägte, während wir in der wirren Jugend eines metallischen Maschinenzeitalters stehen.[77]

The Eastern towns present an improvised appearance, as if they were temporary market structures, somehow petrified.[78] The culture of the West is, as heir to the cultures of the antique world, above all a culture of *stone*: "unsere Kultur ist ja als die Erbin der antiken Kulturen vor allem eine Steinkultur".[79] Eastern churches are focused on the inner core, the sepulchure, whereas Western church building strives triumphantly heavenwards – the West did different things with stone:

---

[77] Hoffmann, *Hinweis auf Martin Raschke*, p.117.
[78] Ibid., p.91.
[79] Ibid., p.92

> Daß jede Kirche ein Grab ist, wird hier besonders sinnfällig. Doch was hat das Abendland aus dem gleichen Gedanken für eine triumphale Form entwickelt. Unsere Räume glauben an die Himmelfahrt stärker als an die Grabelegung.[80]

At the prospect of a short assignment to Rome, Raschke flees in spirit to the South from the earthy unbuilt-upon vastness of the Eastern landscape, seeking stone, to ingest as it were, as many animals do to aid the digestion:

> fuhr [...] im Geist nach Süden, um mich dort, wie viele Tiere Steine zur Regelung ihrer Verdauung fressen, an dieser Gräberstadt von Stein für die erdigen Erlebnisse des Ostens zu erfrischen.[81]

For another Easter front writer, Josef Leitgeb, the impression was of a land ever widening eastwards and appearing to thrust human settlements ever farther apart. The German *Dorf*, in implicit contrast to the *mir* village communes of prerevolutionary Russia, was a symbol of rural freedom. The *Hof* of the German *Bauer* was his castle, from whence he was master of and had *subdued* the land:

> Das deutsche Dorf ist eine Form der menschlichen Freiheit: der Bauer hat sich das Land unterworfen, und sein Hof ist die Burg, von der aus seine Arbeit herrscht.[82]

The onion-domed Eastern churches in white or light blue stand out from the modest wooden farmhouses much more so than does the German *Dorfkirche* from the stately farmsteads which it serves:

> Die hölzernen, weiß oder hellblau gestrichenenen Kirchen mit ihren vielen Zwiebeltürmen heben sich von den Bäuernhäusern viel deutlicher ab als unsere bescheideneren Gotteshäuser von den stattlichen Höfen.[83]

Nothing here in the East reminds one of structural cohesion, the "bauliche Geschlossenheit", of the German small town, but how should towns in any case be of note in such a landscape which surpasses in extent any in the German experience?

> Aber wie sollten auch Städte gegen eine Landschaft aufkommen, die alle deutschen Landschaften an Weiträumigkeit übertrifft, wie das Meer etwa unsere Voralpenseen?[84]

---

80 Ibid., p.112.
81 Ibid., p.121.
82 Josef Leitgeb, *Am Rande des Krieges. Aufzeichnungen in der Ukraine* (Berlin: Otto Müller,1942), p.9.
83 Ibid., p.10.
84 Ibid., p.11.

An inversion of perspective, in which offensive war against a 'treacherous' enemy is presented as a defensive struggle of the civilised and sensitive against an opponent portrayed as "die Negativfolie der Selbsteinschätzung als offen und ehrlich sowie gutmütig"[85] is a common thread which Peitsch's study divines among even those Eastern front writers which it singles out as being *non* National Socialist.[86] Those writers: Walter Bauer, Günter Böhmer, Walter Henkels, Horst Lange, Josef Leitgeb, Martin Raschke and Hermann Georg Rexroth, may be so-designated, according to Peitsch, essentially because, though functionally complicit in the construction of the Holocaust-legitimising enemy image, the figure of the 'Jewish-Bolshevist kommissar' is absent from their writings.[87] The homesick wistfulness of text and drawings in Walter Henkel's *Östliche Silhouetten* (1943) is indeed beguiling; the last date in the book is August 1942, the worst has not yet come: victorious troopers, *offen* and *ehrlich* and *gutmütig*, offer bread in compensation for poultry slaughtered and root crops ploughed under – the smallholder would have them trample about on the kolkhoz lands instead.[88] Such privatising and aestheticisation of immediate experience as this, at which these writers excelled, were officially sanctioned tendencies which actually served the purpose of the *Propagandakompanie* front reportage – the reports of faschist and non-faschist writers appeared together in the same magazines and newspapers.[89]

Even the gaze of the invading onlookers upon the Russian landscape can be functionally organised: upwards in grasp at the meaning of the war, outwards in terms of conquest and hegemony.[90] Walter Bauer's eulogising of Europa in invocation of the Hellenistic ideal[91] reads readily as humanistic transfiguration of the European mission of the German Reich.[92] The ideologically contested space of the war in the East left little ground for pure, transcending aestheticism. These are perhaps too reductive conclusions: the inspiration for Bauer's flight into the sublime is Hölderlin, with a nod to Emerson,[93] and for Bauer and the others that which seemed to disconnect all prior norms of perception was the incomprehensible vastness of the land. Leitgeb's epiphany, "Wer hier aufwächst, muß anders

---

85 Peitsch, „Am Rande des Krieges"?, loc. cit., p.131.

86 Ibid., pp.128-31.

87 Ibid., pp.142,143.

88 Henkels, *Östliche Silhouetten* (Berlin: Scherl, 1943), pp.31-35, 'Das Dorf'.

89 Ibid., pp.145-46.

90 Ibid., p.136.

91 Walter Bauer, *Tagebuchblätter aus dem Osten* (Dessau: Karl Rauch, 1944), pp.34-38.

92 See Peitsch, '„Am Rande des Krieges"?', loc. cit., p.138.

93 Bauer, *Tagebuchblätter aus dem Osten*, pp.41-48.

sein als wir"[94], is implicit acknowledgement that anyone who would settle and produce progeny in such a landscape could not but adapt and conform to it, rather than attempt to persist with norms evolved elsewhere.

The freedom of form within the generic diary format presumed in Bauer's term, *Tagebuchblätter*, allowed for digressive essay pieces addressed to correspondents, and the introduction of personal memoir; Bauer cast his father's loss of his home village to open-cast mining as a parable on the conquest of land: "die Erde [...] mächtiger ist als der Mensch. Er ist nicht ihr Herr, er ist nur ein Teil von ihr."[95] *Tagebuchblätter aus dem Osten* is a book of two halves: the first, from pages 5 to 79, consisting of reflective essays and of poetry, and only the second half, entitled "Das Octavheft von B", comprising pages 83 to 149, being actually in diary form with dated entries. Writing from a theatre of active military operations, Bauer observes the usual military censorship restrictions on disclosure of locations and identifiable individuals. The soldiers are quartered on the civilian population. Bauer writes of the emotional comfort of lodging with a family of *Volksdeutschen*, of the joy of re-reading Goethe in the surviving volumes of the library of the old schoolteacher paterfamilias.[96] Over the course of a dozen pages at the beginning of the diary section, Bauer writes with some affection on a sojourn in a Russian village: of a retired Russian minor official's love of gardening, of the cleanliness and good housekeeping of his quarters, but also of the incommunicability with the Russian land and language and of a longing for Europe and for *its* cultural motherland, Greece.[97] This echoes an earlier section of the *Tagebuchblätter*, entitled 'Europas Namen und Ihre Herrlichkeit', a eulogy of Europe: "Geburtsland der Menschen."[98] Hearing one who has served there mention Greece, Bauer in fantasy beholds the classical sites that for him constitute Europe, and apostrophises her: "Das Licht, dieses kühne, junge, alle Dinge einigende Licht — es war um mich. So kamst du zu mir, Europa."[99] A recollection echoes Kästner, "im Museo Nazionale in Neapel [...] inmitten griechischer Klarheit,"[100] as does a reflection on the idealisation of youth:

> [...] daß aber bei keinem Volke so wie bei dem deutschen ein solches Hingezogensein zur Gestaltung des jungen Menschen zu erkennen sei, und daß das

---

94 Leitgeb, op. cit., p.47.
95 Bauer, *Tagebuchblätter aus dem Osten*, p.74.
96 Ibid., pp.20-23,30.
97 Ibid., pp.83-95.
98 Ibid., p.36.
99 Ibid., p.37.
100 Ibid., p.54.

Wort ‚Jüngling' etwas Anderes sei, viel mehr umschließe als zum Beispiel ‚jeune homme' im Französischen.[101]

But Bauer could not, like Kästner, write: "Immer wieder kann sich der Deutsche an Heimatliches erinnert fühlen."[102] Bauer could find no *Heimat* in the East. The land, unlike Greece, offered the *Bildungsbürger* German no intellectual refuge from the war.

Bauer's few references to the war in the East are oblique, and references to light serve as motif and as correlative for pacifist yearnings: for the Black Forest of the home country, "…ein Morgen im Schwarzwald [...] Das Licht kennt keine Grenzen, keinen Haß, keine Liebe.";[103] and for France: "dieses klare Licht Frankreichs, das seine Maler beständig feierten"[104] [...] "von Frankreich und seinen lichtüberströmten Feldern."[105] The light of steppes, in contrast, brings clarity of vision and dispels illusions: "Das Licht, dessen Fülle vom Morgen bis zum Abend unerschöpflich war, hat unsere Augen befreit von den letzten Verschwommenheiten."[106]

Peitsch's analysis pronounces the episodic account in H.G. Rexroth's *Der Wermutstrauch*[107] of the July 1942 fighting around Rostov as thoroughly typical of the characterisation by *Propagandakompanie* writers: of the enemy as treacherous and bestial; the negative reverse of the German self-image as open, honourable and good-natured, and further typical of a self-defensive presentation of the German soldier as denatured by the tactics of the enemy.[108] Peitsch selects an episode of the shooting of three Russian civilians who present themselves before German patrols in the middle of a firefight. The incident is described near the end of Rexroth's 46-page account of the taking of Rostov, from which account it is clear that the city had been defended by a civilian militia, formed among the harbour workers, and by military in civilian clothes who passed from strongpoint to strongpoint in that guise. Rexroth likens the city to a primeval forest filled with enraged spectres, and in which all the laws of humanity perish in the fire of a cunning devilry, "im Feuer listiger Teufeleien" (p.143). The grenadiers, whose motorised infantry death's-head collar pins had earlier needlessly alarmed the young girls of the Cossack settlement in the approaches to Rostov (p.137), now re-acquire primeval senses of survival:

---

[101] Ibid., p.42.

[102] Kästner, *Griechenland*, p.269.

[103] Ibid., p.27.

[104] Ibid., p.35.

[105] Ibid., p.137.

[106] Ibid., p.62.

[107] Herman Georg Rexroth, *Der Wermutstrauch* (Hamburg: H. Goverts, 1944).

[108] See Peitsch, '„Am Rande des Krieges"?', loc. cit., pp.130-31.

their mouths open so that the rush of blood in their ears will not muffle their hearing; they close their eyes that they may hear better; their fingers crook like talons around triggers, ready to shoot on reflex. In another account of the shooting of what again appear to be three civilians who have approached the German lines during firing, one is shot down out of hand, as a warning, and then, with apparent relish, the remaining two who have stopped in shock are shot as soon as they turn about and attempt to flee. The vengeful killing is reactive to a scene glimpsed through a window during street fighting: a woman irons clothes unconcernedly and pours tea as a street battle rages about her house. In implicit sub-text, the witnessing soldiers are affronted: the enemy is now committing an outrage against homely values and *Heimat.* The account occurs in Günter Böhmer's book, *Pan am Fenster*,[109] notable for its succession of Russian/Ukrainian interiors where German soldiers are on familial terms with the householders.[110] In place of Rexroth's heat-of-battle psychology Böhmer offers an apologia unassociated with the particular incident, and implicitly acknowledging excesses on the German side:

> Ach, uns war jedes feste Maß entraten, der Raum hatte seine Grenzen verloren, die Zeit ihre Zäsuren gebüßt, all Regel war hin, das Sinnfällige erloschen. Der Geist der dumpfen, furchtbaren Lebensstunde ereiferte sich in der Wut und Willkür eines der Vorstellung entlegenen Waltens, das über ein empfindsames Begreifen und die umfriedeten Gärten des Herzens rasend, stürzend in Katastrophen, Gewalt und Tod hinweggebrochen war.[111]

The atavistic primitivism presented in these instances by Rexroth and Böhmer may be read, *pace* Peitsch, as the product of a de-naturing occurring in reaction to the tactics of the enemy, or otherwise, simply as a direct product of the nature of close-quarter street fighting compounded by the involvement of civilian-clad enemy military and militia.

Peitsch refers to the *Ästhetik der Erfahrungsunmittelbarkeit* which underlay the institutionalisation of the *Propagandakompanien*,[112] the aesthetic of the immediate literary rendering of experience as exemplified in such cinéma vérité accounts. The heightening of sensory experience, "Favorisierung des Sinns vor den Tatsachen"[113] could favour the internalisation of the

---

109 See Günther Böhmer, *Pan am Fenster* (Berlin: Suhrkamp, 1943), pp.35-36.

110 On Böhmer's use of burlesque fantasy in the *Pan* interiors to point up the lost illusions of a civil world, see Curt Hohoff, 'Junge deutsche Erzähler', *Hochland*, 41 (1948/49), 282-88 (p.287).

111 Ibid., p.80.

112 Peitsch, '„Am Rande des Krieges"?', loc. cit., p.145.

113 Ibid., p.146.

propaganda image of the enemy 'other'[114] in that the representation of the self as product of a German and Western culture of the personality contrasted with a politically massed 'barbarity'.[115] The case argued by Peitsch is that the propaganda image of a less civilised and a politically brutalised enemy was sublimated in non-propagandist writing. It has been here contended that this reading is selectively extrapolative and that other, more immediately pragmatic readings also present themselves from the texts. It is here in addition suggested that there was a credible portrayal (Raschke, Rexroth) of an enemy in a more primal relationship to its land, and that references to the indomitability of that land are obliquely pacifist in allusion: "Nie, so schien es uns, würden wir das Herz dieser Erde erreichen, wir würden immer nur am Rande sein." (Bauer);[116] "…was ist noch meßbar in solcher Unermeßlichkeit?" (Leitgeb).[117]

3.4. Applied fictive form

Citing Wolfgang Weyrauch in his championing of Rexroth as forerunner of the 'realism of the immediate' and Alfred Andersch in praise of Bauer, Lange, Raschke and Rexroth in their subtle deployment of art against the parvenu clamour of National Socialism, Peitsch notes Andersch's reservation: that a certain literary escapism was a consequence of censorship and that, in order to be published at all, a choice of esoteric themes led to a slide into prose 'calligraphy'.[118] An examination of Lange and Rexroth's deployments of conventional forms of literary fiction will here contend that these are counter-examples to the charge of calligraphy.

In the case of Rexroth, the aesthetic of a direct rendering of immediate experience finds expression in the episodic novel, *Der Wermutstrauch*, closest among the other *Ostfront* accounts to true novel form. Weyrauch's naming of Rexroth, had he lived, as one among the champions of the *Kahlschlag*, the tabula rasa new movement in German literature, must have taken the achievement of *Der Wermutstrauch* into account in that judgement.[119] It is surprising that a summation sixty years after Weyrauch's can be as tersely reductive as Wallrath-Janssen's (2007), acknowledging Peitsch:

---

[114] Ibid.

[115] Ibid.

[116] Bauer, *Tagebuchblätter aus dem Osten*, p.60.

[117] Leitgeb, *Am Rande des Krieges*, p.91.

[118] Ibid., p.127.

[119] See Weyrauch, *Tausendgramm*, afterword (Reinbek bei Hamburg: Rowolt, 1989).

> ...auf eine Handlung ganz verzichtet: Einzelszenen aus dem Krieg in der Ukraine werden dargestellt. Der Krieg erscheint als Naturschicksal, der Feind als kämpfendes Untier oder duldsamer Flüchtling.[120]

Without implying a comparison in literary achievement, E.M. Forster's observation on *War and Peace* may here be cited: the great chords that a novel strikes come not from the story or plot, but "come from the immense area of Russia, over which episodes and characters have been scattered."[121] That is pertinent to the choice facing any author concerned with a similar scale of events. As Forster has it, the plot in a novel, the *Handlung*, "is the novel in its logical intellectual aspect."[122] A pattern must emerge, Forster insists, though it need not be so constricting of characters as with Henry James.[123] Pattern, Forster notes, may *itself* be plot.[124]

There is a pattern in *Der Wermutstrauch* of fates overtaking characters individually, as the random consequence of a planned wider pattern of events. The book opens in the summer of 1942, on the Sea of Azov, for the moment a military backwater. Northwards and eastwards, the battles for Kharkov and Rostov are imminent. In the course of an evening drinks party the withdrawn and malaria-stricken Lieutenant Thomas is casually requested by the admiral, after first a considerate enquiry as to the adequacy of his physical health, to command a night sortie of Croatian-manned coastal patrol boats. In a fog-bound chance encounter with an enemy flotilla Thomas is the only casualty. This occurs after weeks of inactivity: refugees are returning to the towns and the land; there is produce in abundance on sale, though most of the refugees are penniless. The women work as domestics for the Germans, the able-bodied men are gone. The self-engaged handyman at the base, "Ivan", a deserter, fusses to trim the coffin he has fashioned for the fallen Lieutenant.

The construction of a *Feindbild* of an antithetical enemy as photographic negative of an honourable and good-natured self-image did not, as Peitsch has also pointed out, exclude the attribution of humanity in depictions of Russian civilians: on the contrary; such private scenes served to contrast the brutality of the military opponent.[125] Though Rexroth's novel begins with a description of general desolation following on the Russian withdrawal, of abandoned houses deliberately rendered uninhabitable, and *soiled*, as though

---

[120] Anne M. Wallrath-Janssen, *Der Verlag H.Goverts im Dritten Reich*, pp.357-58.
[121] E.M. Forster, *Aspects of the Novel* (London: Penguin, 1990), p.51.
[122] Ibid., p.95.
[123] Ibid., p.143.
[124] Ibid., Appendix A, p.160.
[125] Forster, *Aspects of the Novel*, pp.133-34.

the enemy had wished to show his contempt,[126] the sympathetic portraits which populate the scene thereafter are individualised, and not mere types. "Ivan", the absent-without-leave Russian serviceman, makes himself useful about the base as a competent handyman, but salutes the German officers without any loss of his soldierly pride; a hapless Tatar, on the other hand, is scarcely tolerated by the Ukrainians and openly despised by the Russian Ivan. Among the Ukrainian working women, *Lisaweta*, Elizabeth, is portrayed as withdrawn and timid among the others and, unlike the rest, seemingly utterly without goods or shelter: she dies, by unlucky chance, in a bombing raid on the nearby city. Random fate and random death, for the Ukrainian Lisaweta as for Lieutenant Thomas, would seem to be Rexroth's motif and the novel's recurring theme.

Thus far, chapters I and II, the Lieutenant Thomas episode is a self-contained Novella within the novel: it is the story of "a fated life already essentially past"[127] mediated through the viewpoint of a narrator (who is present only once as an individual, as witness at the funeral, otherwise collectively, as "wir"). The Lieutenant Thomas character does not make the ethical choice of the tragic hero, but displays instead an inner spiritual passivity,[128] as when he readily accepts the unfamiliar, water-borne night mission sprung upon him in an off-hand way in the middle of an off-duty interlude. Active and speaking characters surround the 'absent' character of Thomas[129] and it is the presentation of these, as witnesses to the Thomas story, which emphasises the distance of this temporary, conditional, war-determined, transitory society from the security, hindsight and social stability of the Novella's audience.[130]

A flat character, the grenadier Stockmann, is the focaliser for chapter III; introduced without background, a character whose simple thoughts and words are supplied by the narrator. Stockmann's casual charity of half a loaf of bread is ignored by a roadside refugee too far gone in despair. The description of the refugee exodus is unsparing: they look the advancing Germans apprehensively in the face, or down at the ground like frightened animals looking for someplace to hide.[131] Both Germans and refugees are portrayed as equally exhausted from the march, though the Germans in contrast look upwards to the sky, for the relief from the empty land and fields, *which seem to extend up into the sky*, "die geradeaus in den Himmel zu

---

[126] Rexroth, *Der Wermutstrauch*, p.9.

[127] See Graham Good, 'Notes on the Novella', in *The New Short Story Theories*, ed. by Charles E. May (Athens, Ohio: Ohio Unv.Press, 1994), pp.147-64 (p.155).

[128] Ibid.

[129] Ibid., p.162.

[130] Ibid., p.161.

[131] Rexroth, *Der Wermutstrauch*, pp.37,40.

ziehen schienen",[132] and for the mental stimulus the cloudplay offers when sleep threatens to overcome them.[133] Citing reflective passages in Günter Böhmer's *Pan am Fenster* and Josef Leitgeb's *Am Rande des Krieges*, Peitsch (1984) writes: "Der Blick des schreibenden Soldaten geht nach oben, um den Sinn des Kriegs zu erfassen. [...] Der Sinn, den die schreibenden Soldaten finden, wenn sie nicht nach oben, sondern in die Weite blicken, meint Eroberung und Herrschaft."[134] The optical pragmatism of Rexroth's weary soldiers is convincingly vital where Peitsch's metaphors are tenuous inferences. Rexroth's disjointed narrative of the fates of individuals is disjointed by authorial intention, because disjuncture is the circumstance of all the lives in the narrative. In such circumstances the focus is neither upwards nor outwards, but inwards, on re-connection, on survival.

In chapter IV, a pair of twenty-one year old junior officers is introduced: separated in age by less than a year, but widely in temperament and acquired attitude. Wallis, the younger, is a company commander and company-seeking, but an outsider; Holzhausen, the elder, is battalion adjutant and reserved, yet of whose popularity his friend Wallis is envious. The two are loosely followed through the prelude to the attack on Rostov and the attack itself and its aftermath, are separated for four days in the confusion of the action and then reunited; thereafter not further mentioned. The pair's role as focalisers is more important in the peaceful interludes, as when Wallis visits the Russian theatre in Taganrog where the performers play the costumed roles of Ukrainians, Cossacks and Tatars: races some of whom are encountered and identified soon afterwards not far from the theatre in their reality as armed opponents, prisoners, and refugees. Holzhausen is placed in a set-piece interior scene where he is quartered on a fatherless family of a mother and two girls, of possible Tatar or Turkish extraction, and to whom he displays courtesy and consideration. It is conceivable that the scene is constructed for propaganda purposes to contrast humanity, cleanliness and cultivation (the girls sing, dance and play the guitar with accomplishment; the interior is poor, but clean) with the political brutality of the enemy regime. Peitsch maintains that this is a characteristic presentation for the non National Socialist writers writing in remit of the *Propagandakompanien*, and one exclusively played out in the interiors of Russian houses; moreover, that the cunning and brutality of the military actions contrasted with the tenderness of the familial scenes could be integrated into a picture which explained Russia as a riddle.[135] The ascription of such insidious motives to Rexroth's drawing of the character of Holzhausen would, however, be out

[132] Ibid., p.35.
[133] Ibid., p.34.
[134] Peitsch, '„Am Rande des Krieges"?', loc. cit., pp.136,137.
[135] Ibid., pp.133,134.

of balance: the family encounter occurs as epilogue to the Rostov action, includes a reverie of home on Holzhausen's part, and precedes shortly his reunion with Wallis, whose four-day disappearance is foremost on the character Holzhausen's mind.

The character of the grenadier Stockmann is reintroduced in chapter VII, on the march to Rostov, and is given a companion in Fährenberg, a fellow other-ranker. Stockmann is now given a background and some traits of character: he has been a market gardener in civilian life, is practical, and is the first of the two to learn the skills of survival. Fährenberg has been a lawyer, is not practical, and leaves the chores to Stockmann. The two, though older men, are new draftees, replacements, and junior in experience to the young soldiers in the troop. Then a change occurs: Stockmann, the married man with two daughters, puts aside thoughts of home; Fährenberg becomes the solicitous one. They are become dependent on one another. Yet, they are shunned and excluded: they have replaced two to whom in action they owed their own inexperienced lives, and as substitutes they are not accepted. Their isolation and feeling of inferiority produces a death-wish, and the others seem to view them with eyes which say that death will come to them as to their forerunners, "Kommt, Freunde…"[136] All this is succinctly conveyed within chapter VII. Nothing more is heard of either until the roadside grave of Stockmann is mentioned at the close of chapter XIII. The chapter VII psychology of unwitting self-alienation acting upon two minor characters is placed at the point in the narrative where the battle for Rostov culminates, and stands for the enclosed and self-referential order of thinking which detaches the active-service soldier from conventional norms. The aftermath of the initial armoured breakthrough of the Russian lines and the build-up to the fierce street-fighting forms for the *Ich Erzähler* an apocalyptic vision in chapter VIII.[137] A stiffly sprawled dead Russian soldier by the roadside at the beginning of chapter IX becomes "der Künder des Todes", the harbinger of random death which has already selected grenadier Stockmann, and so heralds the extended battle-sequence that forms the dramatic main movement which swells and then ebbs, spawning illuminating sub-scenes and bringing the narrative to a close.

The intermittent narrative thread of all the characters' progress is in fact subordinate to the long, detailed account of the street fighting in Rostov and the successive tableau scenes which depict the aftermath: the mineral water warehouse rewarding the thirsty troops with what the population must now draw from the Don, the wine warehouse where the soldiers indulge in an orgy of drunkenness, the looted grain warehouse where children sink

---

136 Rexroth, *Der Wermutstrauch*, p.100.

137 Ibid., pp.107-8.

without trace in the rush and suffocate; these scenes, and cameos of shantytown improvisation, starvation, and madness. The frank depiction of the nature of the fighting and of its effects on Germans and the Soviet civilians alike does correspond in that respect to the 'heroic realism' approved of by Goebbels after the winter of 1941-42,[138] but its detail is stark and un-heroic and without the presumption of moral superiority implicit in the propaganda projection of an enemy that fought with the "Bestialität einer primitiven Rasse."[139]

Horst Lange's novella, *Die Leuchtkugeln*,[140] published in a collection of three stories under that title in January 1944, accords with the formal principle of the novella: it is intensive in regard to character rather than (socially) extensive as with the novel. The fate of the foredoomed central character, the symbolically named "Hermes", is private and exceptional and is preceded by an inner spiritual passivity.[141] Some autobiographical parallels may be drawn with the author: Lange, frustrated by desk work as writer in a training unit, willingly accepted a posting as soldier-reporter to a 6th Army pioneer unit in September 1941.[142] Hermes is a successful organist-composer who has volunteered for front duty following a creative crisis.[143]

The unifying symbol of the title, the flare or star shell, is laboured in the narrative and only at the end given narrative point, when the character attains redemption through his self-sacrificing discharge of flares into the night sky to deceive the encircling enemy. There is no transformative individual epiphany or narratively decisive *Wendepunkt*;[144] rather, the whole frontline experience is for the character a revelatory detour on an already begun journey of self discovery. Hermes, the psychopomp, guide to the underworld (the character discusses eternity at one point) and as Hermes Trismegistos patron of astrology, and so of comets, '*Leuchtkugeln*', does have a moment of epiphanic premonition in claiming to hear in the signs of the coming battle, "eine klare, stille Wintermusik."[145] An allusion here to a Pythagorean 'music of the spheres' may loosely be inferred from the earlier reference to Hermes Trismegistos, through whom: "das Leben war nicht mehr vom Tod getrennt, er spielte damit wie mit Kugeln",[146] and the later reference to the character, 'Hermes', as one such as "jemand, der es [Musik]

---

138 Peitsch, '„Am Rande des Krieges"?', loc. cit., p.141.

139 Ibid.

140 Horst Lange, *Die Leuchtkugeln. Drei Erzählungen* (Hamburg: H.Goverts, 1944).

141 Cf. Good, 'Notes on the Novella', loc. cit., p.155.

142 Wallrath-Janssen, *Der Verlag H. Goverts im Dritten Reich*, p.363.

143 Lange, *Die Leuchtkugeln* (1944), pp.206-9.

144 Cf. Good, 'Notes on the Novella', loc. cit., p.155.

145 Lange, *Die Leuchtkugeln* (1944), p.171.

146 Ibid., p.97.

mißbraucht, um etwas zu glorifizieren, das der Ewigkeit widerstrebt."[147] The musical perfection which the character hears internally had remained unattainable to him in his musical career because he allowed himself to be seduced by musically hedonist digressions, and is now clearly distinguishable only in premonition of his own death. The narrator, observing the reserved and taciturn Hermes become talkative like others who somehow sense their own impending deaths, sees in the photographs he now passes around that the sensuous, 'fleshly' music which brought him acclaim had choked off "den reinen, kristallen Grundton [...] der alle Melodien zusammenhält wie eine zentrale Kraft, die auch das noch an sich zieht, was schon auf der Flucht ist...".[148] The allusion here is formulated in the thoughts of the narrator character. Earlier, on reaching an abandoned church that is an observation point in their reconnaissance, the narrator character exclaims, "Die Kirche!", which elicits the typically cryptic response from 'Hermes', "Ja, der Kontrapunkt! Der Grundton, man muß ihn hörbar machen. Um ihn kreisen alle Melodien der Welt."[149] The expressions here, the latter explicitly to 'orbiting music', are clearly Pythagorean, and allude therefore to more than the life of a single fictional character. Consistent with German novella theory, the fatalism is of the narrator's mood, the central character beset by an inner spiritual passivity rather than displaying a heroic assertion of the will, the tragedy bourgeois-sentimental.[150] The novella here, as with the short story, reveals through a crisis the essence of a way of life removed from the mainstream of society.[151] What, then, of its function or appropriateness in the context of the clash of *Weltanschauung*?

The premise, stated in the opening paragraph of the story, is that for all the others, but possibly not, implicitly, for the solitary 'Hermes', the war was first accepted in a wave of childishly exaggerated emotions of "Opfermut, Heroismus und dunklen, ungewissen Gefühlen, die uns beinahe den Atem abdrückten." As in all the other accounts, the seeming endlessness and emptiness of the vast land produces feelings of disorientation: "Angesichts dieser unbegrenzten Leere verlor man das Gefühl seiner selbst, man wurde unwichtig und bekam andere Dimensionen."[152] The narrator finds himself "nur durch eine winzige Entfernung von der Wirklichkeit getrennt", but this sense of being separated from reality by only a tiny distance suffices to make him feel as though he were standing outside his surroundings. He thinks on a fallen fellow NCO, a seed-collecting amateur botanist: "Er hatte ein Stück

---

[147] Ibid., p.207.

[148] Ibid., p.188, pp.189-90.

[149] Ibid., p.178.

[150] Cf. Good, 'Notes on the Novella', loc. cit., p.155.

[151] Ibid., citing Frank O'Connor's *The Lonely Voice*.

[152] Lange, *Die Leuchtkugeln* (1944), p.80.

Zukunft bei sich".[153] The fateful symbolism in the name of the routine replacement, 'Hermes', is recognised cynically by the commanding lieutenant and with foreboding by the narrator, 'Friedrich': "ein unsteter, schweifender Sendling, der selten das Glück mitbringt."[154] Hermes, unlike the others, does not curse the land, but urges that they respect it, as a sailor respects the sea: "Ein Ozean aus Erde, das ist auch ein Gegner."[155] He accords the same respect to a pilgrim vagrant as do the Russian locals.[156] He reasons successfully with the farmers who have protested at being compelled to demolish their own barn to furnish logs for an improvised causeway, whereas their appeal for an "Offizier!" had first produced a racist retort from another trooper, "Halt's Maul, gegen dich sind wir alle Offiziere!"[157] On another occasion, however, understanding Russian and hearing the mixed workforce of men and women impressed for snow-clearance duty mock the futility of the effort, Hermes, too, reacts with pejorative fury, but speaking of them, not to them: "Verdammte Bestien! Luderzeug! Aasbande!" [158] On forward patrol, the narrator encounters on the outskirts of a village the flitting figure of a farmer who "grau und gebückt, wie eine große Ratte über den Weg huschte."[159] Here, echoes of propaganda construction of the brutish *Feindbild*. The Russian population en masse is encountered only in its womenfolk in the shape of displaced city refugees.[160] Scenes of fraternisation, with accordion playing and communal singing, despite the security risk of which the narrator is keenly aware, serve the narrative purpose only of portraying the mental state of the death-resigned 'Hermes'.[161] It is here not so much, as Peitsch has posited,[162] the collective self-image of the Germans as inherently open, honourable and good natured and projected by inversion against the cunning of an enemy operating with guerrilla tactics in the rear, but, rather, their insecurity and incomprehension as individuals. Hermes forms a friendship, not with the reflective and insightful 'Friedrich' narrator, but with another, one of two like-named, an innocent, the gaunt figured and talkative "der hagere Max". Hermes, the knowing, bonds himself with the guileless innocent: the one of them careless of survival, the other willingly seeking death. The novella can only hint at

---

153 Ibid., pp.81,85.
154 Ibid., p.96.
155 Ibid., p.113.
156 Ibid., pp.142-43.
157 Ibid., p.136.
158 Ibid., p.166.
159 Ibid., p.203.
160 Ibid., pp.162,181.
161 Ibid., pp.162-63,190.
162 Peitsch, '„Am Rande des Krieges"?', loc. cit., p.131.

wider topics in the portrayal of its single, central character and then only through the recollections and reflections of its narrator. Its scope cannot be that of the novel, such as Rexroth's *Der Wermutstrauch*, and that latter itself, even without its disclaiming sub-title, 'Aufzeichnungen aus dem Kriege', could not be quite a novel since the ultimate social outcome of the events was not known and could not be predicted at the time of writing. The attempt to apply literary form to fluid events could ultimately be wholly successful only in the depiction of character, while incident, unresolved, lost its social character and occupied a temporary space between symbolism and reportage.

The interpretation of Rexroth's novel and Lange's novella offered here is contrary to the negative conclusions of Peitsch (1984) and to those of Wallrath-Jannsen's (2007) appraisal of the wartime work of authors contracted to the H. Goverts publishing house. The latter study concludes that the approach to the war of Rexroth and others, but especially of Lange, and their publishers, Goverts, revealed contradictions:

> ...Widersprüche deutlich, die zwischen der persönlichen Ablehnung des gegenwärtigen Kriegs einerseits und gleichzeitig der Bereitschaft der Verleger und Autoren bestand, diesen aktuellen Lebensbereich als individuelle Bewährungssituation wahrzunehmen, literarisch zu verarbeiten und diese Werke zu veröffentlichen.[163]

Advised by his publishers that the propaganda ministry would look favourably on a collection of freely written short stories from the front, Lange's indignant initial reaction was that the very choice of war-stories as genre was already an extensive concession to the wishes and purposes of the ministry. Lange's own appraisal of the nature of this work: "Zwitterding zwischen Literatur und Propaganda militärischer Art".[164] In response to criticism from Gottfried Benn,[165] however, Lange's vehement refutation of any political intent in the *Die Leuchtkugeln* trilogy of stories must argue for these, and in particular the title story considered here, to be judged not on their commissioning, but on their merits, from the text, as attempted here, as also in the case of Rexroth. The judgement of Wallrath-Jannsen in this regard seems sweeping:

> Weder der Autor [Lange] noch die Verleger wollten einsehen, daß Autoren wie Lange, genauso wie Rexroth und Schnabel, mit der Entwirklichung und Mythologisierung des Kriegsgeschehens in ihren Erzählungen mit dazu beitrugen,

---

163 Wallrath-Janssen, *Der Verlag H. Goverts im Dritten Reich*, p.358.
164 Ibid., pp.365-66,368.
165 Ibid., p.370.

> den Greueln des aktuellen Krieges eine Aura tranzendenter Sinnhaftigkeit zu unterlegen.[166]

Rexroth's sixty-five page stark account of the storming of Rostov,[167] as discussed in this and in the preceding section, cannot be summed up as *Entwirklichung* and *Mythologisierung*. Also, Lange's choice of the novella form preordains the principle of intensity rather than extensity and, with regard to character, dramatic or symbolic revelation rather than gradual development,[168] in which some degree of transcendental intensification of meaning, *Sinnhaftigkeit*, is not out of place. It is argued here that these two works avoid through literary rigour, at least in considerable degree, that general embroilment in propaganda divined by Peitsch and Wallrath-Jannsen. Denkler (2000) goes so far as to pronounce the *Der Wermutstrauch* and *Die Leuchtkugeln* as the two works of highest literary merit on the German side to emerge from the Eastern Front,[169] not least for their integrity, in that Rexroth and Lange do not shy away from attributing the trail of turmoil, death and destruction – "Bahnen des Todes" and "Wüste der Vernichtung" are Rexroth's phrases[170] – to the actions of the invading forces.[171] As to the literary qualities of the works, Denkler notes that the shortcomings of the fiction which Lange in his war diaries had feared, "das Unausgewogene, Lückenhafte, Fragmentarische, schlecht Gebaute und den „den großen Fluß" Verfehlende", and the formal deficiencies of Rexroth's events-driven, loosely figural and casually connected episodic novel, actually translated into an aesthetically innovative authenticity. Denkler points to changing narratorial perspectives, a subversive weakening of the auctorial narrative stance and, notably in Lange's case, the endowment of laconic and unadorned speech with the capacity for allusion and ambivalence, all as literary achievements which on the one hand helped to undermine the epigonic bombast of National Socialist writing and on the other to surmount the tiring monotony of classical-elitist escapism.[172] The sceptical and laconically cryptic anti-hero, 'Hermes', the cynical, at one point

---

166 Ibid.

167 Rexroth, *Der Wermutstrauch*, pp.110-176.

168 Cf. Good, 'Notes on the Novella' loc. cit., p.162.

169 Horst Denkler, ' "*So war der Krieg noch nie.*" Neues von der Ostfront', in *Literatur und Demokratie. Festschrift für Hartmut Steinecke zum* 60.Geburtstag, ed. by Alo Allkemper and Norbert O. Eke (Berlin: Erich Schmidt, 2000) pp.185-95 (p.192). See also Denkler, 'Was war und was bleibt? Versuch einer Bestandsaufnahme der erzählenden Literatur aus dem ‚Dritten Reich' ', *Zeitschrift für Germanistik*, vol.IX-2 (1999), 279-93 (p.292).

170 Rexroth, *Der Wermutstrauch*, p.192.

171 Denkler, in Allkemper & Eke (2000), p.193.

172 Ibid., pp.194-95.

defeatist,[173] commanding lieutenant of *Die Leuchtkugeln*, and the campaign-weary soldiers of *Der Wermutstrauch* who wonder, forgetting all indoctrination, how they are come to be there at all[174] – these are indicators of narratives intent, under the eye of the censor, on a non-conformist sub-text.[175]

---

173 Lange, *Die Leuchtkugeln* (1944), p.167.
174 Rexroth, *Der Wermutstrauch*, pp.43,159.
175 after Denkler, in Allkemper & Eke (2000), p.195.

4. Aesthetic dissidence

4.1. Erhard Göpel's *Die Normandie* and *Die Bretagne*

Already in 1940, two years before the appearance of *Frankreich*, Erhard Göpel's *Die Normandie* had appeared, printed in Paris by Curial-Archereau and with its publishing origin cited as "herausgegeben von einem Armee-Oberkommando". The publication is consistent with the educational and art-historical brief and activities of the *Kunstschutz* service of the military. The early publication date of *Die Normandie* testifies to the immediacy with which the purposes of the *Kunstschutz* service were set in motion. A second army-published edition appeared in Paris in 1941 and a third, civilian edition was published by Staackmann publishers in Göpel's native Leipzig in 1942, this latter with some substitution of woodcut illustrations, some of these at the expense of text,[1] and again with print and gravure from the Curial-Archereau press of Paris, with the author, discovered only on the back flyleaf of the military editions, now credited on the title page. The art historian Erhard Göpel had presented his doctoral dissertation entitled 'Ein Bildnisauftrag für Van Dyck, Antonius van Dyck, Philipp le Roy und die Kupferstecher' at Leipzig in 1940.[2] The prewar engagement of German scholars with the Norman and early Gothic architecture of Northern France, and notably that of Professor Hamann who had already established a photographic collection at Marburg, is acknowledged by Göpel.[3] The book's 90-page text is illustrated, the author's choice,[4] with fine-detailed woodcuts from Janin's *La Normandie*, Paris 1842, courtesy of the city library of Rouen, which also furnished the pull-out antique map of Normandy, *editions Merian*, 1663. The book has also an appendix of thirty-two numbered photographic plates. Twelve of the plates are credited separately and individually to French sources. Three plates are from prewar German collections and eleven plates from current German sources, all fourteen by courtesy of Count Metternich of the *Kunstschutz* service. The six remaining plates are, so Göpel expressly notes, *Propagandakompanie* photographs, several of these illustrating features of traditional Normandy architecture. Of all the plates, just three are not of exclusively architectural or topographical interest: one is of German sentries silhouetted in the portcullis gate of William the Conqueror's stronghold at Caen; another, whose caption makes reference to Seine bridges in the distant background rebuilt after the fighting of 1940, has the figure of an off-duty German serviceman in the foreground;

---

[1] See Göpel, *Die Normandie* (1940/1942), pp.39/40.
[2] See Blume, *Erhard Göpel*, p.7 and note 7.
[3] Göpel, *Die Normandie* (Paris: 1940), XII.
[4] Ibid., flyleaf.

the third is of booted German servicemen ambling on the shingle beach under the chalk cliffs at Etretat. These plates appear incongruent with the general tenor of the text and with the otherwise distantly historical intra-text illustrative complement. The distant-historic illustrative focus, so Göpel's commentary in the acknowledgments appendix, is that of the twentieth century, "unsere Zeit", which had its focus on the early stages of Norman architecture, whereas the 19th century had favoured the more ornate late Gothic:

> …so hat unsere Zeit ihr Augenmerk besonders auf die frühen Stufen der normannischen Architektur gerichtet, in denen sich der *Geist der einwandernden nordischen Stämme* auf eine eigentümliche Weise mit den überlieferten Formen weltlicher und kirchlicher Baukunst verband. [XII] (Italics added)

Though Duke William and his consort Mathilde piously endowed the abbey churches of St Etienne and Holy Trinity in Caen (plates 4-5, 2), the early Norman promotion of church building, in Normandy and virtually simultaneously in England, was bound up with the Norman purpose of reorganising and controlling the Church as an instrument of state. The imposing three-storey structure of St. Etienne, roofed by transverse vaults, was the influential model. That the bold spirit of its benefactor may well be read from it, Göpel does not doubt:

> Der Nachdruck der Auswahl liegt auf den Bauten, die sich mit der grossen Gestalt Wilhelms des Eroberers unmittelbar verbinden, *Meilensteine seines Werdens und Handelns*, an denen sein Lebensweg abzulesen ist. [...] Darauf folgen Beispiele normannischer Gotik, deren *kühne Bauweise* und deren *gestraffte, bespannte Formen normannischen Geist atmen.* [XII] (italics added)

The spirit of the "einwandernden nordischen Stämme" is admired in the high-tension daring of their church architecture. The attribution may have suited the associative needs of the Germanic expansionists, but its appropriation is denied by Göpel's scrupulous professional stress on the architectural features in themselves, by the particular attention he draws to the skill of the illustrative woodcuts, by the separate commentary he provides on each of these in the appendix (III-X), and by the stress he lays on the instructive coherence of the photographic plates (XI-XIV).

The geology, topography and customs of particular regions of Normandy, and its architecture and frontier strongholds, predominate throughout; also, excluding illustrations, twenty pages of text on its history, centred on its empire-building duke, and a penultimate chapter entitled *Geistige Landschaft der Normandie*, all attest to the author's enthusiasm for his subject. Political content there is. The Ehrke-Rotermunds (1999) have noted that because of the reading habits of the literary censors,[5] the beginning and the end of an oppositional work were particularly susceptible to scrutiny and that consequently a variation on the rhetorical rearrangement and transposition device of *transmutatio* – they suggest instead a "Platzwechsel", the simple shifting of a complete text to a less conspicuous position within a work – could serve to camouflage the true message of an author.[6] It is notable that the overt political content in Göpel's *Normandie* occurs on its opening and closing pages. The book opens with the sound of hoofs signalling the approach of a party of armed riders in a mist out of which a church spire appears to be launched as an arrow into the sky: "Reiter kamen näher, braunglänzende Pferdeleiber tauchten auf, ein Leutnant und sein Begleiter grüssten. [...] Waffen schlugen im wiegenden Takt der Reiter zusammen".[7] The fantasy is encouraged by a woodcut of a mounted knight in armour. Göpel cautions, however, that it is "ein weiter Weg", a long way, before land and people in their essence, "in ihrem Wesen" can rise up and take shape, "erstehen" before us, and that the reader must first gain knowledge of the historical springs before the Roman legions of Gaul and the adventurers, the "Reisigen", of William the Conqueror can in the imagination ride by with the apparent substance of the German cavalrymen encountered in the morning mist:

> Es ist ein weiter Weg, bis Land und Leute in ihrem Wesen vor uns erstehen, bis die Kenntnis der geschichtlichen Quellen vor unseren Augen die Legionäre Caesars und die Reisigen Wilhelm des Eroberers, des grössten Normannenfürsten, so lebendig vorüberziehen lässt, wie die deutschen Reiter, denen wir in den Morgennebeln eines Tages im Frühherbst des Jahres 1940, zwischen den Türmen von Norrey und Bretteville in der fruchtbaren Ebene um Caen begegneten.[8]

The association of the latter-day conquerors with their historic counterparts is therefore expressly qualified by the stipulation that for the conjured historical imagery to acquire living association, *lebendig vorüberziehen*, appreciative historical knowledge on the German side is required.

The closing paragraphs of the book hail the call to greatness, "der Zug zur Grösse", that the daring architecture and even more daring overseas ventures of the Normans, to England, to Sicily and to Constantinople itself, summon up. German soldiers stand watch in Normandy only because, for once, "die Volkskraft zusammen genommen worden ist in einer Hand." The

---

[5] On the overlap between propaganda ministry and military censorship in the occupied countries see von Wedel, *Die Propagandatruppen der deutschen Wehrmacht*, pp.71-76.

[6] Heidrun Ehrke-Rotermund and Erwin Rotermund, *Zwischenreiche und Gegenwelten.Texten und Vorstudien zur ‚Verdeckten Schreibweise' im „Dritten Reich"* (Munich: Fink,1999), p.18.

[7] Göpel, *Die Normandie* (1940), p.5.

[8] Ibid., p.6.

allusion here could not be more obvious, but again, Göpel utters a caution: that the memory of Norman greatness, won abroad and lost at home, "diese verwehende Erinnerung", should be a warning not to become bewitched by success but to remain "zum Handeln bereit".[9] The substantive may denote action or negotiation, according to context, and the latent ambiguity may conceal a warning against foreign expansion won at too high a cost. The formulation of the short final paragraph deserves examination:

> Der Zauber, den das Land für uns hat, ist seine grosse Vergangenheit. Diese verwehende Erinnerung spricht zu uns. Lassen wir uns nicht verzaubern, sondern bleiben wir zum Handeln bereit, ohne uns je, wie die Normannen es taten, in der Fremde zu verlieren.

The interpretation of Gordon (1996) that this is an admonition "to avoid the mistake of the early Normans and not lose their identity among the foreign peoples they conquered" seems too flatly literal.[10] Göpel's admonition has already occupied the whole of the two-page final chapter: it points to population decline, absentee landlords, Flemish immigration, the lure of Paris, to a dissipation and enervation of prudent, *contained* patriotism – and warns of a parallel.

Between the opening injunction to study the land and the closing admonition to take a lesson from that study, the content of the book is apolitical, except for the perhaps undue stress in so slight a book on the moulding influence of William of Normandy, and for a tilt at French coyness on the subject of Count Arthur de Gobineau, the founder of a new race doctrine, "einer neuen Rassenlehre".[11] The text is without the soaring lyric passages of Kästner's *Griechenland* and *Kreta*, but one paragraph on the character that the Norman weather imparts to the landscape is the equal of any in Kästner and for comparison deserves to be quoted in full:

> Ein unablässig wechselnder, von Seewinden bewegter Wolkenhimmel spannt sich über das Land, auch in den entfernteren Landstrichen die Nähe des Meeres erkennen lassend. Sein Atem ist als frischer Wind überall spürbar, der das Laub der hohen Buchen und Ulmen, des Gebüsches und der Hecken leise erzittern lässt, im Luftzug die hellen Innenseiten der Blätter sichtbar macht und so einen silbrig bewegten Ton in das Bild der Landschaft trägt, den auch der eilende Pinsel der Maler des vorigen Jahrhunderts nur selten im Bilde als Impression festzuhalten vermochte. Manchmal fegt der Wind die Wolken vom Himmel, der dann in reiner stählerner Bläue erstrahlt, die an Leuchtkraft den azurnen Himmel des Südens übertrifft.[12]

---

[9] Ibid., p.94.

[10] Gordon (1996), '*Ist Gott Französisch?*', loc. cit., p. 293.

[11] Göpel, *Die Normandie* (1940), p.32.

[12] Ibid., pp.7-8

The claim of superiority for the northern light with its steely blue over the deeper and more sensuous azure of the South parallels Kästner's enthusiasms for the intense Aegean light of Greece. The authors thus each champion their own adopted territory in a form of overarching lyrical depiction that appears to disregard as transitory the circumstances of conquest and occupation. As Eugen Blume's centenary *Denkschrift* address notes,[13] Göpel both directly and between the lines formulates the German occupation of Normandy as the last chapter, for the time being only, *vorläufig*, in the history of Normandy.[14]

Die Bretagne,[15] also "herausgegeben von einem Armee–Oberkommando", does not bear a publication place or date, though the end-piece drawing is dated 1940. Catalogue entries give the publication year variously as 1940 or 'circa 1940'.[16] As with *Die Normandie*, the illustrations are again black-and-white gravure, but from contemporary drawings, accredited to 'A. Conrad'. The press is that of the *Propagandakompanie* of the army newspaper, *West-Front*.[17] The compact format is that which is much enlarged upon in *Die Normandie*. The universal avoidance of the umlaut in the text: e.g., Breton *Haeubchen* and *Baeuerinnen* (though Anne de Bretagne in a ballad translation tours her *Güter* in sabots, and an attribution goes to a Prof. von Bülow), contrasts with scrupulous application of accent in place-name etymology, as in Plancoët and Le Folgoët. Though probably indicative of a scarcity of umlauted type font, this is also indicative of a careful and sensitive attention to orthography in French. Wholly unpretentious in layout, *Die Bretagne* is printed on exactly two quires of handmade paper, thirty two pages; the cover of the same paper in double thickness. A mere pocket booklet in comparison to *Die Normandie*, and a far cry from the lavish presentation volume that is the coffee-table format *Frankreich*, *Die Bretagne*'s appearance on handmade paper is, even so, clearly the work of a lover of the craft of bookbinding.[18]

As a cultural-history travel text, *Die Bretagne* opens with a short etymological explication of the Celtic and Brythonic names, Armorica and Brittany. The historical designation is distinguished from the administrative grouping of five *Departements* which comprise the "geographische und geschichtliche Landschaft."[19] As with *Die Normandie*, the account proceeds

---

[13] Blume, *Erhard Göpel*, p.7.

[14] See Göpel, *Die Normandie* (1940), p.68.

[15] Erhard Göpel, *Die Bretagne. Volkstum, Geschichte, Kunst* (1940).

[16] Cf. *Karlsruher virtuelle Katalog* (*KVK*).

[17] On the front newspapers cf. Eckhardt, op. cit.

[18] See Blume, *Erhard Göpel*, pp.5,7.

[19] Göpel, *Die Bretagne* (1940), p.3.

from a fundament of geology through language, settlement, history, and cultural monuments. Other than with Normandy, there are sections for a still-evident separate and distinctive folk craft tradition, folk poetry and folk music, and for the strong tradition of individualistic thought in Brittany, from Abbot Abelard, to Chateaubriand, to Ernest Renan. At the centre of the book is a catalogue of architectural monuments from Roman through the Gothic, the Renaissance and the Baroque to the contemporary. The format of the whole is that of a conventional, concisely written guidebook, though the elevated register of one paragraph pair in the almost two full pages devoted to Mont St. Michel is remarkable:

> Wer sich dem Michelsberge von ferne naehert, vergisst Stile und Baudaten, denn sein Herz spricht mit. Hebt sich der Berg zu Seiten der Ebbe schwer und massig aus dem weiten Sandmeer, scheint er zu anderer Stunde, von der Hoehe bei Granville gesehen, gleich einem stolzen Schiff durch die Fluten zu ziehen oder von seiner hoechsten Spitze, fast aus der Vogelschau betrachtet, sich als vielstufige Pyramide in einem Punkt zu verjuengen, immer wirkt er traumhaft als Zauberberg. Sinnt man dem Eindruck nach, so steigen Maerchenschloesser aus Kindheitserinnerungen auf, Bilder der himmlischen Stadt auf dem goldenen Grunde der Tafeln mittelalterlicher Maler, endlich die das Heiligtum verwahrende Gralsburg.
>
> Weltliche und geistliche Macht vereinigten sich im Zeichen von St. Michaels Schwert und verwandelten den gewachsenen Fels zu gebauter Architektur, den Elementen, Woge und Sturm zum Trotz; Gott zur Ehre.[20]

The exclusive emphasis which the final expression derives from the preceding semicolon admits of no claims of latter-day conquerors. Pithy and poetic though Göpel's prose here is, it is surpassed in architectural erudition by the propagandist Guido K. Brand's essay, 'Mönche stürmen den Himmel', which is also not inferior in poesy: "Bauliturgie"; "Kyrie eleison in dutzenden von schmalen Türmchen."[21] Apropos of the case of Göpel, Brand's earnest propagandist discourse (e.g., that conscripted labour in the German war effort worthily relieved the unemployment caused throughout Europe by the war itself),[22] yet evident liberal cultivation (e.g., philosophical reflections on the meaning of death, citing Plato, Cicero and Schopenhauer, prompted by the loss of Brand's own son on aerial reconnaissance in Russia),[23] is a polarised example of the ethical contradiction at the heart of neohumanist essays written from occupied soil.

In Göpel's slight booklet there is no reference to the German military presence, or to history-shaping conquests of the past. In *Die Bretagne*, only in

---

[20] Göpel, *Die Bretagne* (1940), p.14.

[21] Brand, *Zwischen Domen und Bunkern*, pp.164-71 (pp.166,165).

[22] Ibid., p.123.

[23] Ibid., pp.127-8,129.

the final paragraph is a comparison drawn with contemporary Germany with the suggestion that if one were seeking in order to understand its character to compare Brittany with a German province, then Westphalia would the most likely to spring to mind, "wo dem Boden eine aehnlich elementare Kraft entwaechst, die alle Lebensaeusserungen durchdringt." Brittany resembles Westphalia therefore in being elementally durable. The choice of parallel may be read as an allusion to Westphalia's former status as a province of Prussia, by which Göpel may be suggesting that transitory political subordination need not diminish the elemental character of a land. Göpel's closing sentence seems even more pointed, "Es ist ein Land, dessen Stein der Granit und dessen Baum die Eiche ist."[24] The German plans to weaken the territorial integrity of France by granting autonomy to Brittany were no secret: Felix Hartlaub had read about such plans, for Burgundy also, and remarks on them in a letter of August 1940.[25] The emphasis throughout *Die Bretagne* is on cultural distinctiveness, though nowhere with an anti-French political overtone.

Blume observes that the incongruity of the publication of two such works as *Die Bretagne* and *Die Normandie* by an *Armee-Oberkommando*, for an intended readership of German servicemen, allows of a reading of them as enlightening texts against the barbarity of the wish to militarily subdue an ancient European cultural power.[26] Not the incongruity of their publication alone, but also the understated by-play in their texts makes them works enlightening against barbarity. Göpel makes it clear that before France itself, Normandy was such a European cultural power. Affection for Brittany is coupled with a strong admiration for Normandy and for the character, enterprise and cultural achievements of its people: it is notable Mont St Michel, the subject of Göpel's lyrical passage, lies on the border between Brittany and Normandy. The play on the role of the Conqueror is an obvious and neutral ploy. Current expansionist political orthodoxy could even be flattered, in a backhanded way:

> In manchem kleinen Ort findet man das Denkmal eines Kolonisators, der nach Uebersee, nach Kanada und anderwärts ging und den französischen Kolonialbesitz aufbauen half. *Noch einmal zeigte sich normannischer Unternehmungsgeist.* [*Die Normandie*, p. 65] (italics added)

An echo of the Wilhelmine ambition to emulate France's colonial empire, re-asserted in the present conflict, albeit in an Easterly direction, may be heard in this, as Göpel would have known. Equally, the formulation

---

[24] Ibid., p.30.
[25] See Ewenz I (2002/2007), pp.422/429.
[26] Blume, *Erhard Göpel*, p.7.

suggests that successful expansion was the product of hard work rather than of offensive war.

Blume's memorial address does not conceal the fact that Göpel's wartime duties after his call-up to the translation service were latterly discharged from Holland where, based in the Hague, he was the agent of Dr. Hans Posse and of Posse's successor, Dr. Hermann Voss, in the project of acquiring artworks for Hitler's project of a 'Centre of European Culture' in Linz, which project also involved Göpel in the *Einsatzstab Rosenberg* activities in France.[27] A telegrammed report from Göpel (to Martin Bormann) in April 1943 gives details of the discovery, in the administrative area of Vichy France, of the art collection of the Jewish Schloss family and of the attempted removal of the collection to German custody. Göpel's report concludes with a recommendation that further 'direct action' be suspended in view of the legality of the situation and pending approaches to the Laval-Petain government.[28] After the Louvre museum authorities had appropriated 49 paintings from the confiscated Schloss collection, Göpel is known to have later appraised remainder and thereafter, presumably on his recommendation, a further 226 paintings were reserved for Hitler's Linz project.[29] To the contrary of this image of Göpel, his friendship while in Holland with the political-exile German expressionist painter Max Beckmann and his help given to members of the circle of friends around Beckmann is cited by Blume, who also suggests that Beckmann's 1944 portrait of Göpel was a token of esteem that would not have been accorded a mere functionary.[30] It is also notable that Göpel, upholding an arrangement of the deceased Posse, continued to protect the life of the Jewish art historian, collector and (in exchange for his life) informant on Jewish collections, Vitale Bloch.[31] Göpel did not later seek to justify or excuse his wartime role and, when urged to by a Dutch friend from the wartime years, declined to claim any credit for himself in a planned book on Beckmann.[32] In consequence of his extended involvement with the Linz project, Göpel failed to re-establish a career in the postwar museums' service. The Dresden art gallery's director, the same Hans Posse, had also engaged Göpel's colleague Erhart Kästner for twenty days in March 1941 to arrange the purchase (at well below market value) for the Linz project of the

---

[27] Blume, *Erhard Göpel*, p.12; cf. Hildegard Brenner, *Die Kunstpolitik des Nationalsozialismus*, p.158.

[28] Hildegard Brenner, op. cit., pp.231-32.

[29] Hans Christian Löhr, *Das Braune Haus der Kunst. Hitler und der »Sonderauftrag Linz«* (Berlin: Akademie Verlag, 2005), pp.142-143.

[30] Blume: *Erhard Göpel*, p.12.

[31] Löhr, op. cit., pp.121(note), 136.

[32] Blume, *Erhard Göpel*, p.12.

private library of Ludwig Töpfer, the Austrian Jewish lawyer and book collector, since 1938 emigrated to Southern France and Switzerland.[33] That the one, Kästner, was by inclination a librarian and the other, Göpel, an art historian, proved fateful for the latter.

Erhard Göpel was appointed to the Linz project on the personal recommendation of Martin Bormann. As the authorised representative in the Netherlands of Voss who, unlike his predecessor Posse, did not travel in person in the pursuit of artworks, Göpel was an energetic acquisitor.[34] Yet, no confiscated artworks can be shown from German or Dutch records to have come into the Linz collection through the agency of Göpel.[35] The high rate of state retention in Holland (65%) and in France (50%) of artworks recovered from the Linz project and the low rate of artworks returned to the original owners (Holland: circa 12%) has been cited as indication that Hitler's agents had recourse for the most part to the art trade,[36] which trade, in Holland as in France, enjoyed a boom and record prices as a result.[37] That Ludwig Töpfer's library did not revert to any heirs, and is today deposited in institutional libraries in Germany, is a counter-comment on such statistics.

4.2. Göpel and Erhart Kästner: freedom of the aesthete

Göpel's *Normandie* was submitted as a model in the proposal for the Kästner/Kaulbach *Griechenland*[38] and its publishing history is similar: two army editions in Paris in 1940 and 1941, followed by the civilian edition in Leipzig in 1942. *Griechenland* also appeared in two army editions, since part of the print-run of the edition of 1943 was reserved for the military.[39] Whereas Hiller von Gaertringen's research in the Kästner archive reveals that Kästner took a continuing interest in *Griechenland*, revising, rewriting, and planning additional chapters,[40] Göpel's *Normandie*, by contrast, shows no sign of authorial revision in its 1941 and 1942 editions at all. Göpel's wartime role thereafter may have precluded further such work, but *Normandie* is in any case not written in the style of a personal memoir, and lends itself less easily to such later interpolations as appear in Kästner's *Ölberge, Weinberge*. It is notable that Kästner's Homeric comparisons, occurring as they do at the start of *Griechenland*, are prefigured in the 'mediaeval riders' opening passage of *Normandie*. Göpel was already a

[33] See Hiller von Gaertringen (1994), p.66.
[34] Löhr, *Das Braune Haus der Kunst*, p.121.
[35] Ibid, pp.121,139.
[36] Ibid., pp.164,166.
[37] Ibid., pp.140,143.
[38] See Hiller von Gaertringen (1994), p.98.
[39] Ibid., p.107.
[40] Ibid., pp.105-8.

professional associate and friend of Kästner, the two having worked together from 1938 to 1940 on a planned Gutenberg exhibition at Leipzig.[41] That Kästner admired Göpel's natural and apparently simple style is clear from his letter to the then dying Göpel in 1966:

> Fast niemand sonst wagt es, Wärme zu zeigen [...] Fast niemand sonst müht sich, einfach zu schreiben; alle schrauben. [...] Dein Schreiben [...] jede Art von Formel verschmäht.[42]

The same letter reveals that the beginning of writing did not come easily to either author, and that both upheld the code that art must conceal art: "es ist der Pour le mérite allen Schreibens, daß es schwerfällt und daß es gelingt, dieses Schwerfallen wie eine Schande geheimzuhalten, der Leser darf es um keinen Preis merken."[43] That Kästner believed that there was a place alongside scholarly discipline for warmth and passion, and which he had admired in Göpel: "Wärme zu zeigen", is clear from this declaration from *Kreta*:

> Ich bedaure es wie viele, daß sich die Wissenschaft den frei geäußerten Strom der Bewunderung und das flammende Gefühl verbot, wie es zu Winckelmanns Zeiten noch üblich war.[44]

Writing to Gerhard Nebel 1950, Kästner admits that he, too, 'flew on the mane of the beast of militarism', "flog ja schließlich dem Untier Militarismus auf Schulter und Haupt", and at times found it a splendid vantage point, "genoß zu Zeiten eine herrliche Aussicht von dort oben."[45] The same admission in the same phrasing occurs in Kästner's *Ölberge, Weinberge* of 1953.[46] Kästner in his letter is chiding Nebel for not acknowledging as much in his published war diaries.[47] As writers, Kästner and Nebel visited the Algerian Sahara together in the winter of 1950-1951, but had not been acquainted with one another before or during the war.[48] Kästner reminded Göpel, on the other hand, that it was the war which provided him and Kästner with the impetus to write: "Seltsamerweise hat dieser Krieg [...] sowohl Dich wie mich zum Schreiben gebracht." Kästner may be referring here to the difficulties of preserving personal integrity while discharging

---

[41] See Raabe, *Erhart Kästner. Briefe*, p.242.
[42] Ibid., pp.191,192.
[43] Ibid., p.192.
[44] Kästner, *Kreta* (1946), p.37.
[45] Raabe, *Erhart Kästner. Briefe*, p.108.
[46] See Kästner, *Ölberge, Weinberge* (Wiesbaden: Insel, 1953), p.21.
[47] See Raabe, *Erhart Kästner. Briefe*, pp.107-8,260.
[48] Ibid., p.260.

commissions to write *Die Bretagne* and *Die Normandie* when he adds, "ohne Zweifel mußtest Du, als du zu schreiben begannest, von einem ganz entgegengesetzten Ort ausgehen."[49] This may also be a tactful allusion to the burden of Göpel's wartime role on his postwar writing career. The continuity evident nonetheless in the postwar writings of Kästner and of Göpel projects backwards onto their wartime works, making these the beginning of a consistent continuum. Göpel, whose doctoral study is echoed in his selection exclusively of nineteenth century woodcuts for the text-illustrations in *Die Normandie*, continued to publish on graphic art, particularly on woodcuts and lithographs, one of his first accredited postwar books being an introduction to and commentary on the works of Gauguin.[50] In the commentary of his 1955 publication on German woodcuts of the twentieth century he sees the woodcuts as starkly confronting the nation, the nation viewed as a living being, a *Lebewesen*, beset with the unexpressed and the avoided, with the *Unausgesprochene* and the *nicht Angeschaute*, with the demons, in fact, which lurked in the national consciousness:

> Faßt man das Volk als Lebewesen und die Äußerungen seiner Künstler als die stellvertretende Aussage für eine bestimmte Lebensstufe, [...] Das Chaotische, ein Bestandteil des deutschen Volkscharakters, kann aber nur besiegt werden, wenn man sich ihm stellt, wenn jeder einzelne es aus dem Bereich des Unausgesprochenen, nicht Angeschauten, aus dem Dunkel der Höhle herausholt, sich in dieser Absicht auch der ursprünglichen Aussage dieser Holzschnitte anvertraut, sein Gefühl durch ihre Bilderwelt wie durch Mühlen hindurchströmen läßt.[51]

The viewer, i.e. the viewing *Lebewesen* of the nation, shall trust the original message of the woodcuts and allow its feelings to be milled through their image-world, for to seek to evade demons is to be condemned to be pursued by them: "denn den drohenden Dämonen, dort, wo sie gebannt worden sind, zu entwischen suchen, heißt in primitiveren Regionen von ihnen wieder und wieder heimgesucht werden."[52] That Göpel's comment here is a post-bellum politically conscious one is unmistakable. It is yet another coincidence that Kästner, too, should make a political statement stemming from a world view presented in woodcuts. Writing the afterword to a selection of Andre Maillol's woodcuts of the pastoral antique, *Hirtenleben*,[53] and borrowing works on Maillol from Göpel for the

---

[49] Ibid., pp.191-92.

[50] See Göpel, *Paul Gauguin* (Munich-Vienna-Basel: Kurt Desch, 1954).

[51] Erhard Göpel, *Deutsche Holzschnitte des XX. Jahrhunderts* (Frankfurt am Main: Insel, 1955), p.49.

[52] Ibid.

[53] Erhart Kästner, *Aristide Maillol. Hirtenleben* (Frankfurt am Main: Insel, 1957).

occasion,[54] the focus for Kästner is on the celebration of the body, as the incarnation of expression:

> Maillol, das ist deutlich, ist der große Erotiker unter den neueren Künstlern [...] *jede Linie brennt.* Jede Linie ist so lange behandelt, bis nur noch ihr Glühendes, nur ihre Liebeskraft bleibt.[55]

And on light, as in *Griechenland/Kreta*:

> Wer sie anschaut, wird sich vom Licht des Südens angestrahlt finden. Ist es nicht, als ob die schwarzen, kraftgeladenen Linien ein Gitterwerk seien, durch welches das Licht aus und ein gehen kann und so nur noch glanzvoller wird?[56]

Kästner's suggestion that the trenched outlines of the woodcuts make a tracery through which the light of the South streams with a greater intensity is fanciful, but no more so than Göpel's darker vision of national demons lurking in inky impressions. Kästner in continuation grounds the many observations of physical beauty which occur in *Griechenland/Kreta*:

> Erotik bedeutet das gleiche wie: sich wohlfühlen in dieser Welt. Hier beheimatet sein. Der Grad des Heimatgefühls wird immer von Eros gemessen, denn Eros ist Heimat. [...] wo Erotik verfehlt oder verdünnt wird [...] da ist Heimat und Ordnung im Schwinden.[57]

The continuation of the text from this point makes an extraordinary political claim: "Das ist ja der Grund, weshalb die modernen Gewaltstaaten der Erotik mißtrauen: wo Eros herrscht, ist nichts zu holen für sie.[58] Eros must here be interpreted in the sense of the life instinct which seeks the uninhibited enjoyment and celebration of life, as in Freudian theory. *Griechenland* and *Kreta* of 1942-1944 affirm and lyricise this life instinct. Göpel, too, had something to say on the political aspect of the erotic, in his editorial foreword to the 1954 re-issue of Otto Julius Bierbaum's *Eine empfindsame Reise im Automobil* of 1903.[59] Göpel, ever conscious of books as craft objects, before reviewing the achievement of Bierbaum's imitation of Sterne's *Sentimental Journey* lauds him first as one of the energetic initiators of

---

[54] See Raabe, *Erhart Kästner. Briefe*, p.132.
[55] Kästner, *Hirtenleben*, p.44.
[56] Ibid.
[57] Ibid., pp.44-45
[58] Ibid., p.45.
[59] See Erhard Göpel (1954), 'Der Dichter im Auto, oder, Die Wendung vom Jugendstil zur technischen Form', reproduced in Göpel (ed.), *Otto Julius Bierbaum. Eine empfindsame Reise im Automobil* (Munich: Langen-Müller, 1979), pp.263-78.

Art Nouveau in typography.[60] Brenner (1997) sees in Bierbaum's allusion to Sterne the difficulties of reconciling the reading public for travel literature in German to such a non-traditional mode of transport.[61] Bierbaum's automobile journey across the Alps and down the Italian peninsula was made in 1902. So early in the automobile era, Bierbaum could ruefully foresee the effects of the coming acceleration of the pace of life and advised that humans should by choice travel slowly in cars.[62] Kästner, forty years on, pronounced in *Kreta* on the car windscreen as barrier to the true travel experiences that only unmediated, in-the-flesh contact brings: "die Windschutzscheibe [...] die wahre Vertreibung aus dem Paradiese aller echten Reiseerlebnisse."[63] Göpel's analysis is that what overwhelmed Bierbaum was not the works of modernity, but the architecture of the antique; Bierbaum sensed that modern man, even when empowered by the automobile, did not possess the greatness of mind, "Seelengröße", appropriate to that architecture.[64] Of Bierbaum's sensuous eye, Göpel noted that Eros who begot beauty and Pan who ensanguined it were his gods, and that so he was alert to beauty in the human form everywhere. Göpel believed that it took two world wars to make it clear that such a free aesthetic view was forbidden and to finally topple the world of the free aesthete:

> Es hat zweier Kriege in Europa bedurft, ehe das Unmögliche, ja Unerlaubte einer solchen Anschaungsweise deutlich wurde, die Welt der Ästheten ein für allemal zusammenstürzte.[65]

Writing in 1967 to a correspondent who had seemed to impute a feeling of guilt to his reticence in republishing *Kreta*, Kästner declares flatly that the book was commissioned by and its research watched over by a commanding general on Crete who was later executed for war crimes (the unfortunate General Bräuer, executed on a 3-2 verdict, contrary to the convention in Greece of royal commutation in such cases),[66] and that the book also *honoured* that general, who had read and approved its manuscript. Kästner

---

[60] Ibid., p.264.

[61] See Peter J. Brenner, *Reisekultur in Deutschland*, p.161.

[62] Göpel, *Otto Julius Bierbaum*, p.269.

[63] Kästner, *Kreta* (1946), p.65.

[64] Göpel, *Otto Julius Bierbaum*, p.267.

[65] Ibid., p.272.

[66] Raabe, *Erhart Kästner. Briefe*, p.193;
cf. Hagen Fleischer, 'Deutsche „Ordnung" in Greichenland in 1941-1944', in *Von Lidice bis Kalavryta. Widerstand und Besatzungsterror*, ed. by Hagen Fleischer and Loukia Droulia (Berlin: Metropol, 1999), pp.151-224 (pp.196,198); and Marlen von Xylander, *Die deutsche Besatzungsherrschaft auf Kreta 1941-1945*, p.139.

adds that because the book was intended in the first instance for a garrison readership which was steeped in arrogance towards what it saw as a backward Cretan population, the war at large and local incidents of war were quite intentionally assigned a minor role. Kästner gives as his reasons for not re-publishing *Kreta*, the book's lack of appropriate literary level, *Niveau*, and of correct approach, *Ansatz*,[67] that is, of scholarly and literary deficiencies on which the war and its incidents had in any case no bearing. This, from Kästner, is a declaration of the freedom of the aesthete, the freedom which his colleague and friend Göpel saw as in the end lost anyway.

4.3. *Griechenland/Kreta*: repossession of classical Greece

Out of the fortuitously prevailing sense of proprietary custodial guardianship of the Greek antique the consent of the commanding general of air operations Europe Southeast, General Wilhelm Mayer, was secured in the Spring of 1942 to the commissioning of an illustrated book on Greece and its classical sites by Erhart Kästner and the psychology student and artist Helmut Kaulbach, both then by chance serving in a psychological-aptitude testing unit of the air force, in Athens. The book was actually the spontaneous idea of Kästner and Kaulbach, conceived on an Aegean voyage, as Kästner recounts in the 1953 *Ölberge*.[68] Their unit commander, Major Bruno Schaar, who had been responsible for bringing Kaulbach to Greece,[69] had responded enthusiastically and presented the type-scripted proposal to General Mayer. At the level of two individuals, therefore, personal literary and graphic interests coincided with military politics. Offering Göpel's *Die Normandie* as example, an element of competition was appealed to, as is clear from the opening lines of the proposal:

> Es wird angeregt, nach dem Muster einiger Armee-Oberkommandos (siehe Anlage "Die Normandie") ein Griechenland Buch des Luftgaues Süd-Ost herauszugeben.[70]

The proposal text goes on to say that the intention of the book is that its servicemen readers will view positively and affirm, "bejahen", their term of duty in Greece. General Mayer's foreword to the service edition of 1942 claimed with evident self-satisfaction (and with some validity)[71] that no classical cultural monument in Greece or on Crete had been damaged by German weapons in the campaign of 1941.[72] Hiller von Gaertringen (1994),

---

[67] See Raabe, loc. cit., p.193.
[68] See Kästner, *Ölberge, Weinberge* (Wiesbaden: Insel, 1953), pp.19,20.
[69] Ibid., p.16.
[70] Cited from photostat reproduced in Hiller von Gaertringen (1994), p.98.
[71] See Günther-Hornig, *Kunstschutz*, pp.76-78.
[72] See Hiller von Gaertringen (1994), p.190.

drawing on the Kästner archive at Wolfenbüttel where Kästner was library director for eighteen years from 1950, recounts the history of the publication of *Griechenland*.[73] Five thousand copies of the book, with the sub-title *Ein Buch aus dem Kriege*, reached Athens on New Year's Day 1943, Kästner himself having accompanied their transport by rail and road all the way from Berlin.[74] A second edition, with part of the print run reserved for civilian readers, was published in Berlin in 1943.[75] The book, while being informative on the classical sites as they then appeared and as they once were, is written in the form of a memoir of Kästner's personal encounters with the sites. Distance is achieved, however, not least through Kaulbach's spare, minimalist pen sketches, especially in their delicate mastery of vanishing point perspective in landscape and townscape scenes. Kästner in his *Kreta* eulogy for Kaulbach applauds the harmony achieved between the drawings, often naïve in technique, and the text of *Griechenland*:

> Er hat viel erreicht in seinen Blättern von Griechenland. Daß einige Fertigkeit fehlt, ist eher ein Vorzug. Dafür hat es die Unschuld. Dafür ist die Lust des Ergreifens darin und das Staunen. Sie haben die Leichte des Lichts und das Karge, und in vielen liegt die ganze griechische Seligkeit.[76]

Though officially sanctioned out of a preening sense of proprietary obligation in matters cultural felt by the occupiers of the 'New Europe', (which concept had still currency, if not credibility, in 1942: Heinrich Böll, tongue-in-cheek, and Felix Hartlaub in mildly sardonic tones, refer to it at the war's outset),[77] the sell-out of the first, service, edition of *Griechenland* evidenced a need of personal connection felt at the level of the individual serviceman.

4.4. Aesthetic of light: Erhart Kästner and Felix Hartlaub

In deploring the housing of Grecian marbles in the dull interiors of northern museum halls as a crime against the Greek spirit, and singling out for particular opprobrium the reassembly of whole temples – a slighting,

---

[73] Ibid., pp.96-107.

[74] Ibid., p.104.

[75] *Griechenland. Ein Buch aus dem Kriege*, (Berlin: Gebrüder Mann, 1943); see Hiller von Gaertringen (1994), p.107.

[76] Kästner, *Kreta* (1946), p.79.

[77] Cf. Böll, *Briefe* I, p.32, "Was schreibt der deutsche Soldat nach Hause? Daß er sich unsagbar glücklich fühlt, dienen zu dürfen an diesem großen Werk, das Europa ein anderes Gesicht geben wird."; also Hartlaub, "Man kann dort [Wilhelmshaven] interessante Studien machen über die neue Nackenlinie im neuen Europa. Dipl. Ing's und Kolbenringe, Gespräche von Brest bis Narwick." (Ewenz, 2002/2007), pp.444/451-52.

certainly, of the prestigious new Pergamon museum in Berlin (*Griechenland*, pp.14-15) – Kästner was going beyond, but with regard to lighting merely echoing, Gerhart Rodenwalt, director of the *Deutsches Archaeologisches Institut*, who expressed the same reservation in his introduction to Walter Hege's *Die Akropolis* (1935).[78] Hege's photography had used coloured lens filters to enhance the contrasts in black-and-white photography, cropping out the modern also, to produce timeless, mythical scenes.[79] Kästner, in the same passage, praises the initiative of Hege or possibly of fellow-photographer Herbert List in photographing sculptures from the Acropolis museum in the open air.[80] But it is far more in Kästner's case than a concern for authentic presentation in the round or in reprographic representation. The extraordinary lyrical outpouring in praise of the qualities of the Greek light and its suffusing of the entire Greek landscape goes to the heart of Kästner's case that here in the present day Greece was a heightened sense of *Dasein* quite beyond that available from the Greek-derived Enlightenment culture of the West itself. Hiller von Gaertringen posits that Kästner came to Greece with a wholly classical preconception, born out of the neohumanist reception of the antique as founded by Johann Joachim Winckelmann (Kästner drafted a text on Winckelmann in 1945-6 during his detention in Egypt),[81] and that he sought after the sensuous intensification of existence, "nach der unmittelbaren, sinnlichen Erfahrung der Daseinssteigerung,"[82] and found it in transcendental landscapes and unworldly worlds formed out of naked rock and sheer transfiguring light:

> Ausgehend von der Hypothese Winckelmanns, dass die klassische Idealität Folge der in der Natur vorgefundenen Schönheit gewesen sei, fand er sie im Erlebnis griechischer Landschaft: zum einen in der magischen Wirkung des Lichts [...] transzendente Landschaften, erdenferne Welten nur aus nacktem Fels und Licht.[83]

---

[78] See Marchand, *Down from Olympus*, pp.338-40.

[79] Ibid.

[80] Ibid., p.340.

[81] See Hiller von Gaertringen (1994), p.268.

[82] Hiller von Gaertringen, 'Erhärt Kästner. Ein Annenser und unbeirrbarer Humanist' (address at St.Anna Gymnasium, Augsburg, 2 July 2006), Lippische Landesbibliothek Detmold Texte , p.7, at http://www.llb-detmold.de/wir-ueber-uns/aus-unserer-arbeit/texte.html [accessed 27 January 2012]. See also Hiller von Gaertringen, "Im Herzen Griechen und im Geiste Christen zu sein, das oder das Garnichts ist unsere Lage". Zum 100. Geburtstag Erhart Kästners, p.8, at http://www.llb-detmold.de/wir-ueber-uns/aus-unserer-arbeit/texte.html [accessed 27 January 2012].

[83] Ibid.

Felix Hartlaub exhibited a similar fixation in occupied Paris with the phenomenon of light and light-produced tonal and hue effects (see here 5.6, 5.10). It is as lyric that Kästner's celebration of the intense yet diffuse Greek light is remarkable. There is an insistent repetition that the perception of light is essential to the Greek experience. In extract, the passages referring to light and light effects in *Griechenland* are remarkably similar in colour ranges and in adjectival phrases to those of Hartlaub's Paris sketches:

> p.13: "Das griechische Licht, es geht nicht einmal nur das Auge an, sondern es ist ein Strom, der den ganzen Menschen durchflutet. Es ist ein flirrendes, belebendes, elektrisch spannendes Element. Es hebt alle Schwere auf. Es trägt."
> p.15: "Kein Maler hat sie noch gemalt, diese griechische Welt im Licht. [...] Der will erst noch kommen, der den Glockenklang der lichten Meeresbläue, den Lichtatem der Ölbaumwälder und die klingende Ferne dieser Berglinien malen kann;"
> p.18: "Jede der griechischen Tempelruinen hat ihre eigene, unvergeßliche Farbe. Die Akropolis ist honigfarben goldgelb, Olympia von uraltem Silbergrau. Korinth hat ein stumpfes, dunkles Braun, Bassai ist bläuchlichgrau und fahl, der Tempel von Aigina hat die Farbe alten Eichenholzes: zwischen Grau und einem rötlichen Braun. Sunion allein ist schneeweiß."
> p.22: "Was attisches Licht vermag, das zeigt sich überall in den Straßen Athens, an den Häuserwänden, in den Gärten"
> p.22-23: "Das Westlicht des Abends endlich schafft den violetten Purpurglanz, der zum Inbegriff der attischen Landschaftschönheit geworden ist."
> p.91: "In der griechischen Landschaft ist das Blaue alles. [...] Dem Blau erfanden denn auch die Griechen einen eigenen Gott, Glaukos Pontios, den Gott der Meeresbläue."
> p.144: "Das Meer! Eine Klippe, weiß beschäumt. Die Inseln, Zante, Kephallenia, in der Bläue wie hingedichtet, hingeträumt, hingeahnt. [...] Wir sind umbraust vom Licht"
> p.155: "Hundert Berge in lichtem Blau, wie aus edlem Metall geschmiedet, wie getrieben; dünn, leicht und klingend. Die Welt ist rein, ganz rein, kein Schleier, kein Nebel, alles, was da ist, ist aus klarem adeligem Stoff."
> p.235: "ein blauschleieriges Geweb aus Licht und Seide, durchzogen von helleren und dunkleren Streifen und Bahnen, die in diesem blauen Gewoge auf- und niederstiegen wie Wolken in einer Flüssigkeit"
> p.259-60: "Das ist das Geheimnis aller Dinge in der griechischen Landschaft, daß Rauhes, Hartes, Rissiges, Sprödes leicht und hauchzart gemacht wird vom Licht. Es ist immer das Zarteste, Feinste und Hellste an Farben. Wer anders malt, lügt."[84]

In *Kreta*, the more personal journal account with much on the customs and mores of the hill-dwelling people on whom he relied for guidance and hospitality, the Grecian light takes on more human aspects, forming a drinking bowl, breathing, and light cast as though from a magic lantern:

> p.29: "Der Ufersaum [...] wie der Rand einer Schale. Ein Trinkrand des Erdteils."
> p.47: "die Kette des Ida, opalenblau überhaucht"

---

[84] Page references to *Griechenland* (Berlin: Gebruder Mann, 1943).

p.135: "Schräg stürzendes Gold aus blaugrauen Wolken! Die Küste leuchtete rotgelb auf wie im Schein einer Zauberlaterne." [85]

It was Pindar, Kästner notes following the comment at p.22-3 of *Griechenland* here above, who first described Athens as 'violet-garlanded'. The metallic, transfiguring and ennobling light at p.155 above is seen from the Parnassus massif, associated with the Muses, but for a publication intended in the first instance for servicemen, the exalted language of the passages on the Grecian light is quite esoteric. The exclamation at the sea, at p.144 above, resembles the many which occur in Böll's letters from Normandy, except that here the sea here is not, as for Böll, the sovereign war-defying element and therefore psychological escape route out of military service, but the route back, out of the chaos of the present, to another order.

Hiller von Gaertringen states that Kästner had the ambition to establish a distinct profile of his own in the literature on Greece and that this corresponded with his choice of an elevated style characterised by condensation, compression and paratactic structures, above all in his descriptive passages.[86] Moreover, for the intensification of nuance he coined a great many new compounds such as *Tagwunder*, *Lichtatem*, *Sonnenschwermut*, *lichtfunkenbestürmt*, *Olivensilbergeflüster*, *Lichtgestöber*, *Sonnenfunkengespinst*, *Lichtkaskaden*,[87] which occur variously in *Griechenland*, *Kreta*, and *Griechische Inseln*.[88] Others, such as *Lichtdonner*, *Lichtgewimmel*, *Lichtgewölb* and *Lichtglanz* also occur. These are found among still other recurring compounds of suffused or intense light, such as *Silberatem*, *Silbergesprüh*, *Silbergewölb*, *Silberglanz*; also *Goldüberperlt*, *Goldüberstaubt*, and the sun-compounds *Sonnenfeuerrund*, *Sonnenschleier* and *Sonnenbesponnen*. The similarity to Hartlaub's use of colour and atmospheric compounds in the Paris Sketches is both striking and significant, as the following instances show; pagination reference is to Ewenz (2002/2007). In 'Ventre des Paris', a piece on *Les Halles*, the façade of St. Eustace is *bone* white, "Knochenweiss" (41), and a row of houses opposite are painted *oxblood* red, "ochsenblutrot" (44/43). In 'Abendspaziergang' the sunset sky is charged with dust and powder particles; the setting sun allows itself to be absorbed by "Dämmerpulver" (55) and again, in 'Quai', a thundery late afternoon sky is filled with "Glanzstaub", the air is "goldstaubhaltig", and zinc mansard roofs are of a "goldblaugrau" *Dixneuvième* (60). In 'Porte Saint Martin' a German civilian's suit is of a dusky "rotbraunviolett" (62). In 'Blick auf Paris – Ile de France' the Pantheon in

---

85 Page references to *Kreta* (Berlin: Gebruder Mann, 1946).

86 Hiller von Gaertringen (1994), pp.168-69

87 Ibid., p.169.

88 In the sequences as listed, in *Griechenland*, p.15,15; *Griechische Inseln*, p.81; *Kreta*, pp.151,175; *Griechische Inseln*, pp.81,154, *Griechenland*, p.13.

the distant silhouette of a wintry forenoon is mole-dark, "maulwurfsdunkel" (74). Then, quite sharply, in 'Blitzmädchen', the piping on the caps of German women auxiliaries strap-hanging in a huddle under the hostile stares of the French is, indicating its perception, poisonous yellow, "giftiggelb" (75), and to the discomfort of their standing in the suburban train is added the oppression of the "Gewitternachmittags" (76). In 'Die Parkmauer', possibly at Fontainebleau, the green of the wood behind the park wall is a negatively qualified substantive, "das stumpfe trockene Ulmengrün", but a broken-arched gateway upliftingly frames a view of a flower-browed, 'blumengestirnt', meadowland (78). 'St. Cloud – Allée des Marnes' opens with the coinage "Mittagsgewölk" (83) – the dictionary gives *gewölkt* as o'erclouded. In 'Hof Hotel Sully. Rue Saint Honoré' the sky above the sunless, overshadowed hotel courtyard is "purpurblaue, golddurchwirkte" (100). The abandoned French foreign ministry, 'Das eroberte Ministerium', has remained unheated all winter and even in July the guard soldiers maintain a fire in the porter's lodge; a painting offers a winter view of the choir of Notre Dame through frosty air, "Blau, Violett, Gelb-Weiss" (118/119), while from the roof of the ministry distant cloud columns in the July sky rise out of a grey tinted 'light-powder', "im grau-blau violetten Lichtpuder" (120/121). These hue and tone constructions are in addition to frequent play on the sea and geology in Hartlaub's many metaphoric compounds on the roofscapes and cloudscapes of Paris, but make it clear that Hartlaub, rather than celebrating light as a defining element of a classic landscape as is the case with Kästner, used colour and light to create present mood. What is common in the metaphoric usages of Hartlaub and Kästner is a striving for a transcending effect which directs the gaze ever outwards and upwards, out of present time. The emphasis on the aesthetic gains pointed effect from the unstated fact of war. Kästner presents a stoic Greek insouciance in the face of wartime circumstances with which his own preferred detachment then appears in accord. The import is that the war is altogether regrettable for both occupier and occupied – the German role as occupying power is elided by allusions to the unpopularity of the *Italian* garrison. Hartlaub, whose focaliser is an anonymous narrating alter ego, affects an equal degree of detachment, but signals a stronger disaffection though sharp vignettes of his fellow-countrymen as estranged from and ill at ease with their surroundings.

Kreta, the manuscript of which was the product of Kästner's journeys through Crete from 6 August 1943 to 4 January 1944,[89] is more free in opinion and figurative expression. Kaulbach, his illustrator, had fallen in Russia even before the first edition of *Griechenland* had appeared and Kästner

[89] See Hiller von Gaertringen (1994), p.178.

was now without a travelling artist-companion. The lack is compensated for by more figurative language, as in this passage from the opening page:

> Da erblickte ich, fern wie aus dem Jenseits, in zartester Bläue, süßester Weiße, einen schneebedeckten Berg. Es war der Ida. Er war schön wie der Atem, wie der Aushauch eines träumenden Gottes im Schlaf, leicht wie der letzte aller Gedanken, rein wie ein Vers, knapp wie der Strich eines Künstlers im Alter.[90]

Again, as in *Griechenland*, the leitmotiv of the play of light is fully indulged:

> Abend für Abend, mit der Gewißheit, in der die Nacht auf den Tag folgt, erlebt der Berg seine Seligsprechung durchs Licht. [...] Es leuchtet der Sockel in rostigem Braun, aber darüber, der obere Bezirk, verharrte eine Weile in einem flammenkernhaften Gelb, das göttlich ist.[91]

A small, lime-washed Christian chapel stands out on a mountainside, and although it turns out on close-up inspection to be somewhat grubby and less than pristine white, the light had transformed it into a beacon:

> Das kleine Gotteshaus leuchtete weit übers Land, als wäre es überaus wichtig. [...] Auch dies war ein Traumbild des griechischen Lichts, das alles erhöht und aus jedem Nichts ein Wunderwas macht.[92]

A physics of light, "Güsse und Stürze von heftigem Licht," is advanced only to emphasise the ephemeral: classics teachers rendering Homer's 'purple sea' had not grasped how this landscape scorned the explicit: "...wie sehr diese Landschaft Eindeutigkeiten verschmäht. Denn es war nur ein Purpurflor, nur Ahnungen, Düfte und leisere Stufen" (*Kreta*, p.184). Surveying the Samaria gorge, light and tectonics become one:

> Hoch droben hingen Geröllfelder gegen die Sonne im Glitzerkies. Die abschirmenden Wände und Gipfel hatten scharfe Lichtkanten gegen die leuchtende Folie des Himmels , wie geschnitten in wahres, in pures Silber hinein. (*Kreta*, p.193)

Kästner's straining after light-effects has become by this point an end in itself, a seeking to fix in verbal imagery not a para-phenomenal, but a meta-phenomenal, in the sense of a transforming, alternate perception of place and aura as one. It is not the present-mood allusive tints and tones of Hartlaub's Paris, but a universal, out-of-time view. Both writers relegate the

---

90 Kästner, *Kreta* (1946), p.7.
91 Ibid., p.9.
92 Ibid., p.36.

war to the periphery, as a temporary aberration. In both cases this is an implicitly pacifist stance.

4.5. Aesthetic of stone: Kästner's appeal for moderation

On recounting the myth of Europa, consort of Zeus, Kästner professes a quite personal faith in the classical ideal which for him is still the lodestar, the "Leuchtgestirn", whose heavenly light bathes Greece, and whose values for him are a reverence for grace, beauty and proportion, evidenced in stone:

> Wirklich ging hier Europa auf, das Leuchtgestirn, an dessen Licht wir uns sättigen unser Leben lang und dessen Schicksalsbahn, wie sie auch sei, die unsere ist.[93]

> Ich sehe lieber einen einzelnen griechischen Quaderstein, als die ragenden Trümmer eines Römerpalastes.[94]

That carved stone can speak, Kästner does not doubt. That inscribed stone can convey more than the chiselled words say, Kästner construes in this passage on the aesthetic of stone calligraphy, with a rhetorical conclusion that is as subtly surprising as the unsuspected freedom he has detected in the execution of the letter of the law:

> Ach, wie wußten sie alles, wie waren sie überall Finder und Treffer und Meister! So gültig die Buchstaben dem Steine eingegraben sind, so wußten sie doch, es müsse der Schrift etwas Flüchtigkeit beiwohnen, ein Momentanes, die Schnelle des Gedankens zu bewahren. Die Zeichen eilen und fliehen, und keines gleicht in der Wiederkehr völlig dem andern. Das macht diese Schrift vollkommen, das gibt diesem redenden Stein den pochenden Herzschlag. Jedem der Zeichen ist der gleiche Raum zugeteilt, immer dasselbe Quadrat für die schmalen und breiten, aber im vorgesehenen Felde gibt sich ein jedes im freien Spiel. Dies ist nun Recht und Gesetz. Aber wo ist in diesem Bilde die Drohung, das Starre, der finstere Ernst?
> Wenn etwas, so ist dies monumental. Aber es kommt auf Taubenfüßen einher.[95]

Why is this conceit of animation in the stone-chiselled characters of two-and-a-half-thousand years old Greek law tablets mounted in the Roman ōideion at Gortyn on Crete so intense? More than admiration for mere calligraphy must have been intended.

In the span of a dozen pages[96] Kästner pronounces on civilised values as these are understood in the cultures that are shaped by Greece, Rome and the Renaissance. A seemingly innocuous observation on proportion, though

---

[93] Ibid., p.31.
[94] Ibid., p.33.
[95] Ibid., p.39.
[96] Ibid., pp.33-45.

ostensibly directed at Wilhelmine pomposity, could be interpreted as an oblique criticism of the monumental Breker/Speer style in sculpture and architecture:

> Alle minoischen Räume sind klein, alle griechischen maßvoll, so wie es die unseres Mittelalters auch sind. Was hätten die Menschen jener Zeit auch dazu gesagt, daß sich die Bürger einer Stadt, wie's nun schon lange üblich ist, Paläste bauen, in denen sie nicht die Herren sind und die sie zu vielen bewohnen, hineingeborgt?[97]

Grace and proportion are applauded, in stone as implicitly in all other things, in a passage of high lyricism prompted by a flight of steps at Phaistos:

> Zwölf Stufen sind es, zwölf vornehme Schwestern, die sich die Hände reichen zum allmählichen Empor. Jede ist nur gering über die andere erhoben, und jede ist in sich eine Schräge, so wie auch die Mündung zuoberst nicht ein Ebenes ist, sondern ein letztes geneigtes Empfangen. Zu beiden Seiten ist die musikalische Leiter bewehrt von festklaren Quadern, damit das Ganze nicht zu weich und schmelzend sei.[98]

Grazie: grace, beauty, Kästner insists, is the starting point of *das Abendlandische*, of Western civilisation. The claim is put in unapologetic terms which speak of the ideal of grace of mind as of body, of the tension between discipline, *Zucht*, and nature; of the stamp, *Prägmal*, of nobility; of a rapier sharpness of intellect, *Gesinnung der Degenklinge*; these all the prerogative, *Vorrecht*, of birth and race among those who cultivate them:

> So begann denn das Abendländische mit Grazie — denen zur Lehre, die Grazie für etwas Weiches halten, das dem Manne entgegen ist. Grazie ist Höchstes in Körper und Geist, Spannung voll Zucht und Natur, Gesinnung der Degenklinge und, wie beim Tier, Prägmal der Edlen, Vorrecht der Angeburt und der Rasse, die gut ist.[99]

Placed as it is, in a discourse on the ideals of a classical civilisation, the reference to birth and race cannot be construed as endorsement of the crude *NS* attempts at appropriation of the Grecian physical ideal, as though that had somehow been bequeathed as inheritance to another people. The plea for grace as exemplified by balanced moderation is echoed when noting that the major sites of classical Greek antiquity, the Acropolis, Delphi, Mycenae, Argos, Sounion, were not sited on the highest and most prominent points in their surroundings, but occupied instead lesser, sometimes overlooked settings, "ich liebe dieses gehaltene Maß, das sich da ausspricht, das

---

[97] Ibid., p.43.
[98] Ibid., p.44.
[99] Ibid., pp.44-5.

menschlich Verbleibende, und sehe etwas Griechisches in diesem Gewarnten, welches das Letzte nicht nimmt."[100] Criticism of totalitarian presumption and excess is implicit.

4.6. Mentioning the war: classical elision

The question of Kästner's selective and oblique references to the war has been addressed by Hiller von Gaertringen (1994) with biographical background and with extensive reference to pre-publication drafts and post-publication revisions from the Kästner archive.[101] Unlike Hartlaub, who says more about the war by avoiding as far as possible any direct references to it, the Kästner of 1942 advances in one instance Homeric parallels, as when at a seaside rail halt meeting a column of troops, shirtless in tropic shorts, en route from Crete to new frontline service:

> Da waren sie, die »blonden Achaier« Homers, die Helden der Ilias. Wie jene stammten sie aus dem Norden, wie jene waren sie groß, hell, jung, ein Geschlecht, strahlend in der Pracht seiner Glieder. [...] Sie kamen vom schwersten Siege. [...] Es wehte homerische Luft.[102]

The full passage suggests that Antenor, Ajax, Diomedes and Achilles could have looked no different, given that the ancient, Dorian Greeks were of northern extraction, than these sun-blonded and bronzed latter-day warriors. They came indeed *vom schwersten Siege*: the costly air-assault on Crete of May 1941, the resistance to which by Cretan civilians, true to old tradition and in support of the reserve Greek forces in the absence on the mainland of the regular Cretan division, had added to the German losses and led to lethal reprisals against the civil population wherever such resistance had been encountered.[103]

Modern, urban Greece is present in the *Griechenland* narrative, but ever as an unfavourable contrast to Kästner's theme: that of an idea of Greece sceptical of German romantic philhellenism and stressing an enduring Homeric stillness and simplicity, "Homerische Einfachheit und Stille, die die Zeiten überdauerte" (*Griechenland*, p.105). Making a rooftop survey of Athens in the chapter 'Athen vom Dach', Kästner discerns the *Weite und Großzügigkeit* of the vision of the German architects who laid the ground

---

[100] Ibid., pp.184-85.

[101] See Hiller von Gaertringen (1994), pp.267-94.

[102] Kästner, *Griechenland* (1943), pp.9,10.

[103] See von Xylander, *Die deutsche Besatzungsherrschaft auf Kreta*, pp.21,28-33; also Fleischer, *Von Lidice bis Kalavryta*, p.154; cf. Hagen Fleischer, *Im Kreuzschatten der Mächte. Griechenland 1941-1944* (Frankfurt am Main: Peter Lang, 1986), p.61; also Ehrengard Schramm, *Ein Hilfswerk für Griechenland*, ed. by Gottfried Schramm and Irene Vasos (Göttingen: Vandenhoeck & Ruprecht, 2003), pp.88-91.

plan of modern Athens and contrasts it with the subsequent urban sprawl (*Griechenland*, pp.34-35). The *Ordnung, Anlage und Reiz* of the new Sparta, laid out by the Wittelsbach monarch a mere hundred years before, is presented as the only exception in a withering dismissal of Greek urban modernity in general (*Griechenland*, pp.237-238). Balancing these reflex observations is a considered chapter on 'Bayerisches Athen' which notes how, a hundred years on, the *tönende Leidenschaftlichkeit* of the Acropolis buildings renders incongruous the mannered bourgeois Bavarian romanticism of the new Athens below (*Griechenland*, p.71). Contemplating Frankish crusader ruins on the way to Olympia, Kästner surmises that those *Nordmänner* felt that only the structurally fantastic was fit to stand amidst the wonders of such a land (*Griechenland*, p.143). At Epidauros, the healing centre of the half-god Asclepius, and therefore a centre of religious belief, Kästner argues that the theatre there, in its tragedies a place of cathartic purging and purification of the emotions, was therapeutic and therefore also a place of religion and of worship (*Griechenland*, p.232). In all, *Griechenland* is coherently focused on a Greece quite out of time, but still as an ethical model relevant to the present time.

Kästner re-published *Griechenland* after the war, in 1953, as *Ölberge, Weinberge: ein Griechenland Buch*, with some additional postwar material, but with some of the original material omitted.[104] Notably, the encounter with the troops returning from the Cretan battles in the introductory chapter is considerably foreshortened in its classical allusions. The assertive "Es wehte homerische Luft." of the original is altered to "*unversehens* wehte homerische Luft" (italics added).[105] The chapter on Sparta which occupied over ten pages of print in the original takes up just two in the postwar edition and omits the comparison with the Wittelsbach-founded new Sparta of the 19th century and much of the critical examination of the Spartan legend. The concluding chapter to the original book, the flight over Greece which sees from above the Alps and the upper Danube valley transplanted onto the landscape below, is also omitted. Imaginative transposition had here brought to mind Goethe's 'Klassische Walpurgnisnacht' and Gerhart Hauptmann's 'Till Eulenspiegel'[106] – Kästner was secretary to Hauptman for eighteen months in 1936-1937. The new edition recounts in conclusion instead a visit to the village of Distomo in the Phokis mountain range, where eight years before the inhabitants had been massacred for their alleged complicity in a partisan ambush. Kästner, mistaken for an Anglo-American, is pressed to attend the village festival, makes an excuse, but finds himself caught up in

---

104 See Hiller von Gaertringen (1994), pp.270-77, 313-19.
105 See Kästner, *Griechenland*, p.10; *Ölberge, Weinberge*, p.15.
106 See Hiller von Gaertringen (1994), p.93.

the spill-over festivities in another village nearby, compelled, as he writes, to partake in an ovation to life and survival, "dem Leben eine Ovation darzubringen, dem Überleben, das die Schrecken der Geschichte verzehrt."[107]

Strohmeyer (2000, 2006) has attacked in particular Kästner's later co-equations without distinction of the aerial bombing horrors of WWII. Hiller von Gaertringen concedes that Kästner's postwar co-equations in *Ölberge, Weinberge* are indeed equivocal,[108] but dismisses Strohmeyer's character attacks on Kästner as selective misreadings of her own 1994 study, made without recourse to its original documents.[109] Conceding also that the original *Griechenland* is problematical in the passages where the Nordic origins of the ancient Greeks are stressed, von Gaertringen adds that the opening chapter in which Homeric comparisons are made to the German soldiers returning from Crete was not written for the censor, as it had already appeared in the *Deutsche Allgemeine Zeitung*, but that it certainly was placed at the start of the book for tactical reasons.[110] The final chapter of *Griechenland*, 'Flug über Griechenland', echoes the opening chapter, 'Fahrt nach Griechenland', both in title and sentiment and contains a blatant claim-by-association:

> Der Deutsche wohnt ohnehin halb in Hellas, solang er in Deutschland ist; kommt er aber nach Griechenland, so ist ihm Deutsches überall um den Weg.[111]

This chapter too, however, had also been previously published in the *Deutsche Allgemeine Zeitung*[112] and so, like the first chapter, must also be considered tactical in its placement. This study would maintain further that the opening chapter of *Griechenland* is consistent with other passages in the book, in which the Greek exaltation of bodily beauty and physical perfection as an expression of a religious ideal is admired. This is evident in the excerpts that follow here. The soldiers, at a train halt by the sea, take the opportunity to bathe:

> … fiel es kaum einem ein, die Badehose, das Abzeichen christlich-neuzeitlicher Körperscham, zu tragen. Unversehens ergab sich ein völlig klassisches Bild.

[107] Kästner, *Ölberge, Weinberge*, p.233.

[108] See Hiller von Gaertringen (1994), pp.333-35, 'Der Umgang mit der historischen Realität in *Ölberge, Weinberge*', and pp.335-43, 'Das Bild des besetzten Griechenland.'

[109] See Hiller von Gaertringen (1996), 'Leserbrief zu dem Artikel "Über dem Krieg schweben" von Wolfram Wette in der Badischen Zeitung vom 28. Juli 2006', at http://www.llb-detmold.de/wir-ueber-uns/aus-unserer-arbeit/texte.html [accessed 15 January 2012].

[110] Hiller von Gaertringen (1994), pp.196,197 and bibliography, p.508.

[111] Kästner, *Griechenland*, p.268.

[112] See Hiller von Gaertringen (1994), p.508.

> Sprühend im Licht dieses Morgens und im Glanz ihrer jungen Nacktheit tummelte sich die Schar dieser Eroberer am fremden Meer. [113]

Hiller von Gaertringen, examining at length Kästner's romantic-classical view of Greece,[114] sees in Kästner's enthusiasm for a pseudo-religious system of belief deriving from the classical Greek an unassailable refuge from wartime reality.[115] Yet, dispelling any popular misconception that the Greek physical contests were athletics in the modern sense, Kästner insists that these activities were in fact central to Greek religious belief. At Olympia, musing on the statues of the victors that once were thick about the arena, he writes:

> es war ein Wald von Statuen in dem wirklichen Wald, eine stille Gesellschaft, die blieb, wenn die laute wieder abzog. [...] Hundert und hundert schönster Menschenbilder, eine strahlende, siegreiche Jugend, Eigentum des Gottes: sein Volk[116]

Expressly, he states that the athletic contest was itself religious ritual:

> Olympia war kein Sportfest, es war Gottesdienst.[117]
> Die Götter waren die stärksten und schönsten. Wer siegte, war ihnen näher. [...] Der Wettkampf war Religion.[118]

and, on nudity:

> Es war das völlige Bekenntnis zum Körper, der letzte Schritt zur Überwindung der Barbarei; denn auch der Wilde verhüllt sich: Die Götter aber sind nackt.[119]

At Delphi, noting that the stadium occupies the highest part of the site, he notes:

> Höher noch liegt das Stadion. Das Klarste, Gesundeste, das unbeschwert Junge, der Gottesdienst des Körpers: er hat das letzte Wort im heiligen Bezirk.[120]

Kästner's eye is also elsewhere alert to the Greek ideal of youthful beauty. Surveying the mosaics at the monastery of Daphni he notices that a diptych

---

113 Kästner, *Griechenland*, p.10.
114 Hiller von Gaertringen (1994), pp.209-24, 'Die zeitlose Idealwelt'.
115 Hiller von Gaertringen (1994), p.253.
116 Kästner, *Griechenland*, p.135.
117 Ibid.
118 Ibid., p.36.
119 Ibid.
120 Ibid., p.173.

of the saints Sergios and Bacchos owes something to the pre-Christian ideal of god-like youth:

> Es sind zwei Jünglinge von geradezu schmetternder Eleganz: weiß starrende Gewänder, goldbehängt, ihre Schwerter halten sie wie Schmuckstücke gerade vor sich hin. Mit ihnen und ihrer glänzenden Erdenpracht flattert in die christliche Kirche plötzlich etwas wie attische Feinheit und griechischer Lobpreis adeliger Jugend.[121]

Disputing the perception of Herakles, the god-founder of the Olympic games, as a muscle-bound strongman, he points out that for the Dorians who had deified him his radiating energy or luminosity, his *Leuchtkraft* was more important and that, tellingly, the otherwise sparing of adjectives Hesiod describes him as the 'slim-ankled' one:

> Den Knöchelschlanken nennt ihn Hesiod, der sonst mit Beiworten kargt. Schlank und sehnig, die Idealfigur eines Jünglings aus dem Gymnasion, gar kein Athlet in unserem Sinn.[122]

Kästner further notes that Herakles, despite his services to the fifty daughters of the king of Tespios, loved his male cousin and friend Jolaos to the point of idolatry.[123] From Tiryns, the birthplace of Herakles, *Griechenland* proceeds via Epidauros to Sparta where Kästner enthuses over Sparta's river, the Eurotas, and sees in the slim poplars lining its banks yet another recollection of the bodily perfection of Herakles, "Die waren ja einst dem Herakles heilig, es paßt gut zu ihrer heroischen Schlankheit und zu ihrem hellstämmigen Lichtgrün."[124]

Kästner's preoccupation with the Greek deification of bodily beauty continues in his following book, *Kreta*, and also in his unfinished third book, on the Greek islands. In *Kreta*, a scene from a Symposium is prompted by the simple appearance of a boy in a doorway:

> Ein Knabe steht im Licht einer Tür, der Umriß des Kopfes ist kühn und voll Ausdruck, er hat einen Weinkrug in Händen, steht hinter den Gästen, schenkt ein, und ungefragt wirft er ein Wort in die Runde, das alle erheitert. Unter der Asche ein Funke. Mir ist lieber, der glimmende Funke, als manches gestellte Vollkommenheitsbild der Antike.[125]

---

121 Ibid., p.111.
122 Ibid., p.220.
123 Ibid., p.221.
124 Ibid., p.241.
125 Kästner, *Kreta* (1946), p.232.

In *Griechische Inseln* there is also an instance of a continuing fascination with the body as object of worship, a thing profane in the Christian view, but not so to Kästner:

> Nie sah ich so unverholen das weibliche Element, das im Bild des Dionysos ohne Zweifel seit Urzeiten ist, ausgeprägt so wie hier. [...] diese Dosis weiblichen Stoffs, welche, der dominierenden Männlichkeit zugesetzt, das Künstlertum macht, dessen Inbegriff dieser Gott ist, — er, der einzige übrigens unter den Göttern, damit man nichts verwechsele, der keine Knabenfreundschaft besaß.[126]

Here, in a statue of Dionysus excavated on the island of Kos, Kästner sees in the sculpted lines of the figure an androgynous strain in the boy god, the more surprising because Dionysus, alone among the gods, did *not* have a homoerotic relationship.

The preoccupation with the Greek physical ideal would seem from all the foregoing extracts to be less pseudo-religious than purely aesthetic, and without suggestion of Nazi eugenics. By the war's end, as Hiller von Gaertringen observes, Kästner had overcome the anti-Christian sentiment, *Affekt*, and developed a new and lively interest in Christian Greece.[127] What the encounter with classical Greece had induced in him was something that defied rational thinking, as he himself well knew:

> Wie können wir glauben wollen an griechische Kunst, an griechischen Marmor, griechische Tragödie und griechischen Geist — aber an griechische Götter nicht?[128]

The thought was prompted at the reputed grave of Zeus, a difficult contradiction for the Greeks, as Greek gods were immortal, living in eternal youth and beauty; a difficult contradiction for Kästner too, as his insistent focus on the aura of the civilisation of classical Greece, something by his own admission without conscious trace in the Greek present, lay open to the charge of mere fantasist escapism from wartime realities. Yet, Kästner's rhetoric in defence is forceful:

> Sollten sie uns nur Sinnbilder sein? So wären's nicht Götter, und aller Glaube an Griechenland wäre nur Schein. Nur Schwärmerei? Das wäre zu wenig; Nur Gedankenspiel? Unwürdig und Frevel; Nur Wissen, nicht Glaube? Zu leer. Nur Klage um ein verlorenes Alter? Zu rückwärtsgewandt. Nur Gleichnis? Zu wenig verpflichtend, zu gottlos.[129]

---

126 Kästner, *Griechische Inseln* (Frankfurt am Main: Insel, 1975), p.143.
127 Hiller von Gaertringen (1994), p.88.
128 Kästner, *Kreta* (1946), pp.139-40.
129 Ibid., p.140.

Mere symbols, mere passionate enthusiasm, mere imagination, mere knowledge, mere nostalgia, mere allegory: all are rejected as insufficient explanations. Kästner adds that the search for the answer to the question besets him: "Sie bleibt mir zu suchen."

Gerhard Nebel's philosophical speculations had by 1940 credited Spengler with having discovered the true weight which attached to the corporeal, the somatic, in the antique as evidenced by the empirical insistence of Aristotle on a psyche, or soul, resident and expiring with the body – a too empirical metaphysics:

> In der Antike erscheint der Raum eingeschränkt auf das Körperhafte, auf die sinnliche Grenze, in der Bevorzugung der Plastik, im Fehlen der Perspektiven, in den somatischen Stadtstaaten, im begrenzten Kosmos des Aristoteles [130]

Nebel goes on, however, to champion the Greek:

> So kommt es, daß [...] der in sich gehaltene, nicht nach außen und oben hinausspringende Raum des Parthenon, unendlicher ist als der Raum der abendländischen Physik, an dessen Unbegrenztheit und Dynamik Spengler sich berauscht.[131]

The *Bevorzugen der Plastik*, the preference for the plastic art, sculpture, coupled with the inward focused spaces of the antique creates a conceptual space, *Raum*, which 'trembles with the secret movements of the divine creative power', "zittert von den geheimen Bewegungen der göttlichen Schöpferkraft,"[132] and is therefore limitless beyond Western physics. Kästner similarly, having deduced that the original, wholly enclosed site of the Parthenon was dictated by its religious nature and that the Greek celebration of the body was a worship of god-like perfection, could not have failed to produce Homeric, and therefore warlike, comparisons on encountering the nude-bathing, modern-day 'blond Achaeans'. He saw them first as god-like antique Greek figures.

4.7. The redundancy of revision

The genesis of *Griechenland*, according to Kästner's own account in *Ölberge, Weinberge* (p.20), was a spontaneous impulse of his and Kaulbach's, his illustrator. The ostensible rationale, concocted as an afterthought, was that of a plain man's guide, for a soldier readership in the first instance, to an appreciation of Greece. The personal rationale, apart from the

---

[130] Nebel, 'Von Inseln, Flüssen und Bergen', in *Von den Elementen*, p.11.

[131] Ibid.

[132] Ibid.

opportunity afforded to acquaint oneself better with the sites of antiquity, was that of a corrective to the views of those VIPs for whom Kästner had had occasionally to serve as tour guide: those who, 'like tin soldiers', carried their standpoint about with them (*Ölberge*, p. 21). Since the whole occupation context could be inferred, the propagation of a personal ethic and philosophy was itself an egregious act, even though comment on occupation policy is absent: the mass deportation of the Salonika Jewish population to Auschwitz-Birkenau between March and August of 1943[133] postdated the first publication of *Griechenland*. The July 1944 deportation of the Jews of Rhodes, however, was witnessed by Kästner, but receives no mention in the 'Rhodos' chapter of *Griechische Inseln*.[134] Hiller von Gaertringen's research notes that Kästner had acknowledged the island commander's efforts to oppose this measure, and later testified in court on the general's behalf. General Kleeman had cordially invited Kästner to the Rhodes early in March 1944, even before Kästner had secured higher approval for the continuation of his *Griechische Inseln* project.[135]

That Kästner was aware also of the so-called 'atonement measures', the *Sühnenmaßnahmen*, the murderously indiscriminate reprisals carried out in reaction to partisan attacks, he acknowledged in 1952, before the publication of *Ölberge, Weinberge*.[136] Taken aback on his first return visit to Crete in 1956 by the resentment of the local population, he was prompted to write for confirmation to the former Major Kessler of General Bräuer's staff and, dissatisfied with the reply, turned to Ehrengard Schramm- von Thadden, who furnished him with the notes of her own enquiries.[137] The letter to Kessler acknowledges that Kästner already knew, as he must have, of the Vianos village massacre near Heraklion in September 1943 during his stay on the island, when according to German reports, 440 inhabitants were killed.[138] While on Crete, Kästner himself encountered the *Wehrmacht* troop approaching to avenge the killing of the entire 27-man complement of the military outpost and agricultural station on the Omalos plateau. In the revised and posthumously published 1975 edition of *Kreta*, Kästner's opinion is one on futility: "jetzt war die übliche, nutzlose, unausbleibliche,

---

133 The Salonika deportations followed on the direct personal initiative of Himmler, supported by Hitler, whose order expressly forbad the Wehrmacht area commander to interfere: see Eberhard Jäckel, *Hitlers Herrschaft* (Stuttgart: Deutsche Verlags-Anstalt, 1986), p.117 and (end note) p.179.

134 See Hiller von Gaertringen (1994), p.207.

135 See Hiller von Gaertringen (1994), pp.121-22,207.

136 See Kästner, 'Enttäuschte Liebe zu den Deutschen', *Schwäbische Landeszeitung*, 31 May 1952.

137 See Hiller von Gaertringen (1994), pp.410-12.

138 Ibid., p.410.

kaum vermeidliche Vergeltung im Gang, die zu nichts führte,"[139] which terms implicitly say that reprisal was understood by one side to be usual, inevitable, unavoidable and scarcely preventable, and by the other to be reflexive and routine, whether or not effectively deterrent.

The hunger catastrophe of the winter of 1941-1942 was witnessed by Kästner in Athens and Piraeus. Such civilian suffering not directly attributable to military action or to expressly punitive measures might be alluded to: "Brot, nach dem Griechenland jetzt im Kriege so bangt, daß es die Tage bis zur Ernte an den Fingern abzählt." (*Griechenland*, p.206). Hiller von Gaertringen divines three strands in Kästner's revisiting of the phenomenon in *Ölberge, Weinberge*: firstly, hunger as a historically recurring affliction, of which, as instance, a female street beggar is merely an image, "die geschlagene Münze der Not", the coin-impress of want (*Ölberge*, p.66); secondly, an Adventist view, drawn from an interpretation of Paul, II Thessalonians, which would cast the conditions as precursors of the rule of the chaos which would precede the Second Coming; thirdly, as three-act tragedy with the 1920s Asia-Minor exodus as the first act, the collapse of the Habsburg empire as the second, and the displacement of populations following upon the end of WWII as the third.[140] These abstruse projections are deduced from Kästner's subsequent preoccupation with Byzantine Christianity and with philosophy. The nexus of causes of the winter famine of 1941-1942 is not analysed in *Griechenland*: that Greece was already before the war no longer self-sufficient in grain, and had then lost its most productive cereal growing provinces in the Northeast to Bulgarian annexation; that general food-supplies were initially commandeered by Axis forces or requisitioned against paper credits, and that the regular landing of relief supplies from neutral ships was not possible until the later relaxation of the Allied naval blockade in Mediterranean.[141] Instead, Kästner repeatedly condemns the immediate causes: speculative hoarding and black-marketeering, as the root evil. In the account of the January 1942 sea visit to Aigina, the German archaeologist, Professor Welter, is hailed as a hero for his altruistic intervention against the black-marketeers on the island (p.86). At the Metropolis convent at Mistra in the Peloponnese an old woman wails in familiar tones, "das Klagelied der Griechen, wir kennen es auswending", about hunger, about the lack even of bread, about the black market and the exorbitant prices (p.248). At the Pantanassa convent, also at Mistra, a young Orthodox nun professes to Kästner that it is not war between the Germans and the Greeks (whatever her private thoughts on this point may have

[139] Kästner, *Kreta* (1975), p.258.
[140] Cf. Hiller von Gaertringen (1994), pp.338-40.
[141] Cf. Fleischer, *Im Kreuzschatten der Mächte*, pp.116-27.

been), but war between the rich and the poor in Greece, aggravated by the black-marketeers (p.252). In fact, Kästner seems to have regarded the 1941-1942 winter famine as the worst of all the calamities to have befallen Greece in that decade, worse than the mass shootings and burnings, worse than the excesses of the civil war:

> Denn es läßt sich nicht leugnen, daß die Geiselerschießungen und Dörferverbrennungen, die die Deutschen vornahmen, einen viel tieferen Eindruck beim Volk hinterließen als alles andere, in den letzten zehn Jahren Erlittene, sogar als der furchtbare Hunger-winter des Jahres 41 auf 42. Das Gedächtnis der Völker ist unlogisch, dagegen läßt sich nichts machen.[142]

Kästner's tag on the memory of peoples, purporting to see an irrationality in the reckoning of fatalities, actually underscores the shock of the deliberation perceived in the mass shootings and burnings perpetrated by the Germans. The same article, however, also appears to offer a mitigating excuse, citing the later civil war experiences of his former guide and interpreter on Crete, Josef Kayales, 'Sifi': "Nur wer die griechischen Berge kennt, weiß, was es bedeutet, dort einen Krieg ohne Fronten zu führen."; further, citing Sifi's own view: "über Vergeltungsmaßnamen dürfe nur richten, wer selber Soldat gewesen sei."[143] The mass famine burials at Piraeus, which Kästner witnessed, appear first in the postwar *Ölberge* (pp.67-71). The shootings and burnings are first mentioned there also, in the parable of forgiveness that is the 'Dorffest' episode on the village of Distomo (*Ölberge*, pp.229-233).

Hagen Fleischer dismisses *Griechenland* as a forum for the presentation of Kästner's 'daydream blend' of antique Greece and occupation reality: "ein Forum zur Popularisierung seiner antikes Hellas mit deutscher Besatzungsaktualität verquickenden Tagträume."[144] This pronouncement is supported by reference only to the 'blond Achaeans' passage in the opening chapter of *Griechenland* and to Kästner's professed dismay at the 'Levantine' decadence of Athens. Professor Fleischer finds Kästner's reference to 'lemur and ape faces' (*Griechenland*, p.84) particularly objectionable. The expression is actually prompted by the discovery among the street children at the Athens Omonoia metro station of a blond-haired, grey-eyed child of mixed Danish and Greek parentage. Spurred to a flight of fancy, Kästner enthuses:

---

142 Kästner, 'Enttäuschte Liebe zu den Deutschen', *Schwäbische Landeszeitung*, 31.5.1952.

143 Ibid.

144 Hagen Fleischer, 'Die „Viehmenschen" und das „Sauvolk". Feindbilder einer dreifachen Okkupation: der Fall Griechenland', in *Kultur-Propaganda-Öffentlichkeit. Intentionen deutscher Besatzungspolitik und Reaktionen auf die Okkupation*, ed. by Wolfgang Benz and others (Berlin, Metropol, 1998), pp.135-69 (pp.163-64).

> Man soll sich nicht irremachen lassen. Woher auch die alten Griechen gekommen sein mögen: dies war ihr Blut. Mit beiden Beinen fest auf der Erde und ums Haupt ein höheres Geleucht. Rein, sauber und klar: die weißen Götter (p.84)

Wherever the blood of the Greeks of the classical era came from, Kästner is saying, it did not come from the South and the East, from the present-day Levant. Racist, Fleischer insists, the more so when taken in conjunction with the pronouncement that:

> Natürlich ist blutmäßig von den alten Griechen verdammt wenig oder nichts übrig geblieben im heutigen Hellas. Es ist eine Sentimentalität, wenn man dies nicht wahrhaben will. (p.45)

But Kästner does add here that, even in antique Greece, the Greek bloodline was a rarity, "Denn schon im Altertum wurde das griechische Blut selten." And already in the same reflections on the idea of Athens and of Greece (p. 43): "Vernünftigerweise ist nicht zu verlangen daß sich in Griechenland dasselbe Blut dreitausend Jahre lang erhalten haben soll." The point, for Kästner, was that, despite the millennia of demographic transitions, *it was all still there*: "Alles noch da"; "Ausgelöscht, ausgelöscht. Und alles noch da."[145]

Kästner, in fact, uses the lemur adjective again in *Griechenland* (pp.103-104), and again in reaction chiefly against Athens, whose urban sprawl encountered on the way to the ferry point contrasts so starkly with the beauty of Salamis: "ein unerwartetes Schönheitsgeschenk [...] so viel blühende Stille." It is because Kästner is in love with the *land* of Greece that he finds its urbanised reality so repellent: "...man an der Haltbarkeit seiner Liebe zum wirklichen Griechenland verzweifelt, so viel *lemurenhafte Verfallenheit* und so viel Schmutz zu sehen: Vorstädte und Dörfer, die sich wie Schorf auf die griechische Landschaft gelegt haben." (italics added). Fleischer is sceptical, suggesting that Kästner himself may have shared the racist views that he purports in *Ölberge Weinberge* to have deplored. Kästner and his like-minded superior, Major Bruno Schaar, availed of their conducted tours for visiting military dignitaries to feed their own curiosity for the antique.[146] It is clear from Kästner's wry accounts in his letters of this tour activity that racist disparagement of the latter-day Greeks was in the common lexicon, despite the official line that prevailed until 1943, which honoured the Greeks' recent valorous defence of their independence: the isle of Makronisi, off Cape Sounion, where Paris and Helen dallied, is dismissed by one newly arrived German potentate as *diese Affeninsel*, and

---

[145] *Kreta* (1946) p.177, *Griechische Inseln*, p.91.
[146] Cf. Hiller von Gaertringen (1994), pp.90,91.

Mycenae and Tiryns as *Affennester.*[147] It is equally clear that Kästner rejects such an attitude founded on ignorance. His later outright condemnation of that attitude is well conveyed in his observation that its holders carried their (mental) standpoint about with them in the manner of tin soldiers:

> ...in der Tat war es widerwärtig, anhören zu müssen, wie sich einer damals *oder immer herrschenden* Geistesverfassung gemäß [...] ohne zu ahnen, daß jeder einzelne Grieche so viel uralte *Erfahrung* im Blute besitzt [...] sie tragen ja doch wie die Zinnsoldaten ihr bißchen Standort mit sich herum. [*Ölberge, Weinberge*, pp.20-21] (italics added)

That mentality may well *still* prevail, so Kästner; but it failed and fails to recognise that the modern-day Greeks, whatever their bloodline, carry in their culture the *experience* of the antique.

In an earlier essay, Fleischer, again singling out the 'Homeric heroes' bathing scene in *Griechenland*, is even more scathing of Kästner, describing him as "ein wahrer »Arno Breker« der Feder".[148] The criticism is accompanied by a photograph of sea-bathing, fig-leaf clad German soldiers posing for the camera (awkwardly, self-consciously, and obviously co-operating in someone's mock-Homeric joke). These are no *blonde Achaier*: all but one is dark-haired, and none of the group of seven strikes any semblance of a Praxitelean pose. Addressing Kästner's subsequent rejection of the preconceptual 'tin soldier' standpoint, Fleischer's criticism continues in an openly derisive tone: "Bravo! Nur an dem »Zinn« für diese Soldaten hat der »Überbau«-Soldat Kästner mitgegossen."[149] Commenting on the same problematic 'Homeric heroes' text in *Griechenland*, Hiller von Gaertringen suggests that Kästner knew that a certain propaganda contribution was expected of him.[150] Though it has been here already argued that that passage is capable of sustaining an apolitical, purely philhellenist reading, Kästner must well have been aware that it would be appropriated to supply ideological superstructure, *Überbau*, to the racial philosophy of the state. The heightened lyricism of Kästner's prose otherwise works in *Griechenland* to frustrate direct appropriation of his text by the propagandists.

Some formally stylistic rendering of experience was the only one *at the time* that could raise the account above that of reportage, whether conformist or conscientious. The works, particularly *Griechenland*, it will be

---

147 Ibid.

148 Hagen Fleischer, 'Siegfried in Hellas. Das nationalsozialistische Griechenlandbild und die Behandlung der griechischen Zivilbevölkerung seitens der deutschen Besatzungsbehörden, 1941-1944', in *Griechenland – Entfernungen in die Wirklichkeit. Ein Lesebuch*, ed. by Armin Kerker (Hamburg: Argument, 1988), pp.26-48 (pp.35,36,37).

149 Ibid., p.37.

150 Hiller von Gaertringen (1994), p.199.

argued, actually benefited from this non-realist treatment. Already in 1944, Gerhart Hauptmann had cautioned Kästner on learning of his intention to revise *Griechenland*, "Aber Vorsicht mit Veränderungen: ich habe Angst wie bei einer köstlichen zerbrechlichen Glassschale."[151] Hauptmann's caution was against the shattering that might result of a fragile literary creation. Kästner nonetheless set about the revision of the book while interned in Egypt, and had a complete new draft ready by the end of March 1946.[152] *Griechenland* had been a fleeting, wholly immature and hurried sketch, without standpoint, "eine flüchtige, gänzlich unreife, standpunktlose und eilige Skizze." This rejection of admiration for *Griechenland* is contained in a letter to Armin Mohler in 1950,[153] a writer whose thinking Kästner scathingly dismisses in a letter to Gerhard Nebel in the same year.[154] The unwonted vehemence may therefore have had as much to do with his correspondent's misreading of *Griechenland* as with Kästner's own dissatisfaction with the work.

4.8. Kästner, Hauptmann, Heidegger: *Wortwunder*

Kästner's difficulty, and his debt to Hauptmann, are evident in a letter from Greece in March of 1942, "Mir will zumeist der Schwung über die wirklichen Dinge, der Aufflug, den ich bei Ihnen an so vielen Abenden lernte, nicht mehr gelingen."[155] A preceding remark hints at the necessity to somehow vault over present events, "Über das Dunkle wollen wir schweigen."[156] Kästner had need at this time of something of Hauptmann's facility for essays in utopian fiction, such as *Atlantis* or *Die Insel der Großen Mutter*,[157] or contrarily, for that of the dystopian *Die Finsternisse*, for which Kästner took the dictation,[158] and in which the shades of the Old Testament prophets visit the present and foresee the coming catastrophe for mankind: "Wie sehr hat sich der bange Ton dieses Werkes zum vollendeten Bangen erfüllt!" wrote Kästner to Hauptmann's widow on its publication in 1947.[159] Hauptmann's Greek tetralogy, the *Astriden*-cycle, a product of his octogenarian wartime years, obliquely alluded to the horrors of the new Reich, and on the occasion of the staging from that cycle of *Iphigenie in Aulis*

---

[151] Hiller von Gaertringen, *Perseus-Auge Hellblau*, p.300.
[152] Hiller von Gaertringen (1994), p.270ff.
[153] Cited, ibid., p.271.
[154] See Raabe, *Erhart Kästner. Briefe*, pp.108-9.
[155] Ibid., p.49.
[156] Ibid., p.48.
[157] Cf. *A Companion to German Literature*, ed. by Eda Sagarra and Peter Skrine (Oxford: Blackwell, 1999), pp.200,201.
[158] Raabe, *Erhart Kästner. Briefe*, p.200.
[159] Ibid., p.83.

in Vienna in February 1942 Kästner's celebratory 'Brief an Gerhart Hauptmann' appeared in the *Neues Wiener Tageblatt.*[160] Just one month before, Kästner had submitted his proposal for the book that would become *Griechenland.*[161]

Kästner's deferential two-page tribute to Hauptmann in the Delphi chapter of *Griechenland* acknowledges (pp.168-170) the popular influence of Hauptmann's travelogue of his 1907 tour of Greece, *Griechischer Frühling.*[162] The *Griechenland* of 1942, however, advances independent arguments on themes broached in the earlier work. Hauptmann's disdain for the 'bloodless' love of a blanched and therefore 'bloodless' Greekdom lends point to his suggestion that the once shrill colours of the Acropolis shrines expressed a naïve state of relationships between men and their gods and were a call, as that of a street-market crier, to festivity and through that to deeper worship. The dramatist Hauptmann proceeds from this to contend that the Christian churches, particularly the Catholic, are 'mausoleums' glorifying death and the crypt, whereas the theatre, relying neither on suggestion nor fear of death, "Todesangst oder Suggestion", is the most dangerous competitor to the church (*G.F.*, pp.43,44). Kästner, also invoking the contrasting analogies of blanched stone and marketplace colour, vividly conjures up the forest-like sprawl of disordered stone and metal monuments that had covered the sacred precincts before and again after the Periclean rebuilding of the Acropolis (*Griechenland*, pp.51, 55ff.), but eschews any direct comparison to Christian ecclesiology. In the *Deutsches-Archäologisches Institut* in Athens he would have had opportunity to read former *DAI* director Gerhart Rodenwalt's writings, whose essay printed in *Hellas* (1943) stresses that the Acropolis buildings were a political statement, and that the Parthenon itself was both victory monument and temple of thanksgiving for victory.[163] Equally, Hauptmann, reading Pausanias on the eagerness with which the Athenians gave sanctuary to all possible gods, sees a religiosity grounded in fear: fear of misfortune, of a return of the Persians (*G.F.*, p.45). Hauptmann and Kästner agree on the essentially religious nature of Greek athletics (*G.F.*, p.77; *Griechenland*, pp.136,173), and of Greek theatre (*G.F.*, pp.73,95; *Griechenland*, p.232), though Kästner does not echo Hauptmann's gory insistence that Greek tragedy is rooted in human blood-sacrifice (ibid). Hauptmann, however, supplies the specific proposition which underpins

---

[160] Cf. *A Companion to Twentieth Century German Literature*, ed. by Raymond Furness and Malcolm Humble (London: Routledge, 1997), p.118; also Hiller von Gaertringen (1994), pp.94-95.

[161] See Hiller von Gaertringen (1994), p.96.

[162] Gerhart Hauptmann, *Griechischer Frühling,* hereinafter cited from the 1966 Propyläen edition.

[163] Schoenebeck and Kraiker, *Hellas*, pp.74,75.

Kästner's insistence that, for the Greeks, sanctity attached to natural sites before ever temples were built (*Griechenland*, pp.18,87), namely, that religion has its deepest roots in nature and that the gods are pastoral in origin (*G.F.*, pp. 64,75). Kästner agrees in spirit: on the moonlight ascent of Mount Ida, he recalls the story of the birth of Zeus, suckled by the goat Amalthea (*Kreta*, p.14).

These concordances between the two writers are more than simply felicitous, they harmonise with Kästner's concern with reverence for life and nature and his deepest respect for the foci of reverence so elaborately developed by the Greeks. Kästner's formulation that Greek art, sculpture, tragedy, and intellect are unthinkable without the gods (*Kreta*, pp. 139-40) accords with Hauptmann's observation that the Greek gods were not eternal and pre-existing like the Christian god, but gestated (*G.F.*, p.37), and were local rather than omnipresent (*G.F.*, p.49); as Hauptmann puts it, the Greek theatre performances were *for* gods, *before* gods (*G.F.*, p.73). Yet, paradoxically, only the Greek gods, Kästner points out, though the creation of men, live in lofty places, among the elements, untroubled by the cares of humankind (ibid., p.93). The paradox understood by both writers is that of a Humanism devoted to the study of a god-fixated society which in its strivings was supremely humanist.

The unease with which Kästner views archaeological excavation and his outright rejection of speculative reconstruction (cf. *Griechenland*, pp.121-122, 163-164; *Kreta*, pp.116-119) echoes *Griechischer Frühling*, where Hauptmann, suggesting a parallel with the archaeological de-layering undertaken at Mycenae, Troy and Olympia, argues for 'psychic' rather than a physical excavation: "...das Griechentum zwar begraben, doch nicht gestorben [...] nur in den Seelen lebendiger Menschen begraben [...] so kommt auch vielleicht für das lebendige Griechenerbe die große Stunde der Ausgrabung" (*G.F.*, p.57). In extension: without the infinite and well-founded, "unendliche, wohl-gegründete", myth-world of the Greeks, the powers of the imagination are today isolated and fragmented, "vereinzelt und zersplittert", and dependent solely on that which may be brought forth in the short life of the individual (*G.F.*, p.61). In further extension, polytheism and monotheism are not mutually exclusive: in the world we have dealings with countless forms of the Divinity, "Gottheit", and beyond this world with the unity of God, "mit der göttlichen Einheit" (*G.F.*, p.62). Roundly, Hauptmann declares that we live in a world of ideas, of the imagination, or we live not in our world at all, "Wir leben in einer Welt der Vorstellungen, oder wir leben nicht mehr in unserer Welt" (ibid.). Kästner, the bibliophile, regrets rather the loss of the literary imagination to archaeological anatomy, "denn die herrlichsten Gemälde der griechischen Landschaft, diejenigen Goethes und Hölderlins, sind ja von beiden Genien nur mit dem Auge der

Sehnsucht geschaut" (*Griechenland*, p.241); also, "ich bin beschämt, daß ich es in Wirklichheit sehe, was er [Jean Paul], der Gnadengroße, niemals im Leben sah als nur mit dem trunkenen Wahrblick der Sehnsucht und Liebe" (*Kreta*, p.77). Viewing the scattered but otherwise virtually complete remains of the Aphaia temple on Aigina, Kästner seems to disdain the possibility that scholarly diligence, "Gelehrtenfleiß", could faithfully reconstruct it, *even were that reconstruction in graphic form only* (*Griechenland*, p.88). He is reacting to the evidence, seen with his own eyes, of relentless excavation, the result of a lust for knowledge of objects, "die Begierde zu wissen über Dinge" (*Kreta*, p.116). Artworks and buildings of other peoples and other times *have their own life and rights*, "ihr eigenes Leben, ihr eigenes Recht". Scientific knowledge, *Wissenschaft*, is just one way among many, "nur eine der Wege von mehreren", to come into close contact with them (*Kreta*, p.116). He regrets the banishment of the free wonderment and passion of the Romantics, "Ich bedauere es wie viele, daß sich die Wissenschaft den frei geäußerten Strom der Bewunderung und das flammende Gefühl verbot, wie es zu Wincklmanns Zeiten noch üblich war" (*Kreta*, p.37). Kästner is an unashamed Romantic, but a Romantic empiricist. Flying in a *Storch* over Crete, the pilot routinely cutting the engine so he and his passenger may speak, Kästner finds that the experience outstrips human awareness: mankind had experienced flying more intensely when it could still only dream of it, "Die ganze Menscheit hat das Fliegen stärker erlebt, als sie noch bloß davon träumte" (*Kreta*, p.97).

Such lamenting of the passing of Romantic vision might seem whimsical, though not out of place, in sentimental travel-writing. The concern, however, becomes shrill and earnest in Kästner's later works. As did Hauptmann, he acknowledges the illuminating discoveries of the archaeologists: "ohne sie wäre das Versunkene versunken und das Verschollene verschollen geblieben; das bestritt niemand."[164] Although here noting with approval the similarity of modern archaeology to forensic science, the Kästner who celebrated the finds of Byronic philhellene dilettantes on Aigina (*Griechenland*, p.89) continued to uphold his reservation against mere *Wissenschaft*: science and that which it pursues are locked in a debate conducted in mutually unintelligible languages, "die Wissenschaft, und das, dem sie nachjagt: [...] Zusammen- und auseinandergeflucht, zu einander gesperrt, in endlosem Gespräch mit einander, aber in einander unverständlichen Sprachen."[165] Kästner's point is that knowledge pursued acquisitively, without conviction, "ohne Besinnung, auf Mehrwissen

---

[164] Kästner, 'Ein Mann der Wissenschaft', postscript to *Die Lerchenschule* (1964); here cited from *Offener Brief an die Königin von Griechenland* (Frankfurt am Main: Suhrkamp, 1973), p.35.

[165] Ibid., pp.35-36.

erpicht",[166] is won at a loss of the previously freely-imagined history of the things uncovered: "Abhanden, abhanden, abhanden."[167]

Kästner encountered Heidegger as one of the invited audience at Heidegger's first public postwar lecture,[168] on 'Das Ding', given before the Bavarian Academy of Fine Arts in Munich on the 6th of June 1950.[169] They met on that occasion afterwards, in the house of Erhard Göpel, as Heidegger reminds Kästner in a letter of 1973.[170] Kästner's review of Heidegger's lecture appeared in the *Schwäbische Landeszeitung* on 10th June 1950.[171] According to Heidegger, "Gerichtetsein", which in context may be loosely translated as 'the state of being focussed upon' is over-emphasised by other philosophers as the basis of consciousness: "Gerichtetsein als der Grundstruktur des Bewußtseins [...] eine viel zu ausdrückliche und überschärfte Charackteisierung des Seins in der Welt gegeben."[172] Things, "Dinge", remain inconspicuous and strike the consciousness only when absent or otherwise out of place.[173] The material of things becomes conspicuous in a work of art where it is *applied*, "gebraucht", rather than *consumed*, "verbraucht": the leather of Van Gogh's 'Shoes' and the limestone of the Parthenon remain conspicuous, the leather for the nature of its service, revealed by the painting, the limestone for the unity of "Bahnen und Bezüge", 'ways and connections', birth and death, weal and woe, victory and defeat, endurance and decline of a people, which the temple ordains and collects of and in itself.[174] Heidegger's example in the lecture is that of a pitcher whose *Wesen*, its nature or essence, is not its Platonic *eidos* as a container of a certain fluid capacity, but rather its capacity to pour, *im Geschenk*, which Kästner fancies the audience may have misheard and that a Heidegger coinage, *Geschänk* – from *Schänke*, a tavern or inn – may actually have been uttered. In the fluttering and hovering of meaning, "im Flatterschweben", over the double or equivalent meaning of words, Kästner thinks that a nerve of such philosophising, "ein Nerv solchen

166 Ibid., p.35.

167 Ibid., p.36.

168 The lecture had been presented at the *Bremer Club* in 1949: cf. *Heidegger*, ed. by Michael Inwood (Freiburg: Herder, 1999), p.13.

169 Cf. *Martin Heidegger - Erhart Kästner Briefwechsel*, ed. by Heinrich W. Petzet (Frankfurt am Main: Insel, 1986), p.7.

170 Ibid., cf. pp.120,121.

171 Cf. Kästner, *Offener Brief*, p.159.

172 Heidegger, *Gesamtausgabe*, vol.27, p.318, cited in Inwood (1999), p.42.

173 Inwood, ibid.

174 Ibid., p.136.

Philosophierens", may have been touched.[175] Philosophy, so it appears, concludes Kästner, is returning to its roots in poetry.[176]

Such a conclusion is one that accords with the intuitive philosophy of Kästner's *Griechenland* and *Kreta.* The re-written version of *Griechenland* that would appear as *Ölberge, Weinberge*, would have little similarity, so Kästner intended, with "jener viel zu feuilletonistischen zweckbedingten Fassung."[177] The second volume of the planned trilogy, *Kreta*, is the one that Heidegger, acknowledging receipt of a copy of the posthumous 1975 edition from Kästner's widow, describes as Kästner's *Erstling*, his 'first-born child'.[178] It is in *Kreta* that Kästner, with the free-roaming brief allowed him by General Bräuer (who, Kästner attests in *Offener Brief*, loved the island with a secret passion)[179] and writing a more personal account, conjures a still-present immanence of the antique world: his language is Romantic, but his observations are insistent on a Heideggerian *Sein und Zeit* inseparability. The influence of the Romantic is freely acknowledged, as in "Sonnenschleier, wunderbar gestuft, wie sie uns die Bilder der Romantik ins Herz gemalt haben."[180] Flights of Romantic lyric can also serve to screen pointed allusion: as in this reference to Crete as the site of the clash of Zeus and the Olympian gods with the Titans:

> Hier traten ihnen die Olympier entgegen, die Schirmer der Ordnung, die Hüter des Lichts, *die Verächter der bloßen Gewalt.*[181] (italics added)

The long ascent of Mount Ida, with which *Kreta* begins, is Kästner's paean to the classical Greek virtues of order, proportion and moderation: "Das war die Ordnung des Zeus [...] Es war die Setzung der Maße [...] der Aufgang der griechischen Welt."[182] Zeus must here stand for the spirit which inspired the Platonic and Socratic understanding that virtue in the contingencies of life is the apprehension by means of reason of the proper mean. He affirms that his two years in Greece to this point have been a schooling: "In diesem Lande zwei Jahre zu leben, ist eine Schule der maßvollen Maße und der menschlichen Grenzen in allem Gelebten und allem Gebauten."[183] One lesson of this schooling that Kästner expounds is the reverence for the fruits of the earth that occasioned the propitiatory

---

175 Kästner, *Offener Brief*, p.43.
176 Ibid., p.44.
177 Raabe, *Erhart Kästner. Briefe*, p.68.
178 Cf. Petzet, *Heidegger Kästner Briefwechsel*, p.130.
179 Cf. Hiller von Gaertringen (1994), pp.111-2; also Kästner, *Offener Brief*, p.8.
180 Kästner, *Kreta* (1946), p.19.
181 Ibid., p.15.
182 Ibid., p.17.
183 Ibid., p.34.

worship of Demeter and Dionysius and which he found still surviving in the Cretan custom of praising food and drink:

> So hier wird gepflückt, geschenkt und genossen. Demeter und Dionysos werden hier nicht mehr verehrt; ihr Andenken hat sich in nördliche Länder verzogen, die ihr Wesen nur ahnen als blassen Abendschein.
> Hier brauchten sie nur wiederzukehren. Es ist ihnen noch alles bereitet.[184]

The significance of a time is more fundamental than its historical determination or duration.[185] In Heideggerian terms, the Cretans were living examples of a continuing *in-der-Welt-sein* in a departed, yet still lived-in *Welt*, whereas the northern Europeans have become disconnected, perceiving the nature gods only as the twilight glimmer of a departed superstition.

Here in theatrically figurative expression is Kästner's insistence on language as defining of all things, *Dinge*, among which Kästner included humans: "Also, was ist ein Ding? Ich komme zu dem seltsamen Schluß, das die Menschen auch Ding unter Dingen sind."[186] Kästner is writing to his long-standing literary friend Heinrich Gremmels, in an impassioned tone approaching exasperation, in explication of his 1972 lecture, 'Aufstand der Dinge'. As to language, Kästner, writing to Hans Egon Holthusen and dismissing Jaspers' *Von der Wahrheit*, maintains that in Heidegger *Dichtung* can be demonstrated to, indeed, be *Wahrheit*:

> Die Bedeutung Heideggers besteht unter anderem darin, daß er weiß [...] daß sie dasselbe wie Dichtung ist, und er hat dem Denken und dem Philosophieren den Rang und Charakter der Dichtung wiedergegeben.[187]

Kästner's objections are directed at Jasper's later work, and would seem to overlook Jaspers' insistence (in *Philosophy of Existence*, 1938) that scientific *cognition of things* is not *cognition of being*, this prefatory to a call for the recognition of an *Existenz* that is more than the sum of existence, consciousness and spirit, which concept would supplant the 'deceptive idea' of a universal, necessary and knowable totality of events.[188] To another correspondent, Kästner stoutly maintains that the older Heidegger would not deny the impossibility of fixing meaning in the sign-and-referent circularity of language:

---

[184] Ibid., p.22.
[185] Inwood, *Heidegger*, p.125.
[186] Raabe, *Erhart Kästner. Briefe*, p.217.
[187] Ibid., p.144.
[188] Cited from *Continental Philosophy*, ed. by William McNeil and Karen S. Feldman (Oxford: Blackwell, 1998), pp.32-40.

> [...] bloß Verstehen, ohne Wortwunder, ohne Bannzauber, das ist platte Wissenschaft, [...] oder schafft der alte Heidegger etwa keinen magischen Raum? Will er behaupten, man könne das, was er sagen will, nicht auch glatter sagen? Doch, wenn er nicht (wie wir) wohl wußte, daß das Glatthingesagte halt nichts mehr ist, Wort ist nicht Nachrichtenübermittlung, Wort ist Wortwunder.[189]

The Nietzschean insistence that epistemological thinking simply does not occur, that 'causality' eludes us in the play between two thoughts of all kinds of affects,[190] corresponds to Kästner's privileging of the aura inseparably surrounding words.

Kästner acknowledged that he had arrived in Greece filled with the conventional enthusiasm for classicism, as received from Schiller, but had come to realise that the modern-day Greeks in no way shared this; they could have had no idea of a Schiller-inspired theory of a *Universalgeschichte*. Kästner's later books, stemming from his postwar visits to Greece, had therefore focused on the transmutation and continuation of the antique world in the Byzantine.[191] In the end, the search that had begun in *Griechenland* and *Kreta* became a strident polemic against the spawning by science of an all-dominant technology. In his 'Aufstand der Dinge' text,[192] Kästner describes scientists as the "Getriebenen", beings driven and pursued by their master, science. While expressing appreciation of a presentation volume of that work with Kästner's handwritten dedication[193] Heidegger is nonetheless compelled to be unwontedly specific in pointing to a misreading on the part of his friend and admirer: "So weit ich sehe, treibt das Wesen der Technik [...] Man meint immer noch, die neuzeitliche Wissenschaft sei der Grund für die Technik, während es sich in Wahrheit so verhält, daß die Wissenschaft im Wesen der modernen Technik grundet." With a concluding caveat, "Doch möchte ich Ihr Buch nicht auf das Feld der »Philosophie« zerren, weil es ein dichterisches Buch aus eigenem Wuchs ist." [194], Heidegger here accords Kästner the status rather of a hilltop prophet from Mount Ida, a prophet of the elusive wonder of language, and therefore forever a recusant in the matter of conformity to methodological (fearing thereby reductive) approaches.

---

189 Raabe, *Erhart Kästner. Briefe*, p.154.

190 Cited from McNeil and Feldman, op. cit., p.82.

191 Cf. Raabe, *Erhart Kästner. Briefe*, pp.193-94.

192 Kästner, 'Aufstand der Dinge,' in *Offener Brief*, pp.134-158 (p.139).

193 See Petzet, *Heidegger Kästner Briefwechsel*, pp.121,124, and 151(note); on variants to the 'Aufstand der Dinge' text, see bibliographic note to Kästner, *Offener Brief*, pp.161-62.

194 Petzet, pp.121-22.

5. Felix Hartlaub: Paris underground

5.1. Formative influences on *Weltanschauung*

The parents of Felix Hartlaub, Gustav Friedrich and Félicie Mathilde, concerned at the sombre content of Felix's drawings (though this content was for the most part illustrative of works he had read)[1] and more so at the fatal conclusions, through suicide, in his juvenile fiction, enrolled him in the liberal *Odenwaldschule* where he was a pupil from April 1928 to September 1932. The school, whose free-spirit ethos owed much to the *Wandervogel and Jugendbewegung* movements, emphasised 'whole person' and group education, self-administration, co-education, and community spirit. This idealistic social model was at variance with the authoritarian cast of post-1933 Germany and ill equipped the young Felix for assimilation into the new political realities. Henri Plard, citing Klaus and Monika Mann, also students at the school, describes its effects on Hartlaub: "cette école de l'Odenwald semble avoir produit [...] une désastreuse incapacité à se défendre de la vie et des hommes."[2] Plard's 1959 study of Hartlaub, concentrating on the Paris sketches, posits that Hartlaub transposed the mundanely detached ethic of the *Odenwaldschule* into a literary aesthetic: "Au fond, il transpose en esthétique l'éthique de l'Odenwaldschule."[3]

Hartlaub was a precocious literary talent, even if, as Wilke has demonstrated, some of his early works were re-drafted by parental hand.[4] An unaided historical work, the novella *Parthenope,* set in Napoleonic Naples, was published posthumously. The long allegorical story, 'Brueghels Affe', is told from the point of view of the chained ape depicted in the Brueghel painting, and is a dark study on the nature of human nature. Wilke notes that the distinctive style of the adult Hartlaub, the mode of seeing and narrating without commentary, breaks through for the first time in the Berlin sketches of his postgraduate studies.[5] 'Brueghels Affe', Hartlaub's most sustained attempt to subject the world to ethical scrutiny, was also his last. Wilke concludes that the real world of the 1930s from which the *Odenwaldschule* had isolated Hartlaub now in turn isolated him. In October 1932, a month after leaving the school, Hartlaub writes to his father from the train station in Zurich telling him that, after a morning toing and froing

---

[1] See *Felix Hartlaub. Die Aufzeichnungen*, ed. by Hellmut Seemann (Frankfurt am Main: Schirn- Kunstalle Verlag, 1993), p.19.

[2] Henri Plard, '»*Tout Seul*«. La conscience de la solitude chez Felix Hartlaub', *Etudes Germaniques, Revue de la Société des Études Germaniques*, Paris (April/June 1959), p.131.

[3] Ibid., p.132.

[4] Cf. Christian-Hartwig Wilke, 'Die Jugendarbeiten Felix Hartlaubs', loc. cit, 263-301.

[5] See Wilke, *Die letzten Aufzeichnungen Felix Hartlaubs*, p.159.

in indecision, he has deliberately missed the train back to Mannheim. He asks if he may be allowed to remain on in Switzerland through November and December so that may overcome "die Kluft zwischen »OSO« und »Leben«".[6] In the event, Hartlaub is allowed to spend the greater part of 1933 in Italy, from February to October;[7] there, he puts down his unease with his Italian acquaintances to what he sees as an un-German shallowness and a dual morality among his Italian fellow students, outwardly subservient to family codes and inwardly hedonistic.[8] Forsaking Naples for a three-month stay in the university town of Perugia, he flees from there in turn to Florence in order to detach himself from the "vor Überintellektualismus gänzlich wert- und wissenschaftsfeindlich" clique among whom, some of them fellow German expatriates, he still feels peripheral.[9] On his return, to Berlin, he found himself no less alienated from his surroundings.[10] Werner Meyer wrote in a recollection that during his doctoral studies in history at the *Friedrich-Wilhelms-Universität* in Berlin, Hartlaub found the critical study of sources more difficult than "die intuitive Erkenntnis aus seiner unnmittelbaren Sehschärfe und die lebendige Darstellung von Menschen und Zeiten."[11] Meyer concluded that this period of formal study in history obstructed Hartlaub's instinctive inclination towards what were his innate creative talents, to which, despite the urgings of his father to produce an academic post-doctoral work, he turned in the end. Meyer attributed to Hartlaub "die Objektivität eines Epikers" and ventured that it could almost be said that Hartlaub had preserved this epical distance to the then ever more pressing "Gegenwartsfragen der Politik," were it not that his truthfulness, sense of justice, and partisanship for weak had activated him.[12] Meyer, Hartlaub's *Odenwaldschule* supervising teacher during his student-exchange visit to Strasbourg in 1930 and tour leader on the month-long school visit to Italy in 1931, had opportunity to observe his student over time and formed a distinct impression. With reference to Hartlaub's penetrating literary style, Meyer remarks that "Dieser Zwang seiner Seele, das jeweils Begegnende aufzunehmen, die Schalen zu durchdringen, nirgends in Halbheiten auszuweichen, ist ihm geblieben."[13] From school

---

[6] Krauss, *Felix Hartlaub: in seinen Briefen*, p.88.

[7] Ibid., see entry for 1933, p.338 and letter dates, pp.89-128.

[8] Ibid., see pp.108-9.

[9] Ibid., see p.123.

[10] See Wilke, *Die letzten Aufzeichnungen Felix Hartlaubs*, pp.150,151,152,159-60.

[11] Werner Meyer, 'Felix Hartlaub in der Odenwaldschule', *Die Sammlung. Zeitschrift für Kultur und Erziehung*, yr.13 (Göttingen:Vandenhoeck & Ruprecht, 1958), pp.623-31, 630.

[12] Ibid., p.630.

[13] Ibid., p.629.

essays, Meyer had noted this facility for expressing the whole through a focalising detail: "seine Art, das Große zu sehen und vom merkwürdigen Einzelnen her das Ganze zu begreifen."[14] Meyer noticed how Hartlaub in the political discussion evenings at the Odenwaldschule affirmed "die offene Auseinandersetzung als menschliche Erscheinung" and how he participated in these discussions "mit einem gelassenen oder grimmigen Humor, wenn nicht mit Bitterkeit."[15] This tinge of bitterness which Meyer noticed may have been transmuted into that amoral distance which characterises Hartlaub's writing thereafter. Balancing this there was his attraction to form and beauty: during the Italian trip something more in the way of enthusiasm was evident than might have been expected even from the son of a museum curator. Meyer was struck by how Hartlaub appeared to be captivated and intoxicated as "eine Trunkenheit des Sehens und Entdeckens nahm ihn in Florenz gefangen."[16] Hartlaub's minute observation of architectural detail is also evident from his fragments written while at university in Berlin and is at its most sustained in the Paris sketches. What to Meyer had seemed a visual intoxication of discovery became a conscious cerebral discipline:

> Zu richtigem konzentrierten Sehen, namentlich von Architektur, bin ich allerdings noch kaum im Stande. Bekomme erst ganz allmählich wieder halbwegs normale Gesichtswerkzeuge.[17]

> ...wie sehr einem das eine Jahr Schlicktown doch anhaftet, leide vor allem sehr an der Unfähigkeit zu konzentriertem Sehen.[18]

> Auch dass ich solange nicht mehr gezeichnet habe, sei es auch nur zur Kontrolle des eigenen Sehens, rächt sich jetzt bös.[19]

Hartlaub was stationed at Wilhelmshaven, 'Schlicktown', for much of the time before his posting to Paris.

Before the move to Paris, postings in October 1939 to the Ruhr mining district of Gelsenkirchen-Scholven and briefly to the industrial settlement of Köln-Knapsack produced observations on Rhineland Catholicism:

> Das Ineinander von westfälischem Bauerntum, Bergbau und Katholizismus zog mich sehr an. [...] Ich würde mich hier gerne mal niederlassen, wenn ich einen anständigen Beruf hätte. [20]

---

[14] Ibid.
[15] Ibid., p.630.
[16] Ibid., p.631.
[17] Ewenz I (2002/2007), pp.452/459.
[18] Ibid., pp.453/460.
[19] Ibid.
[20] Ibid., p.375/381: letter to G.F. Hartlaub, 26 October 1939.

> Knapsack. Vorstellungen von frommen mittelalterlichen Bergmannsknappen, die der Name weckt. Katholizismus, der in seiner Vereinigung mit den Gegebenheiten des Industriearbeitertums den Berlinern sehr fremd ist.[21]

The *Kulturkampf* of the Bismarck era had left its mark in the sense of grievance, still directed at the *Preußentum* (and felt by Heinrich Böll at the social setbacks suffered by his family in Cologne the 1920s). Rheinland industry and enterprise was still overwhelmingly controlled by Protestant, for Böll, 'Prussian', interests.[22] Hartlaub is aware that his own fascination with and attraction to the Westphalian overlap of farming and mining communities, of industrial service in 'Protestant', Prussian industry and a community background in rural Catholicism, seemed at odds, to the bemusement of Hartlaub's Berliner and therefore 'Prussian' fellow servicemen; at odds with his own background also, and presented images with both attracting and repelling aspects:

> Priester und weihräuchernder Chorknabe [...] Nonnen in Ringelreihen mit Arbeiterkindern [...] Kirche und Schule stattliche Bauten. Die Siedlung alle[s] niedrige Arbeiterhäuser [...] Zugänglichkeit der Mädchen. [...] Mädchen mit polnischen, jugoslavischen Namen, die zur Beichte gehen.[23]

The attraction is romantic, in contrast to his attachment to Protestantism which is intellectual, as evidenced by the youthful Hartlaub's reaction to the floridity of the Catholic, Italian baroque:

> Weißt Du, hier unten, wo einen das Heidentum ewig anlächelt oder der katholische Barock seine Hände theatralisch gen Himmel reckt, bekommt man manchmal direkt etwas Sehnsucht nach Protestantismus.[24]

> Der Protestantismus als solcher ist schon etwas Großartiges und auch etwas ungeheuer Modernes. Die erste Tat, die außerhalb des Mittelmeeres, der klassischen Überlieferung getan worden ist. Er gehört mit der Entdeckung Amerikas, der Nauturwissenschaft, alles neueste Dinge, zu den Leitersprossen, die die Menscheit zu besteigen sich erst gerade anschickt;[25]

Amid the heightened language, it is the intellectual independence and sober rigour of Protestantism which Hartlaub is here commending to his brother, from Italy in 1933, on the occasion of the latter's confirmation. Hartlaub's

---

21 Ibid., p.21.

22 See Sagarra & Skrine, *A Companion to German Literature*, p.125, and Böll, *Briefe* II, pp.1139-40.

23 Ewenz I (2002/2007), p.21.

24 Krauss, *Felix Hartlaub: in seinen Briefen*, p.95.

25 Ibid., p.96.

later spare fictional style, characteristically paratactic, may be viewed as a product of his adherence to a code of thought and to an intellectual discipline of restraint in style and expression which he terms 'Protestant'. Ernst Jünger would articulate the elevation of rationality through the Reformation and the shaping legacy of the apotheosis of rationality, the French Revolution, in terms of intellectual eugenics:

> Von einer Seite sprach der Bürgermeister einer kleinen Gemeinde auf mich ein, wohl siebzigjährig, mit dem Ausdruck strenger Rationalität. Mir wurde an ihm physiognomisch deutlich, daß in Frankreich die Revolution gewisse Prozesse der Reformation nachgeholt und weiterentwickelt hat.[26]

Hartlaub's architectural impressions from his Italian sojourn, of classical severity juxtaposed with the 'Catholic' baroque, prompted self-reflective musings, among which was the regret that he had spent too much time at the *Odenwaldschule* on projects for Meyer and for the school community instead of looking to his own maturation: "Ich habe diese Zeit auf der OSO mit nützlicher und weniger nützlicher Arbeit für Meyer und für die Gemeinschaft totgeschlagen, ohne mich viel um mein Alter zu kümmern."[27] Six years later, returning refreshed from a visit to Dresden and perhaps subliminally chafing at the Protestant work-ethic of personal responsibility and career-directed academic diligence of his father's urgings, Berlin is dismissed: "die ganze Kümmerlichkeit der Friderizianik." An appraisal of Dresden's *Frauenkirche*, "ja wohl der einzige wirklich eigenwüchsige protestantische Kirchenbau, die regelbestätigende Ausnahme", acknowledges the Catholic Baroque influence, from Venice, through the apostate Duke Augustus, *August der Starke*. That which was *eigenwüchsig*: self grown, self cultivated, nonconformist, commanded Hartlaub's admiration.[28] Already, on the earlier school group visit to Italy in 1931 and not yet eighteen, Hartlaub had intuited what would become the hallmark of his literary efforts: a visual rendering and ordering of objects and phenomena without authorial comment:

> In meinem Inneren liefern sich wie früher Wissenschaft und einfaches Betrachten der Dinge grimmige Schlachten. Doch wird die Wissenschaft diesmal wohl den Kürzeren ziehen.[29]

The *einfaches Betrachten der Dinge* was what he turned to, despite dutiful attention to a long reading programme and card-index note taking for his

---

[26] Jünger, *Strahlungen I* (Munich: DTV/Klett-Cotta, 1988), p.183.
[27] Krauss, *Felix Hartlaub: in seinen Briefen*, p.96.
[28] Ibid., p.171.
[29] Ibid., p.76.

post-doctoral project on 19th century French literature. To his mentor Rudolf Kieve in December 1938 he wrote presciently, "Das einzige, was ich habe bzw. vielleicht einmal werde haben können: la lingua tedesca und was sich damit anstellen läßt."[30] What Hartlaub would do with *la lingua tedesca* was to foreshorten its strict syntax through paratactic stream-of-consciousness passages and an Austen-like use of focalising characters thinking in interior monologue.

5.2. The migrant *flâneur*

Sketches from the time of Hartlaub's doctoral studies in Berlin are contained in a single handwritten notebook and on typed transcriptions in the *DLA* archive at Marbach. The provenance of the typescripts is not recorded; they are free of the characteristic Hartlaub revisions and insertions and are on white, modern paper dissimilar to the coarser-grained service notepaper of Hartlaub's own later typescripts from the *FHQ*. Non sequiturs in the typescripts point to possible errors of transcription from the notebook MS. Nonetheless, a reading reveals a striking similarity to the Paris sketches in the detached observation of scenes, in the sparsity of dialogue and the absence of any involving the narrator himself, and in a narrating gaze that strays even against the thread of the narration towards skyline and roofscape. In the intervening sketches from the period of service in 1939-1940 with an air-defence balloon unit in Northwest Germany the gaze still seeks out the skyline, as in the sketch, 'Flak': "Nachts bewegen sich die Gestalten der Kanoniere phantastisch vor dem vom Brande der Hochöfen geröteten Himmel." Blast furnace towers, brown-coal excavators, smokestacks and high-tension cable masts dominate the landscape in 'Industrieschutz' where the twin spires of Cologne Cathedral appear only now and again through the smog, between chimney and cable-tower pairs. An impression is conveyed of an already busy landscape complicated by the intrusion of the soldiery and their apparatus. In the Berlin notebook, the observed figures appear as inverted vanishing points in their own perspective: walled in, overlooked from high windows, their plane to the horizon tilted at a steep roofwards angle. The piece 'Der Hund' opens from the perspective of the dog who is busily seeking to play with the Student, the principal perceiving persona of the piece who is, like others of his fellows without money or connections, seeking in vain to find deckchair ease in the summer heat, unable to afford a Sunday afternoon on the Wannsee. A high window opens and the white-bearded face of an elderly Jew looks down, but, seeing himself noticed, immediately withdraws from view, as if extinguished, "blitzschnell zurück, wie ausgelöscht." The setting is the area

[30] Ibid., p.296.

around the Oranienburg Strasse, the Jewish quarter of the Berlin *Altstadt*.[31] The fear and furtiveness is conveyed without authorial comment. The concluding section of the piece gently mocks the morbid juvenile melancholy of the student which strains upwards and away from lived-in street level to symbolic silhouettes and motifs in bronze and stone:

> Heimweg. Die grünen Kupferkuppeln vom Dom, über die die Milch der Dämmerung fliesst, sie blassen ab oder werden bläulich. Die grünen lampentragenden Statuen von Handel und Wandel auf der Brücke [...]. Die "Puppenbrücke ", der Held und Minerva, die ihm Speerwerfen, Bogenschiessen, Flötespielen lernt und den Gefallenen huldvoll wegschleppt. Die Studenten haben weder eine Göttin zur Lehrmeisterin noch solch netten frühen Tod zu gewärtigen. Aufblickend gewahrt man das Leben der Statuen auf den Dächern. Die hohlen Panzer und leerklaffenden Helme in Garben von Fulmen und Lanzen auf den Dächern von Zeughaus und Prinzessinnenpalais. Die moskowitisch endlose Fassade des Schlosses, an der der wohlgezielte Stoss der Lindenallee zerschellt, der Verkehr rinnt an der schrägen Front ab.[32]

The direction of the gaze along facades and across parapets is, as in the sketches from Paris that would follow, a device to depopulate the scene, which Hartlaub then re-animates with armoured statuary. In extension of the conceit of an inner conflict the Unter den Linden dashes its traffic against the façade of the Berlin *Schloss*.

It is perhaps another Berlin piece which is the quintessential *flâneur* essay. 'Holsteinufer'[33] describes an apartment house; more accurately, a tenement of six stairwells with a walled-in, refuse-strewn garden of bare berry bushes and yew, so dark the birds do not venture into it, and a narrow courtyard. The tenantry is eclectic: "Frau Sch. angeblich Türkin,"; "Herr M.," almost 80 years old, shares a lodging with a "Frau A.", lives by uncertain, allegedly shady means, reeks of garlic soap, has a classical library, many dictionaries, and is reputed to speak many languages. The somewhat sinister figure is nonetheless shy and retreats into his room when encountered. Indeterminate noises from adjoining apartments disturb by night. The landlady, a Polish Jew, lives with her partner, once her 'gentleman' lodger: "war möblierter Herr bei Ihr". The whole house is full of such women partnered by come-down, broken-down men, "meist ältlichen und irgendwie lädierten, schwer zu ertragenden, unvermeidlich dummen, frechen,

---

[31] Cf. Geno Hartlaub, *Das Gesamtwerk* (Frankfurt am Main: Fischer, 1955), p.17; also, *DeutschesLiteratur Archiv* Marbach, typescript 93.17.6, p.9.

[32] See *Das Gesamtwerk*, p.18; here cited from *Deutsches Literatur Archiv* typescript 93.17.6, p.11.

[33] See *Das Gesamtwerk*, pp.31-33; here cited from *Deutsches Literatur Archiv* typescript 93.17.6, pp.28-30.

verrückten Männer." Here begins Hartlaub's prose poetry, a succession of poetic oppositions describing the man, whom the woman holds onto as to a security, a pledge, "er ist nur das Pfand", a never-used credit, "nie benutzter Gutschein", against life: "ein Kranker, der gepflegt, ein Erpresser, der hingehalten, ein Rasender, der beschwichtigt werden muss. [...] frech und feig wie ein Dieb, geil und lustlos, gewalttätig und wehleidig." First, Hartlaub writes, it was just the women within these damp walls; then came the man. The man portrayed stands for them all; he lives under the terms of the *Matriarchat der modernen Grosstadt*. The latter phrase forms a full sentence and is Hartlaub's sovereign pronouncement, as *flâneur* of interiors, on age and dependency in the modern metropolis.

The Paris sketches with their surrogate point of view are a direct continuation of the Berlin impressions. Hartlaub was not satisfied with their fluctuation between prose poetry and reportage.[34] *Prosagedicht* Hartlaub saw as one pole, with reportage, of a Scylla and Charybdis of stylistic uncertainty. The lyrical praise of Paris itself alternates with sharp-eyed and witty vignettes of the uniformed tourists and of the citizens in whose way they came. Hartlaub, in addition, in interposing the alter ego of "Er" allowed the reader to be at times also the *flâneur*, watching the *flâneur*. The "Er" *flâneur* is not yet quite developed in the Berlin sketches and there is still something of the schoolboy fixation with the Gothic in his penchant for the surreal, as the concluding section of 'Holsteinufer' exemplifies. Death claims the decayed tenement gent with a Faustian panache:

> Die Seele an einem endlosen Vormittag auf einem Bett, dessen Pfosten im Sumpf und Moder versinken. Halb angekleidet, halb ausgezogen, auf grauen unordentlichen Laken. Das eine Bein hängt aus dem Bett, der eine Arm hinterm Nacken, üppiges Haar, graue Fäden, mit dem andern bedeckt er sich die Augen. Zerbrochene Spiegel, umgeworfene Flacons. Sie wollte aufstehen, fand nicht die Kraft und den Mut, ist wieder zurückgesunken. Wollte sich töten, sich verbrennen – das Feuer erstickte, sich ersäufen – die Wanne leckte, das Pulver war nass, der Dolch stumpf, aus den durchschnittenen Adern floss kein Blut. Das Leben, pantoffelschürfende hastende Haushälterin, klopft ab und zu an die Tür, an die Wände, kratzt ans Bett. Der Tod tritt ein als tadellos eleganter Kavalier, runder Hut, weisses Halstuch. Die trübe Klinke glänzt, nachdem er sie angefasst, das matte Linoleum, wo er es betreten. Legt Hut, Stock und Handschuhe auf den Tisch, setzt sein spitzes Knie, darüber die messerscharfe Bügelfalte, auf das zerwühlte Lager.[35]

This passage is omitted from *Das Gesamtwerk*, perhaps deemed immature in being too like the fantasy pieces of Hartlaub's juvenilia. Death's entrance

[34] Ewenz I (2002/2007), pp.483/491; Ewenz II (2002/2007), pp.60/63.
[35] Cited from *Deutsches Literatur Archiv* Marbach typescript 93.17.6, p.30.

and appearance is plausible, however, since he is paying a call on an already surreal human menagerie.

Neumeyer (1999) posits that since directionless roaming is the 'minimum definition' of the *flâneur*, the figure of the *flâneur* is therefore an 'open paradigm': an open pattern of thought and an open philosophical framework. Neumeyer sees the functions assigned to this paradigm as lying within the context of the invention and exposition of the aestheticisation of the modern.[36] Franz Hessel's *Spazieren in Berlin* (1929) is in Neumeyer's view primarily a tour of the literature of the city and a sentimental exercise in *Heimatkunde*, local history, rather than a confrontation of the surreality of its present.[37] It is Hessel's later, 1938 manuscript, 'Letzte Heimkehr', which contains his observation on the *sichtbare Vergangenheit* temporarily exposed by the new building in Berlin. Hartlaub, too, noted the interiors of the half-demolished houses, but sentiment is confined to a single remark on the widening of the Spree: "Alt-Berlin entrollt sich am Ufer." Hartlaub notes the practicalities of the new construction: foundations excavated by pneumatic drills, the spoil transported away on barges, white-clad stonemasons chiselling at the new Nazi facades.[38] The sketches and fragments of Hartlaub's Berlin notebook are intense with people-watching: of student, rooming house and boulevard café life. The undercurrent of political ferment is present also: brown shirts make up part of the *Tracht* dress of the student societies; there are *Austrian* refugees (it is pre-*Anschluss*), and Russian émigrés, nicknamed "Nazikosaken".[39] The students and eccentric bibliophiles of the sketches are outsiders, viewed by an outsider. It is this sense of alienation which creates an air of unreality in the sketches.

For Hartlaub, occupied Paris would also acquire an air of unreality, through its abnormally diminished activity:

> Die Baulichkeiten liegen infolge des fehlenden Strassentrubels natürlich in einer aufregenden Weise bloss, ohne aber, wie ich es wenigstens empfinde, an Sichtbarkeit zu gewinnen. Es fehlt das Medium zwischen ihnen und der Netzhaut.[40]

The city was laid bare by the absence of traffic and human commerce, but did not seem to gain thereby in visibility. Just as surreal are the encounters in Hartlaub's interior studies from Paris, of the Hotel d'Orsay, of the abandoned foreign ministry, and of the "Puff"; these forming a kind of

---

[36] *Der Flaneur. Konzeptionen der Moderne*, ed. by Harald Neumeyer (Würzburg: Königshausen & Neumann, 1999), pp.17-19.

[37] Ibid., pp.310-11.

[38] Hartlaub archive, *DLA* Marbach, folder 93:17:6, 'Berlin, Waisenbrücke'.

[39] Ibid., 'Politische Studenten'.

[40] Ewenz I (2002/2007), pp.460/467.

trilogy and containing character portrayals that are fragmentary and putative, drawn from fleeting encounters in corridors, in an elevator, from snatches of conversation overheard, from rumour, from the personal effects of the departed diplomatic staff. The Paris narrator has matured, and the bizarre incongruity of out-of-place people is conveyed through factual observation in the tone of free indirect speech, the tone mocking the characters' own self-accounts or suggesting by flat re-telling the implausibility of the hearsay. The chillingly bizarre magic realism used in the late *FHQ* sketches is a further development of the technique of which the Berlin sketches were trial pieces and the Paris sketches a refinement.

5.3. Idle pursuit? The wartime *flâneur*

The *flâneur* does not philosophise; Benjamin insists that this is not his role: what he must do is to observe acutely and relentlessly, under cover of a pose of idleness, and acquire knowledge of the history and provenance of his subjects, as would any expert collector. The *flâneur*'s study is not speculative physiognomy, but the study of the city as chthonic Labyrinth: "Die Stadt ist die Realisierung des alten Menscheitstraumes vom Labyrinth."[41] Benjamin dismisses the conventional characterisation of the *flâneur*:

> …nichts ist [...] törichter als die konventionelle These, [...] die These: er habe aus der physiognomischen Erscheinung der Menschen sein Studium gemacht, um ihnen Nationalität und Stand, Charakter und Schicksale am Gang, am Körperbau, am Mienenspiel abzulesen.[42]

The true *flâneur*, then, is other than a strolling, aphorism forming Peter Altenberg[43] or an impression gathering and opinion dispensing Robert Walser;[44] though he is, in his study of the labyrinth, a *practitioner* of physiognomy.[45] In that, the necessary precondition for the *flâneur*'s role, idleness, the idleness of the literary term, *Müßigang*, corresponds well to the aimless off-duty time of a serviceman on a foreign posting. Also, the *flâneur* need not necessarily be a native, but must acquire a native's topographical familiarity by walking, aimlessly, without slavishly following the Baedeker (Hartlaub complains of a colleague who does the latter).[46] Severin (1988) has formulated a precondition for *herumlaufende Schrifsteller*, 'strolling writers'. It

---

41 Ibid.

42 Benjamin, in Tiedemann, *Gesammelte Schriften* vol.5.2, p.541.

43 Cf. *Peter Altenberg, Extrakte des Lebens. Gesammelte Skizzen 1898-1919*, 5 vols, II, ed. by Werner J. Schweiger (Vienna/Frankfurt am Main: Löcker/S. Fischer, 1987).

44 Cf. Urs Widmer, 'Über Robert Walser', in *Robert Walser. Der Spaziergang*, ed. by Daniel Keel (Zurich: Diogenes, 1973), pp.145-66.

45 See Tiedemann, *Walter Benjamin. Gesammelte Schriften*, vol.5.2, pp. 526,541,554,559,1027.

46 Ewenz (2002/2007), pp. 477/485.

pertains to the *flâneur* and the city, since one defines the other. Severin explains:

> Der aus dem Zusammenhang des Großstadtalltags herausgelöste einzelne Eindruck erhält in der kleinen Prosa den Status eines eigenständigen literarischen Sujets. Indem damit das Marginale des Alltags zum Zentrum des Textes wird, nähert sich die kleine Prosa in ihrem Wirklichkeitsbezug der Perspektive des Flaneurs.[47]

In paraphrase: the single impressions detached from the weave of the everyday life of the big city become the very *sujet*, plot, to the *flâneur*'s *fabula*, story; the marginal of the everyday then becomes the centre of the *flâneur*'s text. Seibert (1995) maintains that in Hartlaub the attempt to write a *flâneur* literature as the specific literature of city experience under the conditions of occupation, and unmodified, failed. The attempt could not succeed because the code of reference, "Bezugssystem", between the observing *flâneur* subject and the perceivable urban exterior world had become its own threatening opposite, "hat sich in sein bedrohliches Gegenteil verkehrt."[48] The grounding of this opinion need not be challenged, so long as one reads these texts of Hartlaub *only* as *flâneur* literature. Read as *flâneur* literature, Hartlaub's Paris prose returns a detached and surreal image of reality, registering that estrangement which he himself had felt. Benjamin's essay on the *Passages* of Paris speaks of a 'Copernican' change in the principle of historic perception:

> ...man hielt für den fixen Punkt das »Gewesene« und sah die Gegenwart bemüht, an dieses Feste die Erkenntnis tastend heranzuführen. Nun soll sich dieses Verhältnis umkehren und das Gewesene seine dialektische Fixierung von der Synthesis erhalten, die das Erwachen mit den gegensätzlichen Traumbildern vollzieht.[49]

The *Gewesene*, the fixed reference point of 'that which is and has occurred', is quite unfixed in occupied Paris, and Benjamin's *dialektische Fixierung* achieved through dream images, *Traumbildern*, is accreted by Hartlaub from the fixed features of façades, mansards and *œils-de-bœuf*. The dialectical *Fixierung* is much more concrete, achieved through an *Entfremdungseffekt* of an excess of precision, the principle of his 'meticulous art', as divined by Henri Plard: "le principe de son art minutieux, étrange par l'excès de sa précision."[50]

If the forty separate pieces which make up Felix Hartlaub's Paris sketches[51] represent a failed attempt to pursue *flâneur* literature, then it is the

---

[47] Rudiger Severin, *Spuren des Flaneurs in deutschsprachiger Prosa* (Frankfurt am Main: Peter Lang, 1988), p.153.

[48] Seibert, in Drost and others, *Paris sous l'occupation*, p.71.

[49] Benjamin, 'Pariser Passagen II', in Tiedemann, *Gesammelte Schriften*, vol.5.2, p.1057.

[50] Henri Plard, 'tout seul', *Etude Germaniques*, 14 (April/June 1959), p.144.

[51] As published in Ewenz (2002/2007). One additional sketch is a memoir of Rouen.

paradox of a successful failure. The arbitrary sequencing of the Paris sketches in Geno Hartlaub's *Das Gesamtwerk* and *Im Sperrkreis* of 1955, which remained unchanged even in the enlarged 1984 edition of *Im Sperrkreis*, had obscured at least one perception of the evolution of the sketches, that of the *flâneur*'s progress. The two trial 'colour' pieces appearing first in the MS notebooks, 'Ventre de Paris' and 'Hochwasser', are followed in sequence in the MS by a quartet of sketches beginning with 'Rubrik: Tout seul oder: Le civil equivoque' which trace the personal sensations and encounters of the *flâneur*, tentatively identifying him in the first section of 'Tout seul' by the indeterminate *man* and thereafter as "Er". The focalising "Er" is contrasted in his loneliness in 'Place Pigalle' to the groups of night-revellers: he is crowded off the footpath, and coins the word "Begegnungschlacht" for the mass hunger for human companionship; the mirrored interior of a restaurant *séparé* reflects his isolation, and he feels that he himself emanates an aura of alienation and mistrust, "Der eisige Hof von Befremden, Misstrauen, den er um sich verbreitet."[52] The sequence is broken off in 'Die Bergèren, Diwane' by a hurried encounter with a colleague, as if this were for the writing and written-about *flâneur* literarily as well as socially unsatisfactory. There follows a long series of sketches which are depersonalised observations whose narrator is an unidentified seeing eye. The blend of objective point of view for the sketches in general, and of the limited omniscient for the narrator/character "Er" and the fleetingly encountered minor characters, allowed Hartlaub's stance to gravitate from the peripatetic of the *flâneur* towards the incident-and-character focus of the novelist. "Er" is employed in the two further short sketches immediately following 'Place Pigalle', but thereafter this focal character is dispensed with until re-introduced two dozen sketches later in just one more sketch, 'Le Rendezvous manqué – der versetzte Sieger', and then not again until the *flâneur* himself becomes the narrating protagonist, though as ever in the third person, of 'Weltwende im Puff.' Otherwise, characters remain socially distant from one another, merely strangers on a train, as in 'Rückfahrt von Fontainebleau', or penned in, like the cheerless soldier tourists on the Seine steamer in the ironically titled 'Lustbarke'. Even the late sketch, 'Boulevard Montmartre', is a night scene of hurrying figures which empties with the evacuation of the last departing *Metro* train. Character portrayals become more sustained only in the last, long sketches, and the very last, 'Paar auf Montmartre,' is written entirely from within the consciousness of its single thinking character. Character-limited omniscience is further limited in this instance for comic effect: the disgruntled off-duty serviceman half of the 'Paar auf Montmartre' is at a loss to know quite why Paris is getting under

---

[52] Ewenz I (2002/2007), p.51.

his skin. With similar comic effect the omniscience of the madam in 'Weltwende im Puff' is limited by her cloistered dependence on hearsay: bereft of clientele through the lassitude of the late June heat, she is half credulous of the rumour of an expeditionary exodus of Napoleonic proportions from Paris to Russia. The comic bewilderment of these characters undercuts the official high seriousness of the German presence in Paris. Accounts of the early experience of the Occupation such as that in Irène Némirovsky's novel, *Suite française*,[53] may be critically fêted for their vivid verisimilitude, but Hartlaub's staccato succession of scenes and of characters who feel out of place in their surroundings says more about the times: the madam of the *Puff* is unsure of her now de-familiarised surroundings and the preoccupations of her narrator client are entirely introspective and detached from all thought of a *Weltwende*. Eschewal of any attempt to offer rounded characters or character-bound *fabula* narrative more successfully conveys that very lack of or disruption of a *Bezugssystem*, that necessary frame of civic and societal reference, felt by the occupiers and the occupied alike. In Seibert's analysis, following Severin, the metropolis occasions a constitutive fragmentation of plot structure in *flâneur* literature. The German quest for regulated order went to un-Gallic extremes, as Tewes (1998) has outlined,[54] hence Seibert reads in Hartlaub's sketches a text-immanent sympathy for the resistance potential of the Parisians, which is literarily transmuted into plot disorder, "Sujet-Chaos".[55] Hartlaub's Paris oeuvre is thus seen to contain another, infra-textual, level of subversion.

5.4. Hartlaub: the writing persona

Hartlaub enjoyed the privacy of a hotel room during his foreign ministry assignment in Paris, twice extended, from the beginning of December 1940 until the beginning of September 1941 when he was recalled to field military duties. Habitually from his student days in Italy and in Berlin a solitary observer, and in Paris impecunious because of currency restrictions,[56] the leisure time occupation of *flâneur* beckoned, not, as Ewenz has pointed out, that of the pleasure seeking bohemian known from the literature of the nineteenth century, but, rather, "immer der einsame Melancholiker, der sich die Stadt auf seinen Streifzügen eroberte."[57] The letters and sharply observed sketches, in contrast to the anecdotes in Böll's letters, contain almost no exchanges between the observing narrator and the observed.

[53] Irène Némirovsky, *Suite française* (Munich: BTB, 2007).
[54] See Tewes, *Frankreich in der Besatzungszeit*, p.136.
[55] Seibert, in Drost and others, *Paris sous l'occupation*, p.71.
[56] Cf. Ewenz II (2002/2007), pp.177/202-3.
[57] Ewenz II (2002/2007), p.32, 'Einführung in Leben und Werk'.

Hartlaub's civilian attire made Parisians wary of one such who spoke French too well and who might be a member of the plain-clothes security services:

> Während der d[eutsche] Zivil, im Freien immer als suspekt empfunden (besonders ich mit meiner sprachlichen Versiertheit und meinem unklaren Phänotyp, in dem man einen ganz besonders ekligen spy und Niemandsländler wittert)[58]

Here, in addition, his Semitic-seeming appearance attracted no less suspicion from his own countrymen: "von den Landsleuten [...] ernte ich nicht minder atomzertrümmernde Blicke ob meines Phänotyps."[59] He wonders, before the mirror, if anything is left of himself from this continual grinding between two millstones, "bei dieser dauernden Bearbeitung durch zwei Mühlsteine."[60] On his eventual return to uniformed service, at first in Berlin, Hartlaub remarked with relief that "in Uniform kann ich mich unbefangen in die Gegend mischen, bin nicht mehr ein aus- und abgekapselter verfehmter Bazillus etc."[61] That the characteristic distance in his literary perception and the oscillation in narrator identity between the fictionally denoted "Er" and the biographical self should give his narrative at times a tone of out-of-body quality, cannot be unconnected with the estrangement he felt from his own his physical exterior. His portrayals of city scenes are correspondingly bleak and desolate; people are singled out only by quirks of behaviour, the people en masse are heard by their silence, in their behaviour a collective organism:

> Das Wetzen, schleifen der vielen Spaziergängerfüsse auf der Brücke, den Kais. Die Menschen sprechen wenig. Die Kästen der Bouquinisten sind alle geöffnet, verursachen Klumpenbildung im Strom.[62]

Marianne Feuersenger, a secretary in the war diary section, although finding him charming and open on a casual meeting, saw in Hartlaub "ein verschlossener, zurückhaltender Mensch" and expresses much sympathy for the lowly, put-upon situation of "dieser schmale, nachdenklich-melancholische Mann", though adding revealingly that the whole apparatus of the *FHQ* fascinated him.[63] The inverse parallels of engagement and estrangement in the writings from France of Böll and Hartlaub mirror their respective personalities and contain the sad irony that the latter was the convinced Francophile.

---

58 Ewenz I (2002/2007), pp.472/480.

59 Ewenz I (2002/2007), pp.476/483-4.

60 Ibid., pp.476/484.

61 Ibid., (2002/2007), pp.495-6/503-4.

62 Ewenz I (2002/2007), p.70, 'Dimanche – Île Saint Louis'.

63 Feuersenger, *Mein Kriegstagebuch*, pp.164,165.

Hartlaub was not unique in being an 'other ranks' writer or artist in occupied France: Jünger mentions the writers Gerhardt Nebel, Eberhard Kretzchmar, the Schiller biographer Erich Müller, and the painters Hans Kuhn and Ernst Wilhelm Nay, all in the rank of corporal, who were stationed in or about the Paris area.[64] It is what Hartlaub and Hartlaub alone wrote out of that experience that has a claim to literary uniqueness, in that it evades categorisation as journal, fiction or reportage, and is instead an original application of the insouciant form of *flâneur* literature to point up the bizarre continuity of civil life as franchised under an alien regime. Jünger expresses the paradox:

> Die Verwaltung eines eroberten Landes ist um so einfacher, je kultivierter, durchgebildeter es ist. Das erklärt den Erfolg Alexanders im persischen Großreich, den Mißerfolg Napoleons in Rußland und Spanien.[65]

In this view, education and a cultivated culture facilitated an accommodation with the occupier. Though accommodated, there was for the cultured occupier no modern precedent for presenting *his* experience in creative literary form. Hartlaub's alter ego is un-named, and the minor occupation figures he observes are animated only briefly and identified only vaguely; the narrating character narrates as though outside the society of his observed characters, as they in turn appear, and are, outside the society which they seek.

5.5. Doppelgänger: Hartlaub and "Er"

G.F. Hartlaub in 1933 furnished a Hartlaub family tree to Werner Meyer of the *Odenwaldschule*, concerned that Geno and Michael should not suffer there from the same suspicion of Jewish heritage as had their older brother, Felix. GFH insisted that the possibility of *great-great* grandfather Adolph Meyer being of Jewish extraction was 'pure hypothesis.'[66] Hartlaub's sallow complexion may well have been attributable to a French Creole maternal grandmother.[67] This 'non-Aryan' forebear alone was sufficient to deny him promotion even to higher non-commissioned rank. Walter Dietz remarks: "Nur daß er nicht Unteroffizier werden konnte, das bedrückte ihn sehr. Er hatte nur eine der beiden vorgeschriebenen arischen Großmütter."[68] Geno

---

[64] Jünger, *Strahlungen II* (Munich: DTV/Klett-Cotta, 1988), pp.10,55,88,107,374.

[65] Ibid., p.551.

[66] See Ewenz II (2002/2007), pp.105/127.

[67] Cf. Hartlaub's *Ahnen Nachweis* of 1934 from Heidelberg University, reproduced in the appendix to Marose, 'Das Eigentliche ist unsichtbar'; also, Krauss, *Felix Hartlaub: in seinen Briefen*, p.296.

[68] Walter Dietz, typescript (28 pages), *DLA* Marbach folder reference 95.76.3, p.7.

Hartlaub is more definite on the point: "Besonders unter der Judenverfolgung litt er fast physisch, zumal da er selbst von der Mutter her einen wenn auch nur geringen jüdischen Blutseinschlag hatte."[69] In any event, his complexion and profile gave his fellow Germans in Paris cause to look askance at him.[70] For them, if the possibility of full Jewish blood was discounted as improbable, the alternative possibility of partial Jewish descent was even more problematic. His Semitic-like appearance was marked, his prominent ears adding even more to the 'non-Aryan' stereotype. Circulating while in prewar Berlin chiefly among Jewish and half-Jewish acquaintances known from the *Odenwaldschule*,[71] he remarks that "Am nettesten sind wie immer die Juden, nur daß sie mich für einen Verräter halten und mir mein Abzeichen nicht glauben."[72] The *Abzeichen* was the certificate of full Aryan descent, a requisite for any public appointment and for registration at university. The unease of the strolling civilian, incorporated in the title of the sketch 'Rubrik: Tout seul oder: Le civil equivoque', is acute when he is obliged to show his pass to the French officials in the *Métro*. The pass is entirely in order; no questions necessary; nonetheless, the mistrust is all the deeper and its signs, for being subtle, felt the more: "Frauen als Schaffnerinnen: Eine kleine Ebbe im Gesicht, ein unmerkliches Engerwerden, die Augen erweitern sich eine Spur, weichen langsam zur Seite."[73]

Despite seeking above all else not to attract attention, the unidentified narrator notes that: "man fühlt Blicke in den Schultern". Even though adopting a shrinking posture, his hunched, meagre, "dürftige", shoulders clad "in dem vagen, impeccablen Pariser Frühlingsmantel", seem "mitleidheischend" to implore pitying glances.[74] This silent admirer of the defiantly stylish Parisians[75] is reluctant to reveal his full identity to the German soldiers manning the exit barrier at the Metro and opts after hesitation to address them "mit einem wohltemperierten, diskret soldatischem Deutsch."[76] In cafés, eager to quickly establish a routine German identity, "Er" speaks deliberately bad French and flourishes a

---

69 Geno Hartlaub in interview with Thilo Koch, 'Der Mann im Sperrkreis', Norddeutscher Rundfunk Drittes Program, 14 April 1957, 20.15 - 21.20 (script transcript in Hartlaub archive, *DLA* Marbach).

70 Cf. Ewenz I (2002/2007), p.51, 'Place Pigalle'.

71 See Geno Hartlaub, *Im Sperrkreis* (Frankfurt am Main: Fischer, 1984), afterword, p.217.

72 Krauss, *Felix Hartlaub: in seinen Briefen*, p.142.

73 Ewenz I (2002/2007), p.45.

74 Ibid.

75 See. ibid. (2002/2007), pp.450/457.

76 Ibid., p.46.

German newspaper and a Baedeker.[77] The Paris Hartlaub attracted a wary attention unwished for by the strolling *flâneur*. The 'Er' figure clearly shares the same inhibitions as Hartlaub and, watcher, feels himself to be the watched one. Seibert sees in the suspicion which the civilian-clothed Hartlaub aroused in Parisians the loss of that residuum of individuality which the *flâneur* had preserved amid the dissolution occasioned by the modern metropolis of traditional patterns of experience and order, and in just those situations where the roles of viewer and viewed are reversed, an 'Er' figure is occasionally introduced.[78] Literarily for a writing *flâneur* and personally for the real-life Hartlaub an inconspicuous anonymity was a circumstantial desideratum.

The *flâneur*, to observe unobserved, must appear to have no particular business in mind; equally so the *flâneur* among his own *Landsleute*, especially so one of 'non-Aryan' appearance:

> Da ich [...] mit meinem gesamten Kontur und Habitus so gänzlich aus dem Schosse meiner Landsleute herausfalle, muss ich mindestens in Puncto Garderobe völlig einwandfrei dastehen.[79]

Painfully aware of the conspicuous inadequacy of his civilian wardrobe among the smart diplomats of the foreign ministry, even for his role of lowly archivist, he expresses the discomfort with droll self-mockery:

> Déjeuner im ehemaligen Palais Talleyrand (jetzt deutsches Kulturinstitut) brachte ich es fertig, im braunen Strassenanzug zu erscheinen (ich selbst hätte mich unbedingt hinauswerfen lassen).[80]

The stroller in the sketches, with the same inhibitions as Hartlaub, is withdrawn, shuns contact, and maintains a voyeuristic distance. A night scene in the blackout borrows lighting from neon signs: "Abends, totale Verdunkelung [...] nur am Anfang einige gedämpfte, erblasste Transparente: Hotel." In the same piece, 'Place Pigalle',[81] drunken privates crowded around a single girl are steadied by her purposeful stride in tripping high heels, "die Zielstrebigkeit der trippelnden Stöckelschuhe". These are contrasted in the same *noir* cinematic frame with the stumbling boots which strike sparks from the cobblestones, "das Stolpern, Schleifen, Funkenschlagen der Nagelstiefel." The soldiers crash in and out of the cafés in search of excitement. Swept into one in a crush he, the anonymous "Er",

[77] Ibid., pp.48,51.
[78] Drost and others, *Paris sous l'occupation*, pp.71,72.
[79] Ewenz I (2002/2007), pp.446/454.
[80] Ewenz I (2002/2007), pp.446/453.
[81] Ibid., pp.47/46,47.

finds himself alone at the bar. The mirrored walls give back his unprepossessing appearance. He orders a drink in deliberately faulty French and then, as if to test his own confidence, invites a drunken soldier newly stumbled in to drink with him. The private stares at the black-haired 'jungle boy', at "dieser schwarzlockige Jangelknabe", astonished to be addressed in fluent German. Here the night-stroller shares distinctive physical characteristics with Hartlaub and also his pain at the racial prejudice registered upon faces at every encounter. The pointed parallel to the author's self suggests an alienation borne as physical affliction. If German war literature of World War II is more that of the *Obergefreite*, the lance-corporal, and that of World War I that of the *Oberleutnant*, as Hans Schwab-Felisch *cum grano salis* suggests,[82] Felix Hartlaub, denied the commission to which his social class would otherwise have provided entry, had the added disadvantage, unlike Böll, of not fitting physically or figuratively into the camouflage of a corporal's uniform or rank.

5.6. Phenomenology of a city

5.6.1. Paris: elemental transmutation

Avoiding thematisation or historical reflection, as Seibert has noted,[83] Hartlaub's observing, narrating *flâneur* rarely engages personally with his subjects, but in substitution endows objects and phenomena with characteristics symptomatic of the population he is so intently studying. In 'Ventre de Paris', Hartlaub endows clouds with organs: stomachs, hearts and kidneys, in allusion to the setting, Les Halles, and sees them like dray horses straining forward with steaming necks, moving in a north-easterly direction – also a possible allusion to war and slaughter in that quarter of France:

> ...der Blick auf die Fassade von St.Eustache. [...] Das grosse Stück Himmel zwischen den Türmen – leuchtende feuchte saftige Wolken auf der Fahrt nach Nordosten, meist richtige Wolken mit Bäuchen, Herz und Nieren, dazwischen manchmal auch blosse Tücher und Fahnen. Mit gebeugtem Nakken [sic], rauchenden Stirnen nach vorne geworfenen Kämmen, Mähnen.[84]

Tücher, cloths, contains a suggestion of the clouds as meat-porters. Even the sun appears stooped, "sie treibt sich herum, niedrig, über den Kuppeln, in den Wolken."[85] The citizens in queue for their meat rations are similarly

---

[82] See Hans Schwab-Felisch, 'Die Literatur der Obergefreiten', *Der Monat*, year 4, vol.42 (March 1952), 644-651, (p.645).

[83] Seibert, in Drost and others, *Paris sous l'occupation*, p.65.

[84] Ewenz I (2002/2007), p.41.

[85] Ibid.

carnalised into a multi-headed snake, "die vielköpfige Schlange"[86] The whimsically bestial comicality is one of lowliness, of *burden*, the burden of the Occupation.

The cloud-laden studies of the Paris skyline and rooftop topography can seem overworked and in their pastel variations merely imagist prose-poetry, were it not for the dominant metaphor of a powerful natural element, the open sea, which Hartlaub himself had not seen since Naples in 1933:

> die Hügel*welle* des *Dächermeers* ('Blick auf Paris – Ile de France')
> eine leicht *gewellte* Dächerflur (ibid.)
> Der Hügelfuss liegt im Wolkenschatten, im *Tintenmeer.* (ibid.)
> Das *Dächermeer flirrt* und *kocht* ('Das eroberte Ministerium')
> dieses weisse Marmorgebirge [...] vorne *zerrte* dieses unmögliche,
> unmenschliche *Dächermeer* an den Kalkdaunen ('Paar auf Montmartre')

The geology of *Marmorgebirge* and *Kalkdaunen* (the latter, literally: chalk-white feather down, though here, in the plural, also a coining for the English sense of 'chalk downs') is sea-formed. Elsewhere, earth-bound natural forms agitate in the sea metaphor of *Brandung der Blätter* (in 'Sommer, Wind'). Perhaps in an echo of his doctoral dissertation on Lepanto, a class distinction in living figures, promenading Parisiennes, is rendered in a lavish maritime simile:

> die richtigen »Poules« [...] wie hochbordige stolze Karavellen unter kommunen Fischkuttern. ('Boulevard Montmartre')

Even a lake metaphor, employed to describe a chilly Spring downpour, is banked as though by sea-formed mud flats, *wattigen Ufern*, and the water is figuratively corrosive, *angesäuert*, like seawater:

> Ein grosser See angesäuertes Blau mit wattigen Ufern kommt angetrieben. Der Regen hört auf. ('Autre Promenade')

Reflections on nature which go beyond the merely descriptive are a common reaction to battlefront trauma, as evidenced in *Feldpost* letters.[87] Sensing the unseen trauma of the city, Hartlaub offers in word-pictures an impersonal, abstract construct as an alternate and opposing realm.

An example of Hartlaub consciously using atmospherics to underscore a socio-economic view is to be found in an infernal night-scene of Köln-Knapsack in 1939, from the sketch entitled 'Industrieschutz':

---

86 Ibid., p.42.

87 See Peter Knoch, *Kriegsalltag* (Stuttgart: Metzler, 1989), p.230.

> Im Hintergrunde, das Industrie-Kombinat filmkulissenhaft zusammengetürmt. [...] Irgendwo dringt wagrecht eine rote Flamme heraus. Nachts scheint sie zu wandern, ertrinkt im Nebel [...] Nie ist klares Wetter. [...] Von den Dächern der Siedlung muss man den Dreck mit Schaufeln abtragen.[88]

The scene is constructed as on a film set, *filmkulissenhaft*, with hellish lighting. Hearing bell peals and seeing occasionally through the haze the twin spires of Cologne cathedral, Hartlaub suggests a remarkable ecclesiastical expression of sympathy for Warsaw, though may be expressing simply his own dismay at the architectural and cultural loss of the Polish capital:

> Die Türme des Kölner Münsters kommen manchmal durch die trübe Luft. [...] Das Glockenläuten für Warschau.[89]

He later expresses the same regret for Cologne itself, distancing himself at the same time from the war-makers at the *FHQ*:

> Über die Wirkung der Luftangriffe bin ich mir leider sehr im Klaren. [...] allerdings interessieren die kunsthistorischen Verluste hier weniger. – Ich bedauere sehr, daß ich Köln nicht einmal ausführlich angesehen habe.[90]

In the fragment 'Wiesen', the son of the art museum director appreciates a fortuitous trompe l'oeil offered by a passing ship on the Kiel canal:

> Die Kriegsschiffe, die unendlich langsam durch den Kanal fahren, scheinen unmittelbar durch die Wiesen zu reisen.[91]

He dryly observes that "ein Fischerfahrzeug dort nach alle den Kriegsschiffen ist ein Erlebnis."[92] A fishing boat motif is used by Böll as an escapist, romantic fantasy:

> ...es wird mir bitter sein, morgen in einem häßlichen Industriedorf zu schlafen, in einem Mauergewirr, ohne das Meer in der Nähe und ohne die berauschend schönen Morgen und Abende, ohne die demütig schöne Parade der Fischerboote die Küste entlang.[93]

Hartlaub applies the same motif as a single emblem of absence.

---

[88] Ewenz I (2002/2007), p.20.
[89] Ibid., p.22.
[90] Ibid., pp.544/552-53.
[91] Ibid., p.15.
[92] Ibid.
[93] Böll, *Briefe* I, p.488.

5.6.2. The body municipal

In Hartlaub's figurative representations of Paris anthropomorphosis and its inversions are a recurring trope by which the city is likened to a living body. The city as it appears in the 'exterior' sketches, that is, in virtually all except the three long 'interiors', is continually anthropomorphised. The result is that the reader feels for the citizens through animate attributes assigned to house fronts, roof-slate and quay walls and, curiously converse, through inanimate petrifications or metallisations of living things. Geological, marine and, in one instance, lacustrine metaphor ('Autre Promenade') is applied to sustain the conceit of a city of natural forms, one thereby animate in cycles outliving any disruptive human intervention.

At ground level, the inanimate surfaces are rendered tactile and fleshly: the facade of St.Eustache has incomplete flanking towers, one described as being of stunted growth, "nicht zu Ende gewachsen", a thinner stump than the other, "ein magerer Stumpf" ('Ventre de Paris'). The Seine quay walls are large-pored, *grossporig*, ('Hochwasser', 'Quai'). Stones breathe ('Abendspaziergang', 'Nachts, Wind'), and sweat ('Il fait lourd'); have *égout* mouths ('Lustbarke'), though this latter is a silent, "strömt lautlos", hard-lipped, cemented mouth – a barque of German soldier tourists is passing by. Mineral surfaces are endowed with humanoid features: houses with steep-slated roofs appear to have brows, *Stirnfläche* ('Die Häuser des Quai de Béthune'); zinc-sheeted roof surfaces appear to have bulging ribs, *weissliche Wülste-Rippen*, suggestive of skeletal undernourishment ('Dächer – Quartier Saint Germain'). Where it pierces the mist, the roof terrain appears as something dermal: a crust, *Dächerschorf*, with scars and furrows, *Narben*, *Furchen*; when embedded in mist it is a gently rolling meadow, *eine leicht gewellte Dächerflur* ('Blick auf Paris – Île de France') – this latter metaphor is part of the general terrestrial shift to a liberated and defended zone above ground level: chimney cowls become helmets, *Helmen*; chimney shafts become halberds, *Hellebarden* ('Dächer – Quartier Saint Germain').

Natural forms are animated or rendered inanimate according to contextual mood: meadowland appears benignly 'flower-browed', *blumengestirnt* ('Die Parkmauer'). Contrastingly, in sultry parkland flowers appear narrow-eyed, to have *engen Blumenaugen*; heavy leafed canopy appears as oppressive *Blattgebirge*, and tree screens appear chiselled and petrified, *wie gemeisselten Baumwände*; even the goldfish in the fountain are lignified into *totes Holz* ('St Cloud – Allée des Marnes'). Sylvan metaphor, as in *Laubdach*, *Kastaniendach*, *Kaminwald*, is also part of the terrestrial shift upwards ('Dächer – Quartier Saint Germain'). This transposition of Paris to a suspended 'space world', *Raumwelt*, is accompanied by much marine and geological metaphor. Slate cliffs, *Schieferklippen*, appear; houses appear to surge, *branden*, upwards against St Etienne du Mont, causing it, unlike the longer-hulled

Pantheon, to ride less surely on the *Dächermeer*, but the long pontoon of its slated roof at least, appearing as though clad with *Eisenblech*, looks unsinkable ('Abendspaziergang'). The late-gothic Tour Saint Jacques appears as a weathered, hewn piece of coral reef ('Quai'). About the bluff of Montmartre, a reef of houses appears to subside into an inky sea, *Tintenmeer*; Montmartre itself appears as a marble reef, *Marmorriff* ('Blick auf Paris – Île de France'). The sky, as *wattiger Himmel* ('Dimanche – Île Saint Louis') has the dully luminous quality of mudflats; elsewhere it is compared to the cotton wool quality of fine ash, *Wattehimmel* ('Schwarze Bestien').

As if to render them as part of the city statuary, human figures are in places gilded, bronzed or silvered, while flora borrows human features. The effect is that of stilling human activity and of allowing vegetable or mineral forms to take its place. The moonlight reflection of a small-statured German officer becomes a blurred, silvered manikin ('Mitteleuropäische Mondscheinidylle'). An abbé is gilded about the shoulders by a tongue of bronze sunlight, *eine Zunge Bronzelicht* ('Dächer – Quartier Saint Germain'). Through the railings of the Jardin du Luxembourg two *Bronze-Tänzerinnen*, sharing a twisted towel, are seen to hurry with glistening flanks into the interior of the garden ('Autre Promenade') – none of the park's permanent sculptures correspond, and the railings and gates are plain. Meanwhile, many-tongued ivy clambers over the Seine quay walls ('Hochwasser'). The Spring chestnuts have already acquired finger-long leaves ('Die Bergéren, Diwane'); in high summer they have grown to *Blätterhänden* ('St. Cloud – Allée des Marnes'), and in April, the grass, too, is *fingerlang* ('Buttes Chaumont'). Tree trunks appear to sigh, limbs occasionally to groan or laugh ('Sommer, Wind'). House rows appear to move in whole-body parts: *Bauch*, *Hüfte*, *Hohlbrust* ('Quai'). Antiquated, *vorgestrige*, house fronts appear faceless, *ohne Gesicht*, their window glass turned to sullen looking, *air renfrogné*, spar ('Porte Saint Martin'). Clouds are leaden-bellied ('Die Parkmauer'), or attenuated and bodiless ('Ufer, draussen'). These exchanges of vitality allegorise the city as an organism, disturbed and uncomfortable in it parts, but everywhere manifesting life.

5.6.3. Anthropometric ironies

Marko (1987) suggests that Hartlaub's letters and ironic fictional portrayals offer a more penetrating understanding of that time than that of later well-meaning but ill-understanding *Vergangenheitsbewältigung* literature, or of what Marko terms the blackmailing hypocrisy/cant of literary-psychological grieving, "erpresserische Trauerarbeitsheuchelei."[94] Geno Hartlaub was aware that the editions of her brother's work which she brought to

---

[94] See Kurt Marko, loc. cit., (see note 172), p.289.

publication in the 1950's remained not without influence on postwar literature in West Germany, particularly on the 'so-called' *Kahlschlag* literature, "nicht ohne Einfluß auf die Nachkriegsaliteratur in der Bundesrepublik, besonders die des sogenannten „Kahlschlags", geblieben."[95]

Hartlaub on a summer-term visit to the Alps in 1935 was already a practised observer in the manner of the detached, non-participating *flâneur*:

> Ich sitze meist in der Gaststube und studiere den homo alpinus in allen Aggregatzuständen [...] die meisten ein klein wenig spinnig wegen dem vielen Alleinsein in den Bergen.[96]

In the same year, from Hanseatic Bremen, his sociological and anthropogeographic curiosity is confronted by what appears to him to be a real physiognomic paradox:

> Alles Leute, die ihr halbes Leben in Schanghai oder Valparaiso verbracht haben, ohne auch nur den winzigsten Zug davon in ihren ausdruckslosen Gesichtern zurückbehalten zu haben. [...] Mein sonst immer reges soziologisches und anthropogeographisches Interesse stößt hier auf eine Gleichförmigkeit der Gesichter, Gestalten , der Sprache und Mimik [...] ich bin irgendwie über die Grenzen meiner Seelenlandschaft hinausgeraten.[97]

Here, at the age 22, is a detached sociological and *anthropogeographical* frame of observation. The mature Hartlaub retained that same intense visual curiosity which saw people as figures, shaped by their surroundings. When accounting to his father from Paris for his diffidence in approaching the opposite sex, a street scene conveys his feelings of loss and isolation:

> ... hier kaum je einmal über die Strasse gehen kann, ohne eine weibl. Gestalt zu sehen, die mich nicht ganz unmittelbar ergreift, deren Entschwinden ein Gefühl unwiederbringlichen Verlustes hervorruft.[98]

The passage describes in uncannily similar terms the same feeling of illogical instant infatuation and fleeting but irrecoverable loss of Baudelaire's *À une passante*:

> Un éclair . . . puis la nuit! — Fugitive beauté

[95] Geno Hartlaub, 'Antifaschistische Literatur im „Dritten Reich" ', *Sammlung 5. Jahrbuch für antifaschistische Literatur und Kunst* (Frankfurt am Main: Roderberg, 1982), 16-18, (p.17).

[96] Krauss, *Felix Hartlaub: in seinen Briefen*, pp.144,147.

[97] Ibid., p.149.

[98] Ewenz I (2002/2007), pp.482/490.

> Dont le regard m'a fait soudainement renaître,
> Ne te verrai-je plus que dans l'éternité? [99]

The anthropogeographical fascination is applied once more, to the population of Holstein, in the first months of what for the conscripted millions would become the *Europatourismus*, as yet still largely an internal tourism:

> Die beste Schülerin mit dem mächtigen Stirnkopf auf dem unausgewachsenen Körper. [...] Die weissen Blondköpfe der Kinder unter den Händen der Berliner Flaksoldaten. [...] Sind wir hier noch in Deutschland – nicht in Dänemark, Holland? Wo Deutschland aufhört, fangen die richtigen Germanen erst an.[100]

Hartlaub lets us hear this racial irony from out of the mouths of the "Berliner Flaksoldaten". The allusion to Nazi phrenology goes almost unnoticed in the casual observation on "Die beste Schülerin", and the fatuousness of the whole Nazi racial theory exploded by the concluding remark.

Hartlaub's etching-like ink drawings of macabre and grotesque figures reveal his deficiency of formal training in life drawing; nonetheless, his gaze is that of the painter. Conscious perhaps of his own hapless appearance in uniform, "Hartlaub ist ein Mensch, zu dem die Uniform einfach nicht paßt" was the comment of Marianne Feuersenger,[101] he is attracted by becoming appearance in others, as evident from this closely observed scene:

> Und Matrosen von den grossen Schiffen. [...] In Gruppen zu zweien, dreien. In der eisigen Kälte mit offener Brust, die sich durch die knappe Jacke modelliert. Einer jünger als der andere, schlank, sie wirken im Gegensatz zu den in unförmigen Waffenröcken, faltigen Stiefeln versinkenden Landsoldaten alle merkwürdig zierlich, schmalbrüstig. Wie sie sich gegenseitig beim Anziehen der Collanis helfen, die Exerzierkragen dürfen nicht dabei heraufrutschen.[102]

The technique is cinematic: the frame containing figures first in full-figure, then in upper body and head-and-shoulders close-up, *die Exerzierkragen dürfen nicht dabei heraufrutschen.* There is more here expressed than the simple envy of the baggily clad and clumsily booted soldier for the graceful uniforms of the *Kriegsmarine.* Something of an androgynous beauty is rendered in

---

[99] Cited from Ciaran Carson, *The Alexandrine Plan* (Loughcrew, Oldcastle: The Gallery Press, 1998), p.38.

[100] Ewenz I (2002/2007), pp.17-18.

[101] Feuersenger, *Mein Kriegstagebuch*, p.165.

[102] Ewenz I (2002/2007), p.38.

addition. A similarly unabashed observation is found in a letter to his father and stepmother from his Naples lodgings with distant relatives in 1933:

> Der ältere von den beiden Jungens, Luigi, ist ein bezaubernd hübscher, sehr mädchenhafter, tiefdunkler Neapolitaner, der andere ein strohblonder krähender Bengel deutschester Artung.[103]

A precocious twelve year old is studied loitering by a café table in 'Boulevard Montmartre':

> Ein hübscher, fast kokett gekleideter Knabe steht reglos an einem der Tische, [...] Tiefschwarzes seidiges Haar, ein grosser Wirbel am Hinterkopf, Ponyfransen fast bis auf die Brauen herab.[104]

A prewar literary observation from Italy, however, is unequivocal:

> Ich dachte an eine dichterische Nachgestaltung der letzten Tage Winckelmanns in Trieste. Doch fehlt mir da eine entscheidende Voraussetzung, Verständnis für die gleichgeschlechtige Liebe, die ja dabei das Grundmotiv war.[105]

It is not sexual orientation which prompts the studies of youthful beauty, but a mastery, now in words, of the sure-stroked and minimalist technique of the sketch that was not his in the fiercely inked and cross-hatched drawings of his boyhood.

Writing to Melita Laenebach after she had to his delight and to the admiration of his colleagues made the rail journey from Berlin to Rastenburg, the now thirty-year old Hartlaub choreographs an apparition of peach-coloured style emerging from out the armpit proximity and fleshly shortcomings of the thrusting platform throng:

> Die ganze amorphe, aus dem Gleis geworfene, überanstrengte Menge, die nun leider für unsere Zeit bezeichnend ist. [...] Da erschien, angetan mit einem grossen Hut und allen möglichen distinguierten Pfirsichfarben, still wie der Mond, mit grossen traurigen, aber sehr gutmütigen und zutraulichen Augen ein ausgesprochenes Nicht-Dirndl.[106]

The negative stress of "Nicht-Dirndl" can be read as tongue-in-cheek comment on the straight-laced folk image of German womanhood idealised in family-directed regime propaganda which belied an active and

---

[103] Krauss, *Felix Hartlaub: in seinen Briefen*, p.91.
[104] Ewenz I (2002/2007), p.106.
[105] Krauss, *Felix Hartlaub: in seinen Briefen*, p.103.
[106] Ewenz I (2002/2007). pp.621/629-30.

independent feminist movement.[107] Hartlaub's letters from France are, like the sketches, piquantly terse in their observations. Hartlaub would later become romantically involved with Melita Laenebach, an acquaintance of his friends Klaus and Irene Gysi, and his letters to her would reveal his admiration for her individual style in femininity,[108] but his letters *about* her would give paramount place to intellectual parity.[109] The philologue Hartlaub can switch to the mellifluent when the topic, romance, requires it, but cannot resist a grammatical tag:

> Jetzt ein Brief an einen Einzelnen Menschen wie Dich ist etwas seit langem Ungewohntes, wie ein Schwimmen in einem anderen Wasser, mit einer leichtflüssigen gleitenden Tinte, mit wenig Hauptwörtern und vielen Verben.[110]

In Hartlaub's mode of observation the narrator does not report on personal encounters. Incipient encounters are bungled affairs: a coat caught in a train-door, an abortive attempt to engage a soldier in conversation at a bar.[111] Hartlaub's narrator confines himself to comments on groups or types. The meat-market maids at Les Halles, in 'Ventre de Paris', are depicted in the cold, dark light of their surroundings and are completely un-romanticised:

> Einzelne Lehrmädchen, in knapp sitzenden weisen Kitteln und Schaftstiefeln, die Hände in den Taschen, unter den Männern, rauchend, sie scharren an dem kühlen, dunkeln Holperpflaster.[112]

In the same sketch a pair of nuns is observed; again, no dialogue ensues or is overheard:

> Zwei Nonnen schleppen einen schweren Sack zwischen sich, er streift den Boden. Ihre staubigen, unbequemen Kutten. Die eine, Jüngere, trägt den Kopf im Nakken [sic] mit einem mühsamen, entschuldigenden Lächeln. Sie hat rote Backen und eine schwarze Hornbrille. Von der Anderen, Gebeugten hört man nur das Keuchen.[113]

---

107 Cf. Christine Wittrock, 'Das Frauenbild in faschistischen Texten und seine Vorläufer in der bürgerlichen Frauenbewegung der zwanziger Jahre' [dissertation] (Frankfurt am Main: Johann Wolfgang von Goethe Universität, 1981 – also as *Weiblichkeitsmythen*, Frankfurt am Main: Vervuert, 1988).

108 See Ewenz I (2002/2007), pp.621/630.

109 Ibid., pp.549,565/557,573.

110 Ibid., pp.563/571.

111 Ibid., pp.46,49.

112 Ibid., p.43.

113 Ibid., p.43.

A thumbnail sketch of the pair by Hartlaub in the notebook MS is comically accurate,[114] but the word-picture is hard-edged; femininity portrayed through its obverse. In the indicatively titled 'Autre' half a page is devoted to the close and unsparing physiognomic study of an Oriental, demurely dressed, seemingly Islamic female on the Metro. It is the narrator who observes:

> Über der Stirn ist ein Fünfmarkstück-grosser silberner Halbmond angeheftet. Sie hält die langbewimperten Lider beständig gesenkt, ohne Flattern. [...] die wilde Bitternis der Mundwinkel erinnern an ein edles Kamelsgesicht.[115]

The phonetically rendered coarse speculations the pair of German soldiers sitting opposite contain the prevailing racist attitude: one of them would not be averse to what propaganda has told him would be "Rassenschande", with the woman. In 'Place Pigalle' the drunkenly explicit but shocked description of witnessed depravity related by the German *Landser* at the bar reads as implicit condemnation the pleasure-seeking soldiery.[116] The superior confidence, but also abandon, of the French female in the company of German admirers is conveyed in a metonymy of footsteps in 'Place Pigalle' and 'Mitteleuropäische Mondscheinidylle':

> Mehrere Soldaten um ein Mädchen, die der kreisenden, stockenden Bewegung Halt und Richtung gibt. [...] Die Zielstrebigkeit der trippelnden Stöckelschuhe, das Stolpern, Schleifen, Funkenschlagen der Nagelstiefel.[117]

> ...dreimal schwarzer Schatten [...] Im Marschtritt kommt es heran, die Seidenstrumpfbeine in der Mitte fliegen am höchsten.[118]

Balancing that, German Occupation females out of uniform are seen to give *consumerist* scandal:

> Schräg den Fahrdamm querend, hinter einem gereckten Zeigefinger her, steuern drei deutsche Bürodamen auf eine gehäkelte Bluse zu: Preis hat schon wieder aufgeschlagen.[119]

Even where correct behaviour on the part of the occupiers is manifestly evident, it is no less objectionable to the French, who see it as a presumption. A group of German female auxiliaries, known by their

---

[114] See reproduction in *Felix Hartlaub. Kriegsaufzeichnungen aus Paris*, p.9.
[115] Ewenz I (2002/2007), p.67
[116] Ibid., p.49
[117] Ibid., p.47.
[118] Ibid., pp.69/69-70.
[119] Ibid., p.80.

nickname, "Blitzmädchen" or "Blitzmädel",[120] are strap-hanging on a Paris suburban train, without appropriating seating places. The seats are occupied exclusively by the French. When places become free, the group seat themselves all at once, quickly and quietly; all but one girl, who sits down heavily and blushes with embarrassment as a result. A few more such gaffs, Hartlaub suggests, would relieve the suffocating tension, because "Gerade das im Grunde völlig einwandfreie Benehmen der Mädchen ist für die Franzosen der eigentliche Skandal."[121]

The acerbic clarity of these vignettes, particularly where at the expense of his fellow countrymen and women, is in accord with Hartlaub's elective view for his study of Paris: that of a city put-upon, its innate civility strained, its dignity slighted. It is the unwavering view, sombre, tinged with a wry wit that penetrates below the charged ephemera of the occupation showpiece. In contrast, Hartlaub's future co-worker at the war-history/war-diary unit of the *OKW*, Marianne Feursenger, heard from a colleague returning from Paris in August 1941 that "Unseren Offizieren sollen die Pariserinnen doch zu gut gefallen und unsere Mädels bemühen sich eifrigst, es an Eleganz und so weiter den Französinnen gleichzutun." It was all too much for the colleague: "Die Kameradschaftlichkeit soll darunter leiden."[122] Another lady, Luise von Benda, a career secretary at the army general staff headquarters, the *OKH*, had been in Paris immediately after the armistice, had seen the returning columns of refugees, and been astounded at the rapid revivification of the city:

> War dies noch dieselbe Stadt wie vor knapp drei Wochen? Mir schien, als habe sie sich in dieser kurzen Zeit von einer trauernden Witwe in eine strahlende und lebensfrohe Frau verwandelt. Die Läden boten alles an, was ein Frauenherz begehrte, wozu der Wehrsold aber nicht reichte."[123]

Luise von Benda would later become the wife of General Alfred Jodl.

The Paris sketches culminate in the longer, overtly satirical studies of Hartlaub's own milieu at the Hôtel d'Orsay where German foreign ministry officialdom was quartered, of the vacated foreign ministry at the Quai d'Orsay, as well in the surreal episode of the 'Puff', or brothel, and conclude with the short story in interior monologue, 'Paar auf Montmartre'. These latter sketches are interiors, the last of all interior to the mind of the character-narrator. These sketches are more densely peopled, and their

---

[120] Ewenz II (2002/2007), notes, pp.61/67-68.

[121] Ewenz I (2002/2007), p.76.

[122] Feuersenger, *Mein Kriegstagebuch*, p.63.

[123] Luise Jodl, *Jenseits des Endes. Leben und Sterben des Generaloberst Alfred Jodl* (Vienna-Munich: Molden, 1978), p.45.

characters are more assertive. In the earlier sketches, the cold-coloured skyscapes, roofscapes and streetscapes were a metaphorical commentary on the frigid quality of urban life under the occupation. Switching to interior observation, posture, mannerisms and foibles are observed as the outer architecture of character. One of the German residents of the "Hochburg" – Hartlaub's term for the Hôtel d'Orsay – is Fräulein X, an embassy secretary who keeps a parrot, white mice, and various dogs. This character is never seen, but "eine deutliche Nuance von Menagerie" at her door adds to the already musty smell in the corridors of the hotel, itself "nicht mehr ersten Ranges."[124] Fräulein X is unique in being the only secondary character to be mentioned in more than one sketch; she is referred to again for comic effect in 'Weltwende im Puff', because of her surname, which sounds like that of an apple variety, "Boskopp, Mostkopp oder so" – the hearer isn't sure.[125] The young Hartlaub had holidayed with relatives at Kreuzlingen on the Bodensee, a renowned apple-growing region, and may be enjoying a private joke. 'Weltwende im Puff' is unique among the Hartlaub Paris sketches in having a named supporting character, "Zitsche", a self-important embassy functionary, and also for the promotion of the Hartlaub-like narrating character to diplomatic status. The latter decides on a brothel visit alone. The tête-à-tête with champagne conducted by the brothel madam for the benefit of her sole client on the sultry afternoon of June 1941 is turned into a parody of diplomatic spying, "Un Du bischt immer noch hier, noch nit Soldat geworre? Isch Dei Tätigkeit hier denn eso wischtig?"[126] The bizarre quality of the dialogue – Madame fears the rumours that her clients, two German divisions, have already entrained for the Russian front – is a lampoon on the historical inversion of a German invasion of Russia from French soil and on the economic perils of this for *France*. The Hartlaub-like character in 'Weltwende' has visited the brothel before as a paying guest. The Böll-like character in his story 'Unsere gute, alte Renée'[127] calls there only for an apéritif. Renée is a small-town amateur, selling drink by her sex-appeal, a suggestion of moral looseness attaching to her, and is a credible character in so far as Böll transfers his own war-weariness to her. The affectedly mannered madam of the *Puff* is by contrast a big-city professional, sharing the stable detachment of Hartlaub's "Er" from the destabilising commotions of the war.

The social superiority of French, of which the French *and* the Germans are convinced, is a subtle weapon of condescension: a cleaning lady at the Quai d'Orsay must endure the rudeness of a German NCO, but wears a fur

124 Ewenz I (2002/2007), pp.108/110.

125 Ibid., pp.127/128.

126 Ibid., pp.131/133.

127 Böll, *Werke 3. Kölner Ausgabe* (Cologne: Kiepenheuer & Witsch, 2003), pp.459-66.

boa to work.[128] The diminutive governess of the "Hochburg", the Hôtel d'Orsay, neglects to greet most of the German 'guests', but does favour with a small apologetic smile the more elderly diplomats, those who by their age clearly belong to the 'old school' and not the new regime.[129] The sympathies of Hartlaub, too, are clear: just days into his Paris posting he had declared himself unreservedly for the Parisiennes, "die Pariserin ist eben ein »schlechthinniger Inbegriff«, sicher das abendländische Höchstprodukt."[130] Hartlaub has observed a threadbare elegance, in men as in women, that summed up the quietly defiant mood of the population: "Aber auch mit abgetragenen, alten Sachen: der unnachahmliche Schick ist nicht tot zu kriegen."[131] The German policy of correctness is met with an aloofness and a corresponding correctness, not least in dress, that declares it redundant:

> Die Diziplin der Bevölkerung, die weise Haltung durch alle Schichten hindurch, ist ganz einzigartig. Es passiert so gut wie nichts, gerade das ist das eigentlich Unheimliche.[132]

Felix Hartlaub repeatedly asked that his sketches from Paris be removed to safety and considered them, along with the unidentified and lost 'sketches from Elmau', as the most important among his literary papers.[133] By the time of the *FHQ* sketches, the Paris notebooks were already deposited with family friends for safekeeping.[134] The thirteen-page novel draft written amid the late *FHQ* sketches is centred around the exploits, or lack thereof, of the male characters "Gustl", "Herbert", "Schr.[eiber], "Seppl", and Z[eichner]", who have attributes of Hartlaub's war-diary colleagues and of Hartlaub himself.[135] In the final *FHQ* sketch, 'Der Zug in den Abgrund', the sex-starved, overworked and sleep-deprived "Schreiber" must, while lusting after, induct and supervise the female assistants who have replaced his front-mustered male colleagues. In the earlier and longest of the *FHQ* sketches, 'Im Dickicht des Südostens', there is time yet for the narrator to fantasise satirically in dialogue (actually, in the form of interior monologue), with the narcotically named "Fräulein Rauschkohl", in the persona of a poseur and inner émigré of the all-embracing Hellenist 'Third Humanism' as

---

[128] Ewenz I (2002/2007), pp.117/118.
[129] Ibid., pp.111/111-12.
[130] Ibid., pp.450/457.
[131] Ibid.
[132] Ibid.
[133] Ibid., letters numbered 170, 180, 226, 228: pp.619/628,637/646,728/738, 731/741; also Ewenz II (2002/2007), pp.184/210: note to letter no. 93.
[134] See Ewenz II (2002/2007), pp.289/320.
[135] Cf. Wilke, *Die letzten Aufzeichnungen Felix Hartlaubs*, pp.117-19.

propounded by Werner Jaeger.[136] It is a not unreasonable speculation that *Parisiennes* and *Blitzmädels* might similarly have come into the foreground as focalising foils in any reworking of the Paris sketches, had fate permitted.

5.7. *erzählte Zeit:* relegation of chronological time

Henri Plard has noted that one or other of the two poles of the personal journal or diary: passing time and the presence of the author, is almost absent in the writings of Hartlaub.[137] Plard has also noted that Hartlaub's wartime writings contain no dates: occasions can be dated only by incidental references to known events of the period. [138] Seibert (1995) notes that it was Geno Hartlaub in her 1955 edition of her brother's writings, *Das Gesamtwerk*, who dated some of the Paris sketches: "March 1941", "April", "May" and "Summer", but that these can be only assumptions, made from incidental seasonal indications.[139] In fact, some of sketches in the first of the two Paris notebooks do bear such date notations in what appears to be Hartlaub's hand: 'Ventre de Paris' is headed with the date 1. März and the numerals 1.3; 'Quartier Latin' has the word *Avril* under the title; 'Porte Saint Martin' contains a dateable reference to "Karsamstag Abend"; 'Buttes Chaumont' begins with the word April; 'Dimanche – Île Saint Louis' bears the word *Avril* to the right of the title, and 'Dächer – Quartier Saint Germain' begins "Mai _ _ 21h.". Notably, the sketches in the second and later notebook bear no direct date references at all; alone 'Weltwende im Puff' contains just a humorously oblique reference to the date of the German attack on Russia in June of 1941. Seibert suggests that the disregard for time and date indicates a disdain for the victors' relish in this time of conquest and triumph.[140]

Hartlaub does not, in fact, so much suppress or avoid dates as, rather, subordinate time to narrative circumstance. A morose piece dubbed 'Porte Saint Martin' paints an insistently gloomy picture of post-twilight Paris. The tardy darkness fails to seep through, as when a glossy paper resists ink, seeming "nicht hineinfliessen zu können, wie auf zu glattem Papier"; the half-moon appears as a forgotten, weaker imprint of itself, "wie ein vergessener schwächster Ausdruck seiner selbst."[141] These may be meta-similes for the literary difficulty of satisfactorily registering impressions of the pervading mood in the occupied city. A passage in the same sketch dwelling on the imperceptible advance of the darkness, "Nur am dem Düsterwerden der Häuser erkennt man das Fortschreiten der Dämmerung",

---

[136] Ewenz I (2002/2007) pp. 210/212; cf. Marchand, *Down from Olympus*, pp.319-30.

[137] Plard, '»tout seul«', *Etudes Germaniques*, 14 (April/June 1959), p.142.

[138] Ibid., p.141.

[139] Seibert, in Drost and others, *Paris sous l'occupation*, p.64.

[140] Ibid.

[141] Ewenz I (2002/2007), p.62.

opens with the notation "Karsamstag Abend." This is specifically dateable to 12th April 1941,[142] but naming the day is without obvious relevance to the text unless that by indicating the dead hours in the Christian liturgy between Good Friday and the Resurrection on Easter Sunday it is an oblique allusion to the dead hand of the occupation which has yet to be lifted from the spirit of the city. Another fragment, 'Buttes Chaumont', begins similarly with a notation, "April", and goes on to describe the signs of spring in the chestnuts, planes, poplars, and plum. Evergreen thujas "row", *rudern*, on the bank of the lake. A solitary high-school student, a "Pennäler", mane of blond hair blowing in the wind, sits on a bench over a copy of Racine's *Andromaque*; others exchange pubescent gossip, identifiable only by their voices, but it is the solitary figure which is picked out in detail and precisely placed as part of the composition.[143] Time is present, but also, in the sense of people being unaware of it, as Louis MacNeice meant, "away and somewhere else".[144]

In 'Dimanche – Île Saint Louis' the weather is cloudy, already humid; the booksellers' stands are all open, the quays and bridges are thronged. The floodwaters have receded; the remaining mud slick, mixed with plane seeds and bud-husks, covers the stones so that "man fast unhörbar darauf geht". Three children, ranked in size, sit closely together "mucksmäuschenstill" by the side of an angler. The tableau is a fixed focus. Time, except in so far as it is indicated by nature and the stirrings of people, is not of consequence. A preceding piece, 'Mitteleuropäische Mondscheinidylle', contains a reference to "noch nicht weggeräumte Schneehaufen" and bare trees. The Pont Royal appears as if formed out of 'bone-like' marble and 'ashen' snow. It is a warm "Föhnnacht", but for the Parisians a curfew is in force from 23.00 and everything that is moving in the dead still, "totenstillen" streets is "Besatzungsmacht";[145] time thereafter belongs to the occupiers. A searchlight switches on, probes the low cloud cover, dies out in a fraction of a second, "stirbt in einem Sekundenbruchteil ab." Figures are swallowed by moon shadow. Exchanges are conducted by torchlight. The source of an overheard conversation is located by two lighted cigars. The moon itself appears as an inwardly-torn fleeing prisoner of the clouds and in a moment is extinguished again in another cloud. The motif is extinction, as if spring, too, is to be extinguished.

'Dächer – Quartier Saint Germain' is a study in twilight, exclusively at roof-top level; only in a short concluding paragraph is the gaze directed

[142] See Ewenz II (2002/2007), pp.61/66.

[143] See Ewenz I (2002/2007), p.64.

[144] See Louis MacNeice, 'Meeting Point', in *Collected Poems* (London: Faber and Faber, 1979), pp.167-68.

[145] Ewenz I (2002/2007), pp.68-70.

downwards at the street, following a sudden shaft of sunlight. The Paris of mansard roofs and *œils-de-bœuf* is seen as a dwelled-in, frequented space-world, a roof village, a city in itself, "eine bewohnte begangene Raumwelt, ein Dorf, eine Stadt für sich." The appellation is repeated, with variations: "Dächerstadt", "Dächerwelt". Hartlaub's view is taken from a bedroom window in the Hôtel d'Orsay, where he and the staff of the German foreign ministry archives commission were quartered.[146] The narrating viewer is placed at a distance from the city, surveying it from a superior position, aware that he is remote from its life, and presenting the mute, surreal roof architecture as symbol of the city's aloofness to the importunities of Occupation regulations.

Light, colour and temperature indicators of the time of year are interpolated as if by mere convention: "die Helligkeiten noch winterlich fahl" ('Blick auf Paris – Île de France'), "schwüler Spätnachmittag im Hochsummer" ('Le Rendezvous manqué – der versetzte Sieger'), but they are applied as warm or cool hues to tone the mood of each scene. In a piece on the fruit and vegetable gardens below the long terrace at Saint-Germain-en-Laye,[147] a reference to leaves already browning on a cherry tree and to colonies of red-green apples indicates late Summer or Autumn fruiting, but the point is that the gardens are untended, husbandry sacrificed to the exigencies of war. Hartlaub's Dickensian description of the abandoned French foreign ministry building on the Quai d'Orsay, 'Das eroberte Ministerium': papers strewn about, desks ransacked, "in jeder Schublade ein Roman",[148] does not neglect the roof architecture and sees in the zinc-plated roof-terrace of a connecting wing "ein leergefressener Brandaltar der Julisonne." In the tongue-in-cheek satire of the brothel visit in 'Weltwende im Puff' the client because, he thinks, of some caviare consumed from the confiscated stocks of the Russian embassy, is feeling queasy and is uncertain of his capabilities for the occasion. He has not been feeling quite himself since Sunday, "seit die Russlandsache losgegangen war", since Sunday the 22nd of June 1941. With this apocalyptic date are connected stomach aches, "vielleicht dieses bolschewistische Fischzeug?" and, in passion-sapping summer heat, the high farce of Madame's fears that all her clients may have departed for the Russian front. Hartlaub has here just once linked a scene to a significant date in the war and done so only point up the remoteness of 'world-changing' events from the banal but immediate concerns of humans.

The Paris pieces including the excursion to Rouen lack, as Seibert says, the identifying marks of a diary: successive dates, a chronology, and an

---

146 See Ewenz II (2002/2007), pp.62: note 23/p.70: note 30.
147 Ewenz I (2002/2007), p.102.
148 Ibid., pp.119/120.

experiencing and narrating subject.[149] The experiencing *flâneur* figure is unnamed and in only one sketch is a reflector figure introduced with whom he interacts, "Zitsche", a fellow foreign ministry official in 'Weltwende im Puff'. "Er", when he appears in the sketches clearly has education, occupation, appearance and inhibitions in common with Hartlaub. From Paris in April 1941 Hartlaub writes to his father how his "Hunger nach Spaziergängen" is ever more acute, how he devotes most of his free time to this pursuit and how he daily discovers new favourite localities, how intoxicatingly sad is the Paris Spring and how much immeasurable depths of suffering and exhaustion, "unermessliche Tiefen von Leid und Verbrauchtheit", is masked under the little display of colour in "Knospen, Marquisen und Halstüchern." Also, dismissively, he admits to pursuing some 'diary-like' activity, "ein wenig Tagebuchoid führen".[150] Hartlaub has used a diary-like, *tagebuchoid*, mode to record this feeling, but with direct expression of feeling withheld. Interest and feeling is evoked in the reader through observation only. In the stillness of the pieces – there is little street noise and the reserved silence of the citizens is noted – the contrast with the busy tourism of the occupiers is made. The diary-like observations of roofscapes, streetscapes and parklands are ambulatory in true *flâneur* tradition, most of the pieces being set in particular localities. The *flâneur* has time on his hands, or must appear to have; time is not therefore chronological time, but occasional time, to indicate the appropriate activities for the time of day, pursuits for the time of year.

Plard points out that all is with Hartlaub according to the same plan and participates in the same "facticité", a coinage which might be translated literally as 'artificiality', but with a stress here on the *art*, particularly on its visual aspect, in artificiality: what is presented to the senses is recorded without effort at hierarchy, without synthesis or symbolism; the judgement of the author is implicit or absent. All the more so, Plard stresses, do these "témoignages", witness statements, of Hartlaub serve as material for the history of the times.[151] This is, Plard asserts, the very opposite of the objectivity of Hegel.[152] Rather, it might be said that it is the objectivity of the Young Hegelians, who maintained, contrary to Hegel himself, that it is the physical and material life of human beings that determines consciousness.[153]

---

149 Seibert, in Drost and others, *Paris sous l'occupation*, p.64

150 Ewenz I (2002/2007), pp.470/478.

151 Henri Plard, '»tout seul«', *Etudes Germaniques*, 14 (April/June1959), p.142.

152 Ibid.

153 Cf. Diané Collinson, *Fifty major philosophers, a reference guide* (London: Routledge, 1988), p.99.

5.8. Occupation: alien aesthetic

The kinaesthetics of architecture, light, colour and weather in Hartlaub's Paris sketches have a prefiguration in the diary observations of Simone de Beauvoir on the theatrical suspension of disbelief at the unreality of the sudden appearance of a costumed troupe on the streets and in the cafés of Paris. Evacuation and migration, the scarcity of petrol and the scarcity of provisions, all contributed to an impression of lifelessness in the French capital, against which backdrop alien uniforms were foregrounded. De Beauvoir registers both an inner and an outer visual impact. The inner change had already occurred before the Germans were much in evidence: "Paris ist ungewöhnlich leer, [...] von den Deutschen ist nicht viel zu sehen [...] Aber der Unterschied ist vor allem ein innerer, nicht so sehr einer des Straßenbildes."[154] The inner change, the existentialist realises, is the result of the individual's changed relativity to the societal surroundings, by which the individual defines his or her *Existenz* as distinct from the mere continuation of the *Dasein* of one's objective existence. The altered *Straßenbild*, the peopled streetscape, might be conveyed by reportage, but the altered frame of reference in which the familiar, gazed-upon urban exterior now returned a menace would be a problematic even for the detached and non-participant *flâneur*.[155]

The outer, purely optical change has an aesthetic appeal that is paradoxically heightened by it's being emotionally repellent. The ground troops had worn 'Italian' green,[156] but the first steel-grey uniforms do impress: "die ersten stahlgrauen Uniformen [...] Mit ihren schönen Uniformen und den schönen gleichfarbigen Autos gebärdeten sie sich stattlich.[157] Not only the uniforms, but also the sleek, uniformly coloured autos have the appeal of *couture*. In the heady days of late June 1940, in the full flush of their victory, de Beauvoir is struck by the repeated impressions of youth and happiness, and again particularly by the beauty of the more elegantly cut, open-necked, steel-grey (*Luftwaffe*, most probably) uniforms.[158] That was at Le Mans, on the return to Paris after the panic of the first flight. Later, as the Germans invade her favourite café *Dôme*, she finds the phenomenon strangely abstract; they seem like tourists, reserved, foreign. In the previous two days, caught up in convoy with them, de Beauvoir had

---

154 *Simone de Beauvoir, Kriegstagebuch September 1939-Januar 1941*, ed. by Sylvie le Bon de Beauvoir (ed.), German translation by Judith Klein (Rowohlt: Reinbek bei Hamburg, 1994), p.393.

155 See Seibert, in Drost and others, *Paris sous l'occupation*, p.71.

156 de Beauvoir (Sylvie le Bon), op. cit., p.396.

157 Ibid.

158 Ibid., p.401.

actually felt initial feelings of solidarity with the enemy soldiers; the change in her own feelings astonishes her:

> Ich bin darüber erstaunt, denn in den letzten zwei Tagen haben mich heftige Gefühle bewegt. Allerdings waren sie einem da viel näher, unser Leben war mit ihrem verquickt, man fühlte sich solidarisch; und außerdem waren sie in Aktion – hier sind sie wie Touristen, reserviert, fremd.[159]

The sprucely uniformed and be-gloved German officers en route to Paris were, de Beauvoir notes, conscious of their gloves, their beautiful uniforms, their rank, and their politeness, and consequently oozed a dreadful arrogance, "trieften von einer gräßlichen Arroganz."[160] Their punctiliousness had often an angry nuance to it because it was so self-conscious and prescribed, yet frequently also, she notes, full of grace and charm, and among the other ranks, natural and spontaneous.[161] The German truck drivers are lavish with cigarettes, food, and champagne, so de Beauvoir has heard, and one of them is solicitous of her wellbeing after she has been travel-sick while hitching a lift; she finds them in fact to be obliging, tactful and ready with help without, somehow, being aware that they were embodying German magnanimity to the defeated.[162] A troop truck goes by, full of grey-uniformed soldiers sporting splendid red roses on their tunics. The image sticks in her mind. [163]

It was crushing, De Beauvoir writes, amid the refugee flux to see the elated Germans with their spick-and-span field ambulances, their well-groomed appearances, their pronounced politeness, while France was represented by hundreds of fearful, helpless refugees reliant "auf diese schönen Soldaten" for every help.[164] An involuntary attraction to order, to the allure of graceful competence, was the confused but natural reaction to disorder, incompetence, and powerlessness. The rational reaction is negative, against the collaborative propaganda and false tone of sentimental brotherly sympathy for the afflicted French people in the compliant press.[165] The reaction of the senses remains one of a visual fixation which at the same time repels. The Café de la Paix had swarmed with 'very elegant' German officers on Thursday, July 4th, but a notice encountered on entering *Café Dôme* on Saturday proclaimed it out of bounds for German servicemen; a pleasure, De Beauvoir pronounces, not to have to see these uniforms there

---

159 Ibid., p.402.
160 Ibid., p.398.
161 Ibid., pp.399-400.
162 Ibid., p.406.
163 Ibid.
164 Ibid., p.399.
165 Ibid., p.412.

anymore. On Sunday the 7th, on the way to the *Dôme* on foot, a tank convoy goes by, "voll Deutscher in Schwarz und mit großen Mützen, die im Wind flatterten – ziemlich schön und unheilvoll." The black bonnets of the tank crews are rather beautiful, and ominous. On Wednesday the 10th, a small wood is full of exercising Germans, 'really like steel robots'. On Thursday the 11th, the Place de la Concorde is 'full of German sailors and soldiers in black'. And disagreeably, on Bastille Day, Sunday the 14th, the boulevard cafés still swarm unceasingly with Germans.[166] The initial fascination, bordering on admiration, gives way to irritation.

The compulsive fascination with that which rationally repelled was the product of that same estrangement by which art transforms the mundane. This aesthetic appeal of the well-ordered sleekness of the victor is frankly wondered at in the diary. Though for de Beauvoir only a temporary manifestation, it is honestly recorded. The same impressions of the first days of the occupation are retold with hindsight in de Beauvoir's *La force de l'âge*,[167] but without the diary's nuances of involuntary wonderment and attraction and reflexively rational correction. Felix Hartlaub's studied fascination is rather with the departed order, with the demeanour of its erstwhile subjects, contrasted with, in a view from within, the posture of those intruders who had so confronted the imagination of de Beauvoir.

5.9. Sub-texts of subversion

By dwelling on old photographs of colonial occasion and on the pathetically abandoned contents of once officiously quired desks at the Quai D'Orsay ('Das eroberte Ministerium') Hartlaub conveys a sense of the absent world of an overturned order. In the succession of fragments that make up the 'Kriegsaufzeichnungen aus Paris'[168] and written from the point of view of a narrator who at times is bemusedly watching the progress of his own alter ego, a sense of an interrupted and absented civilian world is conveyed. The last and longer sketches from 1944/45 would expose the mad normality of unending war in which sane thinking had atrophied. The Paris sketches, employing a ruefully melancholy tone coupled with wry amusement, expose the same ominous surreality on a municipal scale. Suggesting an endurance and indomitability, Hartlaub refers affectionately to the Parisians as "Lutetier", from Lutetia Parisiorum. The technique is cinematic; the frames those of the travel documentary; stills, shot in close-up and long-shot, cut into one another without syntactic cues; street exteriors are architectonically

---

166 Ibid., pp.425,426,434,436,439.

167 Simone de Beauvoir, *La force de l'âge*, here cited from the German translation, *In den besten Jahren* (Reinbek bei Hamburg: Rowohlt, 1985).

168 Cf. Ewenz I (2002/2007), pp.41-140/41-142.

detailed, passing figures precisely captured in clothing and posture. The technique is already present in the Berlin sketches. The lone student observer of those years is now at one further remove from his surroundings.

The first of the Paris sketches, 'Ventre de Paris', set in Les Halles, is an entirely civil scene; the occupation is evident only through the arrival of a massive, bull-like German marine, "ein richtiger Küchenbulle", in insignia-less fatigues, arrived in an unmarked small vehicle, an "Autochen", to collect meat from a stallholder, whose *leather*-clad shoulder he claps in greeting and whose own neck is blood-red with the exertion of lifting the laden *harasse*.[169] The carnal rendering of the German at once reduces him to a natural, instinctive animal rather than a conscious alien agent, and at the same time alludes to the bloodletting occasioned by that agency which he represents. The oxblood colour of a row of houses in the vicinity of the famous meat market, "Eine Häusergruppe ochsenblutrot angestrichen,"[170] is noted, apparently casually, but only *that* detail is noted. The slight shudder the reader feels at the unfortunate coincidence in colour causes an involuntary look over the shoulder; the bloodiness of the times is inescapably called to mind.

The second sketch in the Paris notebooks sequence, 'Hochwasser', is less than a page long, and describes the Seine in flood:

> Der weisse, grossporige Stein der Quaimauer, mit blauen, gelben Verfärbungen, und das grüne dicke Wasser. Die Stämme der Pappeln, schwärzer als schwarz – lebendige atmende Farbe [...] Der Lärm des Wassers und die Stille der vielen Menschen. Die schweigende Belagerung des Flusses.[171]

The quay walls, white, have flesh-like pores. Though the black of the poplar trunks is *schwärzer als schwarz*, it still, *lebendige atmende*, lives and breathes. The allusion to the city's situation in *Belagerung* is obvious. The silent, *schweigende*, siege made by the river's busy, noisy waters is watched by silent, motionless anglers. Oppositions of noise and silence, of movement and stillness, of animation suspended and transposed, convey a sense of muted, restless discontent. In the spring floods of 1941 the bridge piers stand 'up to their shoulders' in water, "Die Brücken stehen bis an die Schultern im Wasser."[172] The sturdy stonework of the city thus acquires by transference characteristics of its citizenry.

Reticent, nervous signs of the Parisians themselves are transferred to window-blinds and awnings which sigh in a light breeze, "irgendwo

---

169 Cf. Ewenz II (2002/2007), pp.60/65: note 2.

170 Ewenz I (2002/2007), pp.43-44/43.

171 Ibid., p.44.

172 Ibid.

schwingen die Persiennes einwärts, mit leichtem Seufzen", and panic in the sudden gusts, "Panik unter den Fenstermarquisen."[173] Streetwalkers appear as night-figures who merely absorb animation from light, "Licht absorbierend, wartende Mädchen."[174] As though symptomatic of a flight, human features are made to migrate to characteristic features and landmarks of the city; the plane trees acquire hands, "mit grossen Blätterhänden verkleidet", and bodily trunks which appear to hunch their shoulders towards the water of the Seine, "die grossen Leiber [...] und die dem Wasser zugekehrte Schulter".[175] The mansards on the *Quai de Béthune* are steep-browed, "die steile Stirnfläche des Schieferdachs."[176] The *Hotel Dieu* is blue-bespectacled with its own roof-tiles, "mit tausend blauen Brillen."[177] Roofs appear too steep to receive even light, shedding it instead as they would rain, "die Dächer [...] zu abschüssig für das Licht."[178] The houses of Paris appear to surf drunkenly upwards in a sea of roofs, "Die Häuser branden höher hinauf, etwas Schlagseite."[179] The collective impression is of a population turned in upon itself in dark days, reluctant to be seen abroad in the cold light of the occupation.

In place of a subdued and withdrawn citizenry Hartlaub endows the elements with human characteristics. The rising half-moon acquires copper-coloured flesh, "bekommt er kupfernes Fleisch"; on a squally night it has a wet-streaked face, "der Mond, mit zerissenem nassem Gesicht."[180] The night acquires subversive traits, dawdling in the woods, "die im Walde angesammelte Nacht hat es nicht eilig," and swallowing the silver braid of military caps, "die Nacht schluckt Litzensilber."[181] The sky is at times restless, troubled, containing "unruhige Wolkenländer", and night clouds appear as scattered herds of moonlight, "zersprengte Herde von Mondlicht."[182] Clouds themselves appear as leadenly shuffling, tethered animals, "einige Wolken schleppen einen bleiernen Bauch", or as wandering masses across the sky, "Wolkenbank", "Wolkenherden", "Wolkenzug."[183] Light and dark appear to be physically part of the city; a wall of light, "die Mauer des Lichtes", intrudes into the *Place des Vosges*, and the dark descends

---

173 Ibid., p.58, 'Die Häuser des Quai de Béthune', and p.91, 'Nachts, Wind...'.

174 Ibid. (2002/2007): pp.48/47, 'Place Pigalle'.

175 Ibid., p.84, 'St. Cloud – Allée des Marnes', and p.85, 'Sommer, Wind...'.

176 Ibid., p.56, 'Die Häuser des Quai des Béthune'.

177 Ibid., p.58, 'Quai'.

178 Ibid., p.65, 'Place des Vosges'.

179 Ibid., p.55, 'Abendspaziergang'.

180 Ibid., p.62, 'Porte Saint Martin', and p.69, 'Mitteleuropäische Mondscheinidylle'.

181 Ibid., p.87, 'Rückfahrt von Fontainbleu', and p.104, 'Boulevard Montmartre'.

182 Ibid., p.64, 'Buttes Chaumont', and p.68, 'Mitteleuropäische Mondscheinidylle'.

183 Ibid., p.78, 'Die Parkmauer', p.91, 'Nachts, Wind...'.

not from the sky, but is released out of the open pores of the stones in the walls, "eher wie von den Mauern ausgeatmet [...] aus den offenen Poren der Steine."[184] The successive play of metaphor would appear overworked and tedious were it not for the abnormal state of the city portrayed. Hartlaub's own dissatisfaction with the instability of a course steered between prose-poetry and reportage suggests that his impersonal observation of phenomena was a seal against sentimental contamination from the emotive in metaphor.

As with the carved figures of the Hof Hôtel Sully, as with the gilded abbé, figures are placed in the scene as part of a composition. As figure-and-ground the finished piece has the balance of history painting, in which the one figure studied in detail focuses a group portrait. In cinematic technique Hartlaub opens 'Impression'[185] with an establishing shot of the Seine quays, moves to a queue of unemployed at the German *Arbeitsvermittlungsstelle*, and dwells on one female figure, noting her tattered black coat, in shawl, mittens and beret, and her flaking make-up and trace of moustache above the red-painted mouth. Seibert (1995) elaborates the deeply coded criticism of the occupation in this piece: the East-wind cold of the opening line, "Kalter Ostwind den Seinekai entlang," may be read as a metaphor for the occupation; a dust, "vermischt mit flaumigen goldbraunen Platanensamen," is tainted by a lingering odour of fresh horse manure, another metaphor – this is the Spring of 1941, and the occupation army had nine months before come with mounted officers and a baggage train still to a considerable extent horse-drawn. As a smart French limousine rolls by with German uniforms inside, the female figure reacts: "Ein plötzliches Erhärten der Lider, die Pupille verengt sich, ein Glanz von der Seite her." The black-coated figure straining against the cold wind stands for mourning and a readiness to resist. The limousine is a compact French four-seater, an inappropriately sporty model with yellow-walled tyres. Three uniformed Germans inside and their civilian driver are described as having "viermal dieselbe Kinnlinie, dasselbe Rückgrat"; cramped, yet they sit bolt upright despite the danger of banging heads against the roof. Seibert points to the contrast of the intimate portrait of the Frenchwoman and the formulation of the Germans as a mere number of uniforms, whose rigid posture, by extension that of the occupying power, is undermined by the comical incongruity of their conveyance.[186] The scene closes with the blanched, seated figure of Calvin with "sacht gekreuzten Beinen" presiding, as if in ironic detachment, over the traffic scene to which Hartlaub has added a shaky gas-powered truck following immediately upon

---

[184] Ibid., p.65, 'Place des Vosges', and (2002/2007) pp.127/128, 'Weltwende im Puff'.
[185] Ibid., pp.66-67.
[186] Seibert, in Drost and others, *Paris sous l'occupation*, pp.68-69.

the sleek indulgence of the occupiers. Impression is piled upon allusive impression: the tramlines are dead, "Tote Tramgleise."– two words and a full stop; this motif followed by a funereal line of braziers: "Die Mauer vor der Tempelfront trägt auf ihrem Kamm Stachelbuketts". In place of an Akroteion an abandoned shack for a flak MG. The reference is Greek; the allusion is to tragedy. Seibert selects'Impression' as exemplary of how far from lacking in structure and how tightly constructed the Paris sketches actually are.[187]

Hartlaub's expression of dissatisfaction with the sketches, describing them to his father as hesitating "zwischen Prosagedicht und satirischer Reportage",[188] dates from July of 1941. 'Das eroberte Ministerium' and 'Weltwende im Puff', two of the three long subversively satirical interiors of the Paris sequence were not, however, written until six months later, at the beginning of 1942,[189] which would also suggest a date closer to then for 'Die Hochburg', the first of the three interior sketches and separated from the others in the MS only by a 35-line beginning draft of Hartlaub's sketches from his subsequent posting to Romania. 'Paar auf Montmartre' appears last in the MS and is in probability therefore similarly dateable to early 1942. The "Paar" of the title is ironically intended, as the sketch is narrated entirely in the self-reflecting interior monologue of one of the title characters only. It is a short story in setting, characterisation and orientation, but dispenses with the conventional sequence of development, complication, resolution, and coda. Wilke's observation that the action of this sketch falls victim to too much reflection is uttered in the context of appraising Hartlaub's later elaborate weaving of action and reflection in the *FHQ* sketches,[190] but omits to note that the subversive point of the sketch is the alienated state of mind of its out-of-place protagonist. From the growing complexity and mastery in the latter sketches from Paris it may therefore be argued that Hartlaub's much quoted self-criticism of his work there was premature in its utterance.

5.10. Colour as agent

5.10.1. The coded spectrum

Wilke (1967) statistically established that the proportion of metaphorical descriptives to substantives increased continually in progression from the prewar Berlin sketches to the early sketches from Paris, and concluded that Hartlaub thereby increasingly succeeded in writing uninterrupted description

---

187 Ibid., p.67.

188 Ewenz 1 (2002/2007), pp.483/491; Ewenz II (2002/2007), pp.60/63.

189 See Ewenz II (2002/2007), pp.59-60/63.

190 See Wilke, *Die letzten Aufzeichnungen Felix Hartlaubs*, p.38 (note).

without to the need to otherwise comment or analyse.[191] Already, as a 17 year old, Hartlaub while on a student-exchange visit in 1930 with a Jewish family in Strasbourg had presciently written, "Man sieht als Zeichner, weiß als Baedekerleser."[192] In the same year he wrote that "In Paris fand ich mich plötzlich in der Heimat, im Nest und Lebenselement all der Dinge, von denen ich gelesen hatte. Zum ersten Male begriff ich auch etwas vom eigentlichen Schicksal und Dasein einer Stadt, vom Stadtplan und von der Logik seines Werdens"[193] When, ten years later, Hartlaub as ill-shod *flâneur* viewed the city again (the character in 'Le Rendezvous manqué – der versetze Sieger' ['the stood-up victor'] wears the same thin-soled, creaking summer shoes of which Hartlaub complains in a letter),[194] he recorded its confusion and distress in intensely hued miniatures: of randomly studied bric-a-brac in a shop window, of a whole townscape rendered in Impressionist infinity:

> Ein Buddhakopf aus graugrünem, sehr hartem Stein – Granit, Syenit? [...] Oder eine spätmittelalterliche wurmstichige Holzplastik mit dicker Bemalung – rötliches Gold, Karminrot, Dunkelgrün.[195]

> Das unendlich noble Grau und Blau, in das sich die Häusermassen kleiden – unmerklich, rauchartig scheint es ihnen aus den Poren zu atmen.[196]

Relatively few of Hartlaub's drawings, many of them macabre illustrations for historical works he had read; others, equally macabre, of a *Neue Sachlichkeit* social realism, are coloured.[197] In the Paris sketches he could apply colour with a technical confidence he had not attained in the juvenilia of his ink-and-wash sketches. His colours come from the play of light on neutrally coloured roofs, house-fronts, quay walls and paving. In the letter of 10 April 1941 he describes the "Frühlingsstimmungen" of the city as both exciting and intoxicatingly sad, and very difficult to reproduce, "Es lässt sich sehr schwer wiedergeben", but, acknowledging that it gave the colour-key, adds: "Sehr wesentlich ist immer der Himmel."[198] Marose (2000) suggests that the frequency of Hartlaub's mention of grey, "die Farbe der Tristesse",

---

[191] Ibid., p.62.
[192] Krauss, *Felix Hartlaub: in seinen Briefen*, p.57.
[193] Ibid., p.67.
[194] Ewenz (2002/2007), pp.95,96.
[195] Ibid., p.54.
[196] Ibid., p.55.
[197] See Seemann, *Felix Hartlaub. Die Zeichnungen* (Frankfurt am Main: Schirn- Kunsthalle, 1993).
[198] See Ewenz I (2002/2007), pp.470/478, and Krauss, *Felix Hartlaub: in seinen Briefen*, p.200.

and his use of many grey-tinted, "graugetünchte", adjectives creates a mood-picture, a *Stimmungsbild*, in which the highlighting of colour serves all the more as a reminder of the everyday drabness of the Occupation.[199] This reading omits note of Hartlaub's extensive use of anthropomorphosis in his subversive creation of much more than mere mood. His use of colour is also more complex, and three quite separately functional effects wrought through colour may be identified.

5.10.2. Colour as re-animation

Hartlaub, in deciding that the sky was to give the colour key, used dappled colour with pointillist effect, fusing city and sky. In 'Place des Vosges', describing the first really Spring-like evening of the Paris of 1941, "Der erste, reine, ausgegohrene, ausgewogene Frühlingsabend", the sky receives the city's offering of vapour without loss of lustre; the city in turn receives the sky's radiance:

> Der Himmel hoch und zugleich nah, er enthält den Dampf aller Dächer und ist doch nichts als purpurblau, gleichmässig golden durchleuchtet. [...] die noch voll besonnte Ostseite des Platzes [...] Rot und Weiss-gelb, dazu das goldgraue Glimmern der steilen schlichten Schieferdächer.[200]

The sky over the 'Dächer – Quartier Saint Germain' is unreachably far away, a veiled, *breathed-on* opal, "unerreichbar weit weg, ein verschleierter behauchter Opal." In 'Blick auf Paris – Île de France' Sacré Coeur is a natural petrification, "eine gelbe grelle Marmorklippe, ein vereister Termitenbau." The city is rendered as a natural and living organism: sky is breathed upon, *behaucht*; roofs expel vapour, *Dampf*; ants, *Termitenbau*, build. Profiles in the dusk take the form of reefs: "Häuserriff", "Marmorriff"; others that of a bulwark against the sea of roofs, "ein feuchtes dunkles Bollwerk". Everything in the view field of 'Blick auf Paris' is presented as it registers in image on the mind's eye; even the prosaically functional, factories, are noted only for the glinting of their glass roofs.

In 'Quartier Latin' grey and *Violett* dominate "in der Tiefe der Strasse". The vanishing perspective of house fronts appears as a flight, "Häuserflucht", and seems endlessly alive, familiar and intimate, its forms human-like, "unendlich belebt, vertraut, menschenförmig." In 'Abendspaziergang' in an evening sky of muted gold and satin blue, "gedämpftes Gold und Atlasblau"; the setting sun absorbs "Dämmerpulver" and the housing blocks appear to *clothe* themselves, *sich kleiden*, in "unendlich noble Grau und Blau." Although 'Die Häuser des Quai de Béthune' are all

---

[199] Marose, 'Das Eigentliche ist unsichtbar', p.103.
[200] Ewenz I (2002/2007), p.65.

painted in the same milky white, each has taken on another hue, of pink, olive-green, ochre yellow, "jede mit einer anderen zarten Beitönung." Another frontage appears in blinding white, but shot through with blue and purple. The window mouldings are of soft grey-green limestone, "Travertin?" Hartlaub wonders. As the evening light burns out on their façades, the dry, grainy white appears as moist mother-of-pearl, finally flushing pink, "feuchtes Perlmutter, das Rosa blüht." In these sketches the inanimate and stony is rendered soft with colour and imbued with a feminine delicacy. In another twilight scene, the moon over Hartlaub's 'Porte Saint Martin' is copper fleshed, "bekommt kupfernes Fleisch." A crescent on the Rue Aboukir returns a heavier spectrum of gold, bronze and brown; is cluttered, built in upon itself, its pilasters flat-chested, "flachbrüstig", under too many coats of paint. Among the antique furniture stores in 'Quartier Latin' the tension of stretched damask leads the gaze, as in a painting, from the fabric to clawed chair-leg to living limbs, with an erotic tension:

> Rokokobeinen mit gespreizten Krallen. Blaurosane, blassgrüne Seidendamastbespannungen. [...] damit verflochten die Beine des Paares, [...] die Kniee [...] schüchterne blinde Hügel in der bewegten Weite der Röcke.[201]

The sky appears to clothe the city, and the figurative animation of the city's physical fabric and even the literal fabric of its interior furnishings, stresses that the city has an independent life of its own, untouchable by any occupation.

5.10.3. Colour as isolation: studies in grey

Drab grey, when Hartlaub chooses to use it, is applied flatly to descriptions of the occupation presence itself, as in "das graue Feld der parkenden Wehrmachtsautos." A heavy, leaden quality attaches to the military colour: "Die Mauern scheinen ein graues schweres Gas auszuschwitzen. [...] Das mischt sich mit dem deutschen Bleibenzindunst" ('Il fait lourd'). Hartlaub here avoids the Böll weakness for flat iteration, and his variations have a compounding effect. Contrasting ironically with the title of another piece, 'Lustbarke', a Seine pleasure steamer, "ein kleiner Touristendampfer" is "voll grauer Soldaten"; even its sun-awning is grey: "ein graues Sonnensegel." Military greyness is applied aurally also, by extension: in 'Blitzmädchen', a group of German female auxiliaries is strap-hanging in a Paris suburban train. Their speech is toneless, "klanglos"; only some Bavarian dialects lend any colour, "bringt sparsame Farbe hinein". The

[201] Ewenz I (2002/2007), p.53.

dissonance is projected by Hartlaub onto the mismatch of their lustreless dark-blond hair with the sharp, 'poisonously' yellow piping on their service caps, "Dasselbe glanzlose dunkelblonde Haar, in keinerlei Zusammenhang mit der giftiggelben Mützenpaspelierung." The seats are occupied by unspeaking French. The Germans are equally ill at ease. Hartlaub conveys the gulf between the parties: the speech of the German females is without resonance, as though emanating from a birdcage hung from the ceiling of the compartment; not the alien language itself, but its dull grey and water-blue tone (as though this were picked up from their uniforms) hinders the transmission of sound; the metal and wood of the carriage and the air within refuse to conduct:

> Das Geschwätz ohne jede Resonanz, wie in einem an der Wagendecke aufgehängten Vogelkäfig. Es scheint weniger die fremde Sprache als die Klangfarbe, dieses stumpfe Grau und Wasserblau, was die Ausbreitung der Stimmen verhindert. Die Luft, das Metall und Holz leiten nicht.[202]

The tightly written language conveys the oppressive atmosphere of the scene, and a phenomenon is observed that had affected de Beauvoir in the very first days of the occupation, the repulsive-compulsive fixation on the object of hate and resentment:

> Blicke hängen wie gebannt an den Mädchen, nicht an einzelnen Gesichtern – am Haar, an irgendeinem unmöglichen Detail der Uniform, – ausgeleert, ausgeblasen vor Schrecken, Widerwillen und doch mit einer Art von Unersättlichkeit.[203]

As in a painting, a small detail of intense colour can focus an entire composition: the red fez worn by a pair of native colonial soldiers is the sole complimentary against a mud-flats sky, a complimentary opposite also to the pervading *colourlessness* of the occupied city:

> ... zwei Kameraden in scharlachrotem Fez, [...] auf dem Scheitel der Brücke bleiben sie stehen. [...] Das blühende Rot über dem mittleren Brückenjoch ist völlig allein. Der Wattehimmel, der graue Kalk, der Schiefer, die fahlen Kamine haben nichts dagegen.[204]

The sketch is entitled 'Schwarze Bestien'. The title alludes perhaps, and if so, with Hartlaub's usual irony, to Germany's own African colonial past; possibly also to the affront felt at the stationing of French colonial units in the Rhineland. The piece begins, "Kolonialsoldaten beim Sonntagsausgang",

---

[202] Ibid., p.75.
[203] Ibid., p.76.
[204] Ibid., pp.97-98 .

and the text indicates that these are French colonial troops, on restricted liberty within the French capital itself. A sketch in the MS notebook shows what appears to be a Negroid soldier wearing puttees and the twin-peaked forage cap worn by another group mentioned in the sketch. These solitary, shunned figures, clad in "Graugrün" and themselves doubly alienated – a concierge does not trouble to withdraw his slippered stretched-out feet from their path – compound the sum of sadness pervading the city.

Studies of lone figures emphasise a solitariness and a loss of sociability. The sunset in 'Dächer – Quartier Saint Germain' has enflamed a cloud-mass, "eine grosse Wolkenmenge entflammt" and the setting sun pours a tongue of bronze light, "ergiesst sich eine Zunge Bronzelicht", onto the shoulders of a passing abbé, who becomes a gilded figure, as in a church. In 'Quai', a figure at an open window is portrayed with a crisp economy according with the dapper appearance presented: "Ein gepflegter silberhaariger Mann, mit einem Panama und einer braunen Samtjacke." In 'Ufer, draussen…' the threadbare fashion of a student dandy lounging in a park speaks to Hartlaub's own strainings to keep up an inconspicuously correct dress appearance: "Die einst hochanständige schwarze Jacke ist zu knapp, unter den Achseln aufgeplatzt, die rissigen Spitzen der gelben Halbschuhe haben den Glanz alten Elfenbeins." In 'Hof Hôtel Sully, Rue Saint Honoré', the imagery is that of figures imprisoned in stone. The evening sky appears "unerreichbar hoch" and into the narrow quadrangle of the courtyard no sunlight ever falls on the twin sphinxes guarding the terrace steps. The window gables culminate in garlanded female heads, and two-storey narrow niches above the courtyard main portal constrain carved human figures. The motif of stony imprisonment occurs also in 'Schwarze Bestien', as one of Hartlaub's marine-geological metaphors: "Die Köpfe über den Portalen gleichen [...] im Kalk erblindeten Muscheln."

In 'Hof Hôtel Sully' roof tiles are anthropomorphised into scales, *Schuppen*, and are a population in themselves, varying in their receptivity to light: "Das Dach mit seinen tausend Schieferschuppen, jede empfängt das Licht anders. Einige sind rauh, blind, verschlucken es, andere blank wie Glas." Hartlaub sees a "Dächerstadt", a roof city, which he imagines as a separately inhabited space world, "eine bewohnte begangene Raumwelt." At the level of the "unberührbare Dächerwelt" Paris is still sovereign, indifferent to the Occupation ('Dächer – Quartier Saint Germain').[205] Hartlaub's own intellectual discomfort with the Occupation is evident from irreverent references to the busily fluttering *Hakenkreuzflagge*:

---

[205] Ibid., pp.72-73.

> Die grosse H[aken]k[reuz]flagge steht in mächtiger Welle nach links, wie künstlich mit Heissluft gebläht, die Stange biegt sich.[206]

> Auf der Giebelspitze die vom Wind schon halb aufgrefressene Hakenkr[euz]fahne in dauernder knatternder Ekstase.[207]

The flag of the occupiers may fly over the rooftops, but it is alone, straining against the wind, is in a state of high agitation, and already fretted away.

5.10.4. Colour as myopia: the use of etiolation

The last of the Paris sketches, 'Paar auf Montmartre'[208], nearest resembles a conventional short story in its initial focus on the engagement of two characters, that of a short-statured German private with his casually picked up and taller French lady companion (Hartlaub's ink sketch in the MS well suggests this disparity and the disharmony between the pair).[209] The whole piece is narrated in the interior monologue of the soldier, who in retrospection reveals his own coarse character. The monologist, already at a social disadvantage, senses that Paris fits no German paradigm: it cannot be comprehended, without guidance, with the naked eye, "aber nicht so, mit blossem Auge, so ganz ohne Vermittlung." Reduced to a selection of tourist landmarks, Paris does not add up to anything that is familiar: "die Sowieso Kirche, den Dingsbahnhof" – a long-naved church may just as well be an airship hanger, a "Luftschiffhalle"; the Opera he can manage to identify, dismissively, by its 'half violin case' shape. This other 'Er' observer is out of sympathy with the conquered rival capital and irritated by the landmark-spotting efforts of his fellow countrymen, which provoke him to a passionate interior outburst: "Doofes Volk! Das war ja garnicht zum Entziffern, das sollte zusammengebacken und ineinander verschachtelt bleiben." A copper church roof is *poisonously*, "giftiggrün", green; a train sends up a yellow-white "Rauchpilz", a *toadstool* of smoke. This involuntary, conscripted tourist of 1940-1941 is repelled by the city; its colours strike his eye without resolving into familiar schema. The sky overhead oppresses; is white, blinding, glowing with oppressive heat, "dieser weisse, blendende Gluthimmel." Only a faded butterfly stirs in the air, a cabbage white, a "Kohlweissling". The winding streets are *stony* entrails with *stillborn* squares, "heisse steinerne Därme, totgeborene Plätze." On reaching the terrace before *Sacré-Cœur* the church towers up oppressively as a white marble hill-range, "dieses weisse Marmorgebirge", at the back of his neck, "auf den

---

[206] Ibid., p.61, 'Autre Promenade'.

[207] Ibid., p.67, 'Impression'.

[208] Ibid., pp.135-40/137-42.

[209] Reproduced in the Suhrkamp Hartlaub editions (2002, 2007, 2011).

Nakken" [sic]: from a distance, in 'Blick auf Paris – Île de France', the Hartlaub narrating eye had seen it as a cliff of *brilliant yellow* marble. To the disgruntled soldier the city below is a huge stone cow-pat, floating in a milky haze, a fermentation of limestone, "Gährung des Kalksteins." The 'impossible, inhuman' roof-sea, "Dächermeer", strains towards the *chalk down/downs*, "Kalkdaunen" (a poetic play on the English sense of the word) of the clouds. Colour everywhere, when perceived by the unsympathetic, is viewed as distasteful, malign, blanched, petrified, and lifeless.

5.11. The centrality of the Paris sketches: critical reception

The wartime fictional writings comprise the sketches from the early months of military service with a barrage-balloon unit, the Paris sketches of 1940-1941, sketches from a subsequent interval with the balloon unit, in Romania, and sketches from his service in the war-diary section at the forward headquarters at Winniza in the Ukraine in the late Summer and Autumn of 1942. Wilke has determined a two-year gap thereafter in the surviving sketches, from November 1942 until the appearance of the final long sketches depicting life at the Rastenburg *FHQ* in East Prussia, these tentatively though persuasively dated by Wilke to late September 1944 until early January 1945.[210] Wilke suggests that writings from the 1942-1944 interval may have been lost in the Spring of 1945 through the looting of the Berlin cellar of Melita Laenebach, who had received materials from Hartlaub for safekeeping.[211] That possibility is borne out by the recollection of Hartlaub's war-diary co-worker, Walter Dietz, that Hartlaub was just as busy at his desk during the three-and-half months' stay in the Ukraine in the summer and autumn of 1942, had experienced more in freer surroundings there, and must therefore have written more.[212] The Ukraine notebook[213] does contain two pages of thematic headings: some, like "Abend am Bug" correspond clearly to passages in the notebook text, but one other heading at least, containing the phrase "die Suche nach dem Puff", is just as clearly not realised. As the two Paris notebooks[214] contain similar pages of headings, it seems probable that unless another Winniza notebook existed, the headings, as with the Paris notebooks, indicate a preliminary list only, with some redundancy, of themes to be explored. Dietz's recollection relates to the texts published in Geno Hartlaub's *Im Sperrkreis* (1984). Further material identifiable with the interlude at Winniza neither appears in Ewenz (2002/2007) nor is to be found among the Hartlaub papers at *DLA*

[210] See Wilke, *Die letzten Aufzeichnungen Felix Hartlaubs*, pp.84-99.
[211] Ibid., pp.80-81.
[212] See Walter Dietz typescript, *DLA* Marbach ref. 95.76.3, p.11.
[213] Hartlaub papers at *DLA* Marbach, ref. 93.17.17.
[214] Ibid., ref. 93.17.26, 93.17.38.

Marbach. The longest of the Winniza sketches, 'W[erwolf]', describes life and surroundings at the so-dubbed headquarters with oblique dark humour. This sketch and the other Winniza fragments lack the specific streetscapes and defined interiors of the Berlin and Paris sketches and are crowded with civilians, military construction workers, forced labourers, and nervously energetic and unsettled young soldiers, "die lauten, stets pressierten und unsteten jungen Landser,"[215] and reflect a relative liberty and intensity of local intercourse in the neighbouring hinterland. The fragments read as densely written and hurried and, though acutely observed, are without a focalising character-narrator like the "Er" of the Paris sketches. Nothing more thereafter of Hartlaub's creative work survives until the long last sketches from the *FHQ*. In these, so Wilke has determined, the narrating character is elusive, nowhere a personalised first person, yet never separately and wholly distinguishable from the author.[216] Wilke maintains that an inconsistency in Hartlaub's handling of narrative inversions in characterisation and consciousness led to a drift from ironic authorial intention into the merely fantastic.[217] As the Paris sketches expand from observations in the form of sequences of minutely detailed word-sketches in the manner of film-frames – Hartlaub insisted on the connection between the discipline of drawing and that of the concentrated observation needed for written recall (see 5.1.) – the *FHQ* sketches, much longer, become staccato successions of dialogue, free indirect monologue, and observations on scene, background, and noises off. The Paris characters are not resident and interchangeable as are the small cast of characters in the final *FHQ* sketches, and so may retain their fleeting but distinct identities. In the sardonic detachment of busy night-scene, bizarre interiors (an abandoned ministry, a commandeered hotel, a patron-less brothel), and a mind-interior ('Paar auf Montmartre'), these last and longest of the Paris sketches prefigure the neurally cross-wired multiple and overlapping consciousness, increasingly vertiginous, of the *FHQ* sketches, and are therefore central to the understanding of Hartlaub's development as a writer.

Seibert (Drost et al., 1995)[218] concludes that Hartlaub's Paris 'diaries' were feted by a majority of the West German intelligentsia of the early postwar years to such an extent that this helped to defer further reappraisal of the recent past.[219] Müller's study of 1997[220] traces the critical reception of

---

215 Ewenz I (2002/2007), pp.153/155.

216 Ibid., pp. 41,118,119.

217 Ibid., pp.55-57.

218 See Seibert, in Drost and others, *Paris sous l'occupation*, pp.54-73.

219 Ibid., p.72.

220 See Frederike Müller, 'Felix Hartlaub – Ein 'poeta minor' der Inneren Emigration' [dissertation] (Universität des Saarlandes, 1997), pp.6-17.

Hartlaub from the abbreviated texts in the Geno Hartlaub editions of 1950, 1955 and 1984. The intentional irony of the unstable narrator perspective in Hartlaub's Rastenburg *FHQ* sketches was not wholly apparent from the truncated published texts and was misread, influentially for others, by Holthusen (1951), who saw Hartlaub as an ironist and satirist, but one without ideals.[221] Already by 1952, however, Schwab-Felisch[222] had divined an innovative language technique in the Paris texts printed in Geno Hartlaub's *Von unten gesehen* (1950), though Müller gives the credit for this discovery rather to Ruland (1955).[223] Critical realisation that Hartlaub's writings were not diary-sketches, *Tagebuchaufzeichnungen*, at all, but an entirely new form of prose was first philologically grounded by Wilke (1967)[224] and Schäfer (1976),[225] and Geno Hartlaub herself in her afterword to the 1984 edition of *Im Sperrkreis*[226] completed the change in perspective on her brother.[227] A fuller exposition of that perspective must acknowledge Hartlaub's innovation in hybrid literary form: the *Fragment* of early German Romanticism now written with an unsparing verist concentration on emblematic detail, pointed with apposite neologisms and the *aperçu* of imagist conceits.

Wilke (1967), writing before the publication of the unabridged Hartlaub, had already pointed out that Hartlaub's sketches are attempts to order events otherwise than as an authentic rendering of personal experience,[228] and amount to story narratives, *Erzählungen*, albeit fragmentary, rather than diary excerpts. Taking the selective, and therefore fragmentary, as a given in any authentic account of personal experience, Wilke insists that *unintentional* fragmentariness, leaving aside the intentional fragmentariness of 'free form' writing, is a defect in a literary work, and in Hartlaub's sketches also, these being what Wilke terms *intendierte Wortkunstwerke*.[229] Hartlaub's Paris sketches are certainly intended to be in the first instance verbal artworks, in

---

221 Ibid., pp.7,8.

222 See Hans Schwab-Felisch, 'Die Literatur der Obergefreiten', *Der Monat*, year 4, vol.42 (March 1952), pp.650-51.

223 See Frederike Müller, loc. cit., p.9, note 31.

224 Cf. Wilke, *Die letzten Aufzeichnungen Felix Hartlaubs* (Bad Homburg: Gehlen, 1967).

225 See Hans Dieter Schäfer, 'Die nichtnationalistische Literatur der jungen Generation im Dritten Reich', in *Die deutsche Literatur im Dritten Reich. Themen. Traditionen.Wirkungen*, ed. by Denkler & Prumm (Stuttgart: Reclam, 1976), revised and reprinted in Schäfer, *Das gespaltene Bewußtsein* (Frankfurt am Main: Ullstein, 1981), pp.7-68; on Hartlaub: pp. 45-47.

226 See Geno Hartlaub, *im Sperrkreis* (Frankfurt am Main: Fischer, 1984), afterword, pp.211-18.

227 Frederike Müller, loc. cit., pp.15-16.

228 Wilke, *Die letzten Aufzeichnungen Felix Hartlaubs*, p.141.

229 Ibid., pp.141-42, p.163.

which word sequences are deployed asyndetically, for associative rather than denotative effect. With such an associative primary purpose, a fragmentariness or, rather, a disjunction with regard to denotative content results, but no defect through deficiency, through 'unrealised potential', as Wilke puts it,[230] should be inferred from this (see 5.9., Seibert, on structure in Hartlaub's 'Impression'). That only one in ten of the Paris sketches bear a date in the MS is indication in itself that their author was not concerned with maintaining the chronology of a personal journal. Fewer than half of the sketches contain a specific Paris location in the title, but all except the final four are situated in a particular location or written from a single physical vantage point. Severin (1988) posits that the act of *flânerie* itself can disrupt the character and perspective of the narrative and become the expression of the *flâneur's* disorientation in the big city. Citing the examples of Rilke's *Malte* and Robert Walser's *Räuber*, Severin identifies the prevalence of *écriture automatique* as the resulting most typical technique by which the peregrinating narrator is released from his engagement with the external world.[231] The stream of staccato observations in the Hartlaub Paris sketches does have characteristics of *écriture automatique*, but the precision of observation indicates anything other than an unpremeditated rendering of impressions. That Hartlaub's own inner disorientation was attributable to other factors has already been discussed here (see 5.5.).

His seclusion in the model community of the *Odenwaldschule* had left him ill prepared to adjust to the new society in Germany, in consequence of which he felt estranged from what he saw and experienced as a student in Berlin,[232] but in Paris, Hartlaub's alter ego knows his *Metro* plan better than the natives.[233] Responding to the urgings of his father to avail of the opportunity to engage in cultural promenades, Hartlaub gave the assurance that, though he so did in his scarce free time, and with "aufgerissenen Sehschlitzen", this visual cultural feast was for connoisseurs of a particular kind, "für Geniesser eigener Art".[234] Surprisingly, in view of his meticulous phrasing of architectural detail (e.g., dormer windows having or resembling *aedicula*, temple-like niches, in 'Hof Hotel Sully'), he himself, he felt, had "keinerlei Organ für Architektur, keine Terminologie dafür."[235] He nonetheless became a compulsive *flâneur*: "Mein Hunger nach Spaziergängen wird immer ärger, ihnen widme ich die meiste Freizeit."[236] His 'Boulevard

---

230 Ibid., p.142.

231 See Severin, *Spuren des Flaneurs in deutschprachiger Prosa*, pp.4,151-52.

232 Wilke, *Die letzten Aufzeichnungen Felix Hartlaubs*, pp.151,160.

233 See Ewenz I (2002/2007), p.46, 'Rubrik: Tout seul oder: Le civil équivoque'.

234 Ibid., pp.460/467: letter to parents, 15 January 1941.

235 Ibid., pp.466/474: letter to parents, 24 February 1941.

236 Ibid., pp.470/478: letter to parents, 10 April 1941.

Montmartre' night scene teems with people studies: ladies in *peignoirs* on a balcony; the lead violinist of a lady-orchestra, quickly sketched, "vollreif –, schlank, mit Hornbrille und hoher Stirn"; a man in a beret with the rosette of the *Legion d'Honneur*, 'professors' sporting bamboo canes and too-wide spats; a sharply dressed African gallant; on the fringes, scruffy *clochards*. German military and female auxiliaries join the scene; German civilians alone remain undigested in the throng, "unverschluckt, unverdaut, wie luftgefüllte Schweinblasen auf dem Wasser kugelnd." This densely peopled picture, the fifth last sketch in the Paris series, contrasts with the many ethereal, sky-angled streetscape studies which precede it. Isolation is here also still the theme: "Und das alles schiebt sich durcheinander mit wenigen Zentimern Abstand, und bleibt doch unvermischt unaufgelöst." These reflections of "Er", sporadically surfacing throughout the Paris sketches are, in fact, of the Schlegelian model, embodying in the thoughts expressed a multiple mind (*Geist*) and an ironic, intellectual *Anschauung*.[237] The pieces cohere into a mosaic of city and, in so much, the terms *fragment* or *torso* are not applicable to them in the sense of belonging collectively to an uncompleted whole.

In the last five sketches the average word count approaches three thousand words per sketch and the pieces become a succession of densely described scenes. In 'Boulevard Montmartre' figures are plucked out of the darkness for observation in vignette. The portrait of the Hôtel d'Orsay that is 'Die Hochburg' is claustrophobic in its narrator's impressions of corridors, room interiors, of noises and snatches of conversation overheard through bedroom partitions, of a lift interior, and restaurant and bar scenes. In 'Das eroberte Ministerium' the scenes are set in distinct architectural segments of the ministry building, proceeding from the gilded lances of the external railings to the gate lodge, to the archive wing, up and down stairways, and finally to the basement and exit into the garden again. A significant shift in narrative perspective is then apparent in the final two sketches, 'Weltwende im Puff' and 'Paar auf Montmartre': here, except for passages of dialogue, the narrative in both comes from interior monologue. This is the technique which Hartlaub later applied in his sketches depicting the milieu at the periphery of the *FHQ*. In these, as Wilke's study established, Hartlaub advanced from focalising characters based on himself or on single, observed individuals to composite characters,[238] and to what Wilke has determined as a characteristically for Hartlaub fluctuating migration between the narrating consciousness and that of the focalising

---

237 Cf. Behler, 'Das Fragment,' in Weissenberger (1985), p.139.

238 See Wilke, *Die letzten Aufzeichnungen Felix Hartlaubs*, pp.43,85,119.

character.[239] In fact, Harlaub's late technique of documentary-like presentation of anecdotal detail prefigures Alexander Kluge's *Schlachtbeschreibung*, on Stalingrad, which work, a hybrid of documentary collage and fiction, uses day-by-day pseudo-diary and press-release chronologies as scaffolding for an erratically ordered stream of biographical and circumstantial information. Kluge's biographical sketch of 6th Army commander von Reichenau, for instance, has the bizarre detail and staccato compression of one of Hartlaub's thumbnail figure studies.[240]

How the narration/reflection technique of shifting consciousness might have been maintained for the duration of Hartlaub's planned novel is an intriguing question of innovation in literary form. The beginnings of this innovation in the last two sketches from Paris demonstrate that it could at the same time be satisfyingly entertaining, satirically subtle, and historically illuminating. In the thirteen-page novel outline in typescript with emendations in Hartlaub's hurried handwriting which survives in the MS, a comically irreverent, tongue-in-cheek tone is evident: "Panne mit dem Dienstsiegel, der Sonderführer verfährt sich" (p.1); "Radiergummikonsum auf der Ostkarte" (p.3); "Z.s Buntstiftspektrum reicht nicht aus für die verschiedenen Linien und Auffangsstellungen im W[esten]" (p.9). Characters from the *FHQ* sketches: "Gustl", "Schr.[eiber]", "Seppl", "Sonderführer", and "Z[eichner]", appear repeatedly. "Schreiber" has particular correspondences to Hartlaub: the break in his relationship with Melita Laenebach can be read from p.11; he is assigned, like Hartlaub, the South East theatre in his war-diary duties (p.2), and in an intriguing entry apparently makes (fictional) flights to Budapest, Bucharest and "vor allem nach Ploesti", at which last Hartlaub himself had been stationed; but Schreiber, oddly (in a Hartlaub handwritten insertion), is about to be awarded an Austro-Hungarian, Habsburg decoration, "Er bekommt das K.u.K 1. Klasse" (p.6). The main events of the war from the end of the North African campaign in 1943 to the Ardennes offensive in December 1944 are the subject of brief notes, in sequence, though only as a background chronology. The personal preoccupations of the characters are paramount: "Im Café "Bazar" in Szb.[Salzburg] erlebt Seppl das Einsetzen des Fernkampfs mit. Seine Frauennöte in selbiger Stadt" (p.7). Hartlaub had himself been disquieted by a one-day sojourn in Salzburg in June of 1944:

---

239 Ibid., p. 38 and note no.106, p.61.

240 Alexander Kluge, *Schlachtbeschreibung* (1964, revised 1978); here from Suhrkamp 1983 edition., pp.173-74.

> ...ein beunruhigendes Aufgebot hübscher und dabei intelligent und nicht ohne weiteres anquatschbar aussehender Mädchen, [...] unheimlich viele junge Leute in Zivil und langen Haaren[241]

In the *FHQ* also, Bohemian predilections are adumbrated: "Das Künstlerheim im Bunker 3" (p.3). Reality (in May 1944) begins to detach itself: "Der N.S.F.O. [political officer] muss nebenbei noch ganz allein die russ[ische] Finnlandoff[sive] stoppen und den Druck seiner Regimentsgeschichte überwachen." (p.6). The anti-war, lunatic comedy of Joseph Heller's novel, *Catch-22*, and of Robert Altmann's film, *M*A*S*H*, is anticipated.

Wilke's philological and graphological analysis of the thirteen-page novel outline, "Roman Disposition" is Wilke's term for it, has convincingly argued for the late date of its composition (20th November 1944 to the beginning of January 1945), and for the fact that it post-dates and deconstructs the compressed chronology of the longest of the *FHQ* sketches, 'Im Sperrkreis' (in Ewenz, titled 'Im Dickicht des Südostens'), while pre-dating and serving as template for another: 'Franken II' (in Ewenz: 'Der Zug in den Abgrund').[242] Wilke speculates that, since exposition of the full novel was not something Hartlaub could hope for before the end of the war, he confined himself to reworking the passages concerning the one recurring event of the novel outline, the journeys of the *FHQ* train. It may have been this constraint which creates the extraordinarily sustained surreality evident in the final "Zug" sketch. What richness of irony and what piquant satire might have been expected from the full novel, it is possible to conjecture, thanks to the decrypting of the typescript narrative and of the emendations in Hartlaub's miniscule handwriting, which Wilke fortuitously undertook with the help of personal enquiry of Hartlaub's then still living contemporaries from the War Diary staff: W. Dietz, W. Hubatsch, and P.E. Schramm.[243]

Reviewing his current literary plans and literary efforts in a letter to his father from Paris in July of 1941, Hartlaub doubts if he has the necessary self-confidence and incubatory warmth, "Brutwärme", for a longer "création" and appraises what he himself calls his "tagebuchartigen Aufzeichnungen" as a series of 'word-etchings', "Wortgravüren."[244] Less than a month after leaving Paris he writes: "An die »Aufzeichnungen« erinnere ich mich im Einzelnen nur ungenau. Nur als Materialien gedacht."[245] Even more emphatically, in November of 1941, three months after leaving

---

[241] Ewenz (2002/2007), pp.708/717.
[242] See Wilke, *Die letzten Aufzeichnungen Felix Hartlaubs*, pp.117-31.
[243] Ibid., Wilke's acknowledgement, p.169.
[244] Ewenz I (2002/2007), pp.483/491: letter to G.F. Hartlaub, 22 July 1941.
[245] Ibid., pp.492/500: letter to G.F. Hartlaub, 22 September 1941.

Paris: "Aus meinen »Pariser Fragmenten« ziehst du Wohl zu weitgehende Folgerungen. Ich errinere sie im Übrigen fast garnicht mehr."[246] Wilke (1967) maintains that Hartlaub up until the end had not succeeded in writing sketches that were far enough removed from his own personal experiences as to stand as completely self-contained pieces. Nonetheless, Wilke concedes that Hartlaub gradually attained a sovereignty, "Souveränität", over reality so great that in his last works, the sketches from the *FHQ*, he needed to copy no single real person as a model. Walter Dietz, Hartlaub's immediate work colleague in the War Diary section, confirmed to Wilke that, in relation to Hartlaub's the novel outline, there were no striking correspondences to any single person and that the vaguely identifiable factual details could almost always be attributed to persons other than those described.[247] Wilke, determining the path of Hartlub's progress as a writer, acknowledges a necessary fragmentariness in all attempts at authentic recall of experience, but adds this reservation: "Ein fragmentarisches Wortkunstwerk ist nur in seiner Potenz nach ein Wortkunstwerk, nicht aber seiner Realisierung nach."[248] It is here argued that literary *completeness* is neither necessary nor, any more than in graphic art, appropriate to sketches, particularly so when the fragment occupies such an honoured place in the German literary canon.[249]

Marose (2000) has formulated Hartlaub's style avails of a realism that "in seiner Sachlichkeit um so schonungsloser Unaussprechliches offenbart,"[250] one which in its dispassionate factuality the more unsparingly expressed the inexpressible. What Wilke describes as Hartlaub's "nachgerade leibliche Beziehung zu Worten"[251] gave him, in addition to his facility for sharp imagist observation, a fine-tuned ear for dialogue – here in example turned to good subversive effect in what is written to look like a casually observed Metro scene. The extent of the contamination of the everyday language by racial ideology is pointed by the fact that the exchange between two women-ogling *Landsers* a Metro platform is conducted in *Plattdeutsch*:

> Dolle Weiber gibt det hier …Wat war'n det nu wieder für ne Judenschickse?
> Gloob ick nich. Eher ne Türkin.
> […] Weeste wat, Maxe, sone jesunde kleene Rassenschande – ick
> wäre jarnich abjeneigt…[252]

---

[246] Ibid., pp.499/507: letter to parents, 1 November 1941.
[247] Wilke, *Die letzen Aufzeichnungen Felix Hartlaubs*, pp.43,63,119.
[248] Ibid., p.142.
[249] Cf. Behler, 'Das Fragment', in Weissenberger (1985), pp.125-43.
[250] Marose, 'Das Eigentliche ist unsichtbar', p.130.
[251] Wilke, in *Kritisches Lexikon zur deutschsprachigen Gegenswartliteratur* (Munich: 1983), p.5.
[252] Ewenz I (2002/2007), p.68.

In one sketch, a series of vignettes, 'Mitteleuropäische Mondscheinidylle', tableaus, passing figures, sounds and snatches of dialogue reveal how incongruous, forlorn and *provincial* the occupation soldiers are in night-time Paris. The piece is ironically prefaced by a citation, in parenthesis, from a triumphalist speech broadcast from the Reich:

> (Ein Festredner aus dem Reich nannte das jetzige Paris nichts weiter als eine europ. Provinzstadt; man brauche ihr nicht mehr mit Ehrfurcht zu nahen.)[253]

There follows a series of aural recordings, snippets of overheard night-life dialogue spliced with free indirect speech and interior monologue and devoid of all authorial comment, the hallmark of Hartlaub's style. A small tell-tale sound, a subdued reflex of clicked heels which reaches the ears of the narrator, "eine Spur von Hackenklappen," parodies the Occupation posture of correctness. There is no comment, only the jarring alien sound. Kafka's first published work, *Betrachtung*, contains a passage that expresses the *literary* pace of his *flâneur* wanderings: "ich marschiere und mein Tempo ist das Tempo dieser Gassenseite, dieser Gasse, dieses Viertels".[254] In fact, Hartlaub's observer, though moving on foot or by *Metro*, makes his observations almost always from a static viewpoint. It is the occupiers who move about in busy pursuit of duty or distraction. What appeared to Böll as an exasperating lassitude on the part of the French,[255] Hartlaub gave witness to as a dignified passivity maintained to undermine the self-importance of the usurpers.

Even the high farce of 'Hochburg', 'Das eroberte Ministerium' and 'Weltewende im Puff' is delivered with a restrained succinctness of expression: that which Oehler (1988) terms the 'disciplined impersonality', "disziplinierte Unpersönlichkeit", by which Benjamin and Hartlaub avoided the trap of sentimentality.[256] Moreover, from Hartlaub's Paris texts in general there speaks, so Oehler, the mortification of the coerced fellow-traveller, "Scham des gezwungenen Mitläufers," deadly in the sense of its emphasis, "im emphatischen Sinne tödliche."[257] Oehler, adapting a pronouncement of Ernst Erich Noth, declares that the quality of Hartlaub's Paris 'diary' stems "aus einer die Ohnmacht einer Generation

---

253 Ibid., p.68.

254 Franz Kafka, *Betrachtung* (Leipzig: Rowolt, 1913), p.54.

255 Cf. Böll, *Briefe* I, p.719.

256 Dolf Oehler, 'Autobiographische Paris-Literatur von Rilke und Kafka zu Weiß, Nixon und Handke', in *Rom-Paris-London. Erfahrung und Selbsterfahrung deutscher Schriftsteller und Künstler in den fremden Metropolen; ein Symposion*, ed. by Conrad Wiedemann (Stuttgart: J.B. Metzler, 1988), p.513.

257 Ibid., p.514.

widerspiegelnden Paris-Passion", and (borrowing the title of a work by Peter Weiß) that the 'diary' amounts to a "Dokument einer Ästhetik des Widerstands." Noth's pronouncement, on the impotence and failure of German émigrés of the 1930s in France, "Ohnmacht und Scheitern", exempts the then émigré literary sector.[258] Felix Hartlaub honourably upheld that literary record.

His promotion to officer hindered by an insufficiency of certifiably Aryan forebears on his mother's side,[259] Hartlaub's lowly rank served, in the event, as a camouflage of inconspicuousness for his later project of observing and rendering in surreal parody the insanely meticulous order that attached to the management of Armageddon. Geno Hartlaub believed that the very need for concealment and camouflage begot the unique writing style of the last sketches, and that no one in that war wrote comparable prose.[260]

5.12. Lacunae, resistance speculation, death of a *flâneur*

As Wilke's entry for Hartlaub in the *Kritisches Lexikon zur deutschsprachigen Gegenwartsliteratur* observes, the hope in the postwar years that quantities of such literature as his would be discovered was disappointed. The literature of the *innere Emigration*, Wilke dryly notes, was written by those who had been forced into *external* emigration.[261] The judgement of Geno Hartlaub on the question is unequivocal: her brother did not belong to the writers of the *innere Emigration*; he did not see his task as that of safeguarding Western cultural values in a time of dictatorship, terror and war (*pace* Kästner); his mood was apocalyptic.[262] That is the mood of the late sketches from the war-diary headquarters, in which his despairing hatred of the regime found full expression in an ironically de-familiarised Shakespearian 'porter's view' of great events.[263] Marose (2000) was given to understand in interviews with

[258] Ibid., p.517; also Manfred Briegel, ibid., 'Paris als zweite Heimat? Deutsche Schriftsteller im Exil der 30er Jahre', pp.523-36, here: p.533, citing Noth, *Erinnerungen eines Deutschen* (Hamburg and Düsseldorf, 1971), p.275.

[259] Cf. Walter Dietz, cited in Ewenz II (2002/2007), pp.205/232; also Percy Ernst Schramm, *Kriegstagebuch des Oberkommandos der Wehrmacht*, 8 vols (Munich: Bernard & Graefe, 1982), IV/8, p.1815; also Marose, 'Das Eigentliche ist unsichtbar', appendix.

[260] Geno Hartlaub, 'Antifaschistische Literatur im „Dritten Reich" ', *Sammlung 5. Jahrbuch für antifaschistische Literatur und Kunst*, ed. by Uwe Naumann (Frankfurt am Main: Röderberg, 1982), p. 16, and 'Zum Geleit', foreword to Seeman, *Felix Hartlaub.Die Zeichnungen* (Frankfurt am Main: Schirn- Kunsthalle, 1993).

[261] Wilke, in *Kritisches Lexikon zur deutschsprachigen Gegenswartliteratur* (Munich: 1983), pp.1-6.

[262] Geno Hartlaub, 'Antifaschistische Literatur im „Dritten Reich" ', loc. cit., p.18.

[263] Ibid., p.16.

Hartlaub's intimate friends Klaus and Irene Gysi that although Hartlaub had not passed on any documents from the *FHQ*, he would have discussed important events and occurrences of which he had knowledge with Klaus Gysi, who in a last interview admitted to being active in the information ring of the Soviet spy network, the "Rote Kapelle". Against this information Marose sets the opinion of Geno Hartlaub, who had already stubbornly rejected rumours circulating since the 1950s that her brother had been an anti-fascist conspirator during his service inside the *Sperrkreis* of the *FHQ*. In a 1989 interview with Marose, Geno Hartlaub reaffirmed her opinion that, for her, resistance activity of this nature on the part of her brother was out of character and out of the question.[264] Already, in a radio feature of 1965, Geno Hartlaub had insisted that undercover heroism was simply not in her brother's nature: "Er ist kein Held, nicht einmal ein negativer. Es gelingt ihm auch nicht, als unbeteiligter unter der Tarnkappe zu leben."[265] Also to be weighed against any suspicion of witting indiscretion is the comment of his father, G. F. Hartlaub: "Es ist erstaunlich welche Materialien F[elix] zu sehen bekommt, welche Einblicke er gewinnt. Freilich darf er im Einzelnen nichts sagen und *diese Schweigepflicht hält er sich natürlich eisern*"(italics added).[266] A stroke which robbed Gysi of speech prevented a further scheduled interview with Marose at which he had promised to reveal more on the topic.[267] Marose's inconclusive enquiry does not therefore add to our knowledge of possible ulterior authorial motivation on the part of Felix Hartlaub.

Hartlaub himself in no place evinces a view of the Paris sketches as anything in the nature of covert, dissident, 'desk-drawer', *Schubladenliteratur*; he thought of them merely as trial material for other, as yet unformulated work, "nur als Materialien gedacht."[268] There are no marginal remarks in the Paris notebooks or the Ukraine notebook indicating that they had been read by or discussed with others. A notebook, probably the latter, was relayed for safekeeping to G.F. Hartlaub via Irene Lessing January 1943.[269] Hartlaub's published letters from 1943 and the first half of 1944 seem to indicate very little, if any, creative writing activity in that period. After his return from the Ukraine, Hartlaub met and formed a relationship with Melita Laenebach with whom much of his correspondence from the spring of 1943 is taken up. In March 1943 something he has been reading awakens in him

264 Marose, 'Das Eigentliche ist unsichtbar', p.4.

265 Geno Hartlaub, introductory talk to 'Von Überleben der Literatur. Ein Versuch über Felix Hartlaub von Manfred Francke', (Süddeutscher Rundfunk, 10 November 1965, 23.00-24.00), transcript in *DLA* Marbach.

266 Ewenz II (2002/2007), pp.227/255: extract from Hartlaub family diary.

267 Marose, 'Das Eigentliche ist unsichtbar', p.5.

268 Ewenz I (2002/2007), pp.492/500: letter of 22 September 1941.

269 Ibid., pp. 560/568-69; Ewenz II, pp.235/263.

memories of his boyhood writing efforts: "…das längst begrabene, schon völlig fossile, knabenhafte litterarische Pläne wieder aufgewärmt hat. Ich schriebe so gerne was, was ganz Kleines, Komprimiert-Loses, nur ein Paar Seiten, aber ich brauche immer einen Anstoss von aussen, einen kleinen Auftrag."[270] In April, from Berchtesgaden, he notes that deceptive lulls in the war-diary work have tempted him to draw and write a little again: "Durch trügerische Arbeitsflauten verlockt, habe ich mal wieder versucht, ein wenig zu zeichnen und zu schreiben."[271] By July, complaining of distractions, headaches, eyestrain and sleeplessness, he has abandoned all private creative or scholarly activity: "jegliche private Tätigkeit bis zur Zeitungslektüre […] eingestellt."[272] In August he wishes to look up references from his notes-index on his study of 19th French writers, [273] and in September is preoccupied with a reappraisal of his plans for a book on this theme.[274] In October he reproves Melita Laenebach for having failed to relay university library-loan chits.[275] In November, his friends the Gysis have been suggesting to him that he turn his attention more towards German and contemporary subjects rather than the early 19th century French of his research until then.[276] In December 1943 he is reading Zola and 19th century German history.[277] By February 1944 he is reading Ina Seidel's 1938 novel, *Lennacker*, and writes of stalled literary-historical work.[278] Equally, in May of 1944, he confesses to the Gysis to being stalled in his study of Karl Lamprecht, which subject Schramm had suggested for Hartlaub's *Habilitation* dissertation.[279] At the end of May 1944, writing to his confidant and mentor, Gustav Radbruch, Hartlaub sees as the only task for scholars of his age-group, the forming of a standpoint on current events; he also expresses his disillusionment with the conventional career example of such as his superior, Schramm.[280] He admits to Radbruch to having produced very little: "Persönlich stagniert man ziemlich vor sich hin; gelegentlich kommt man zu einem Buch, einem Entwurf."[281] From the foregoing indications it seems probable that any writings from the period after the return from

---

[270] Ewenz I (2002/2007), pp.585/593: letter to Melita Laenebach, 4 March 1943.
[271] Ibid., pp. 603/612.
[272] Ibid., pp. 618/627.
[273] Ibid., pp. 632/640.
[274] Ibid., pp. 637/646.
[275] Ibid., pp. 646/655.
[276] Ibid., pp. 649/658.
[277] Ibid., pp. 669/678.
[278] Ibid., pp. 684/693.
[279] Ibid. I,II pp. 697-98/706-7, 274-75/304; also Schramm, *Kriegestagebuch des Oberkommandos der Wehrmacht*, vol.IV/8, p.1816.
[280] Ewenz I (2002/2007), pp.706-7/715-16.
[281] Ibid., pp.707/716.

Winniza and presumed among the materials deposited for safekeeping in September 1944 were chiefly notes and drafts for Hartlaub's post-doctoral studies.[282]

In the period after the 20 July 1944 Hartlaub's superior, Schramm, whose sister-in-law was among those implicated and executed,[283] sought refuge in private work for which Hartlaub's help was also enlisted.[284] As late as March of 1945 Hartlaub complains that Schramm's work obsession had now focused back on war-diary duty and had become detail-compulsive in its demands on his assistants.[285] In August of 1944 Hartlaub had complained of Schramm's obsessive preoccupation with primarily private work and of the war-duty responsibilities devolving on him, Hartlaub, in consequence: "…weil die Arbeit nicht weiter kommt, bzw. auf mir hängen bleibt. Ich selbst komme zu gar nichts, [...] Lust hätte ich eigentlich nur zum Schreiben."[286] The stultification and turning towards creative writing again, possibly in reaction additionally against Schramm's urging of *Habilitation* post-doctoral work,[287] bore fruit. Wilke (1967) has dated the resumption of Hartlaub's creative writing, on the last *FHQ* sketches, to no earlier than September of 1944.[288] In October, attributing his re-found energy to the bean coffee issued to night-duty staff, Hartlaub wrote: "habe ich wieder etwas zu schreiben angefangen." The urge to draw returns at the same time: "Zu zeichnen juckt es mich auch mächtig."[289]

In November 1944, writing to Melita Laenebach, Hartlaub muses on what to do with "meinen Manuskripten in Heidelberg", then the Hartlaub family home, and mentions the sketches from Wilhelmshaven, Paris and the Ukraine. He emphatically pronounces them as containing nothing ready for publication, "druckfertiges ist beileibe nicht dabei,"[290] but is at this late point in the war conscious of their potential documentary importance, "…die später einfach auf Grund ihres dokumentarischen Werts Bedeutung gewinnen könnten."[291] Writing to his father days later, and stressing the importance to him of the two Paris notebooks, he adds mention of what he terms, in quotation marks, the "Errinerungen aus Elmau", remarking that if he should not have opportunity to work on these latter again, they could be

---

[282] Cf. Wilke, *Die letzten Aufzeichnungen Felix Hartlaubs*, pp.79-81.

[283] Ibid., p.43.

[284] See Schramm, *Kriegstagebuch des OKW*, vol.IV/8, pp.1810-11; also Ewenz I (2002/2007), pp.732-33/742.

[285] Ewenz I (2002/2007), pp.744/754.

[286] Ibid., pp.716/725: letter to G.F. Hartlaub, 23 August 1944.

[287] See Schramm, *Kriegstagebuch des OKW*, vol.IV/8, p.1816.

[288] See Wilke, *Die letzten Aufzeichnungen Felix Hartlaubs*, pp.79-83.

[289] Ewenz I (2002/2007), pp.728/737-8: letter to G.F. Hartlaub, 17 October 1944.

[290] Ibid., pp. 730/740: letter to Melita Laenebach, 17 November 1944.

[291] Ibid.

of financial value to GFH, but adding a reservation "wegen des Stoffgehalts."[292] He cannot recall if the Elmau writings are complete, but feels that they cannot lack much by way of completion. Hartlaub's own plans to visit Elmau with Melita Laenbach in 1943 never came to fruition, for lack of leave.[293] Already in July 1943, expressing worry about the safekeeping of his notebooks and card-catalogue, and suggesting the *Odenwaldschule* as a possible depository, he conjoins the Elmau writings with those from Paris as "meine Tagebuch Aufzeichnungen aus Paris, Elmau, etc."[294] Again, in September 1943, and again referring to Paris and Elmau sketches: "Ich bitte um grösstmögliche luftschutzmässige Sicherung."[295] Evidently, the 'Elmau' sketches were already written by mid 1943 and were of some exceptional, possibly political, content. Elmau, a resort in Upper Bavaria, was favoured in Nazi circles, and Hartlaub's sister, Geno, had been a guest there a number of times and had made publishing contacts there.[296] Hartlaub himself had never visited there, and researchers in the Hartlaub archive have not found any verification of the existence of 'Elmau' sketches.[297] However, since Hartlaub's satire from the later Paris sketches onwards is interior to the minds of the focalising, not directly narrating, characters, and since these characters themselves cite hearsay, he might have constructed similar satire on the milieu at Elmau from recollections of his sister Geno with whom he remained intermittently in contact throughout the war. Where those particular writings were deposited for safekeeping is not now known, though from the 1943 references suggesting family custody it seems unlikely that they were among the papers consigned to Melita Laenebach in September 1944 and later lost through looting.[298] The loss leaves an intriguing gap in what would have been, taken with the Paris sketches and the *FHQ* sketches, a composite satirical picture of the Paris *Sieger* mentality, of decadence (at Elmau, possibly: Hartlaub makes a reference to such at the *FHQ* also, already in July 1944),[299] and of the meticulously planned delusion to the end.

Through his father's connections Hartlaub was in contact with publishers, with Johannes Maaßen of the Karl Alber publishing house in Munich, who had wished to engage him for historical works, and similarly in

---

[292] Ibid., pp.732/741: letter to G.F. Hartlaub, 30 November 1944.

[293] Ibid., pp.598/606, 635/643.

[294] Ibid., pp.619/628: letter to parents, 2 July 1943.

[295] Ibid., pp.637/646: letter to G.F. Hartlaub, 13 September 1943.

[296] See Ewenz II (2002/2007), pp.225,251/252, 279.

[297] Ibid., pp.252/280. The 'Elmau' sketches are not specifically mentioned in Wilke (1967).

[298] See Ewenz I (2002/2007), pp.723/732; also Wilke, *Die letzten Aufzeichnungen*, pp.80-81.

[299] Ibid, pp.714/723.

a literary historical connection with Hellmut Köster of Koehler & Amelang in Leipzig.[300] To the latter Hartlaub in October 1944 arranged to entrust his notes on a resumed literary-historical project from 1940, on the 19th century French Romantics.[301] He had also, the year before, in September 1943, as an alternative to the 19th century book-project, thought of the Paris sketches and the lost 'Elmau' sketches as material for a series of 'exciting short literary creations', "zündende kleine literarische Schöpfungen", and to this end had requested the return of some of his card-index notes on the theme (the proposal gratified G.F. Hartlaub, who took it for a sign that Felix was finally abandoning his fragmentary experimentations).[302] In January 1945, stationed at Zossen in Berlin, he regrets not having retrieved his Paris notebooks during a visit home to Heidelberg, "hätte auch gerne meine Pariser Aufzeichnungen an mich genommen. Das Paket habe ich in der Ulrichstr. gelassen, ohne dass mich diese Lösung voll befriedigt."[303] His worry is apparently for the safety of the notebooks, last left with a family friend in the Ulrichstrasse, Frankfurt am Main. We cannot know if he had their independent revision in mind. In their original state, the idiosyncratic narrative mode and cryptically ironic language would have been problematic for a contemporary publisher. Thus, thanks ironically to the risk of their destruction, the Paris sketches have been preserved in an unmediated state of very close proximity to the time and perspective of their origination.

Speculation on the circumstances of Hartlaub's disappearance extended to the possibility that he suicidally courted death.[304] Notification of his recall to active duty issued in early April 1945, and after two weeks' leave his orders to report to the Seeckt barracks in Spandau reached him on 20 April at the house of the Gysi's, with whom he had been staying. This latter date corresponds with the final move of the high-command staff within Berlin, from Zossen, where Hartlaub had last been stationed, to Berlin-Wannsee.[305] The length of the ensuing interval until Hartlaub's final parting at the Nikolassee suburban-rail station from Irene Lessing, wife of Klaus Gysi, is unclear from the account in Marose (2000),[306] but if it was as late as May 2nd 1945, the day of Berlin's surrender, then the putative circumstances of his death as supplied in the enlarged commentary in Ewenz (2007) point, rather, to a common misadventure.[307] The reflections of his last letters from Berlin

---

300 Ibid., pp.512/520,723/732-733; also Ewenz II, pp.172/198,178/204,191/218.

301 Ibid. I, pp.723-28/732-33,738.

302 Ibid., pp.632,637/640,646; Ewenz II, pp.258/287.

303 Ibid., I, pp.739/749.

304 Jochen Schimmang, 'Wo warst du, Felix?', *Berliner Morgenpost*, 12 May 2002.

305 Cf. Ewenz II (2002/2007), pp.288/319.

306 See Marose, 'Das Eigentliche ist unsichtbar', pp.173-74.

307 Cf. Ewenz II (2007), pp.321-22.

are illuminating of his wonderment at the enduring aura of the city, even when ruined from the air, and of his high regard in that war for embattled metropolitans, both of Paris and Berlin.

The psychological internalisation of the air war in the consciousness of the German people, a theme for long avoided in postwar German literature,[308] had already engaged Hartlaub. Bomb damage he had encountered on visits to Berlin, and long walks undertaken through the ruins in the course of a four day visit in February 1944 had left a deep impression on him.[309] Actual raids he directly experienced later, after the War Diary section had been relocated to Berlin from Rastenburg in late November 1944. The one aspect of the war that alone seems to have stirred him emotionally was the fortitude of the civilian population under air attack. He is unstinting in his admiration:

> Irgendwie ist das Aushalten der Bevölkerung in den Bombenstädten das Erste, was mich in diesem Krieg begeistert oder wie man es nennen soll. Es ist auch das einzige wirklich Neue und Eigenartige. Wie solche Stadt ein Ganzes ist; was den Menschen für Kräfte zuwachsen. [...] Was hätte man mit diesem Volk alles machen können...[310]

Something singular and new had emerged from the trial by fire, and Hartlaub defines a city here as more than architecture: as a whole, as a concept not existing outside the consciousness of its citizenry. He has difficulty in reifying the ruin landscape and this recognition increases his respect for the Berliners:

> Die Ruinen habe ich trotz ausgedehnter Gänge noch garnicht voll realisiert, hatte nur ein dumpfes Staunen und ungläubiges Kichern dafür und einen masslosen Respekt vor den Bewohnern und der Lebenskraft dieser Stadt. [311]

Hartlaub speculates on the seemingly irrational will to remain: "Verstehen wird das ja später keiner, dieses Bleibenwollen, man wird darin doch eine Art Psychose mit umgekehrten Vorzeichen erblicken."[312] There is in this *Bleibenwollen* a psychosis, with contrary symptoms, that may not be understood later by any who did not live it. Ursula von Kardorff also wondered in her Berlin diary, which was actually real: the ruins or the surviving *plutokratisch-bürgerliche* dining-out social world of the well-to-do.[313] Von Kardorff remarks wryly also that it is the allegedly rootless

---

[308] Cf. W.G. Sebald, *Luftkrieg und Literatur* (Frankfurt am Main: Fischer, 2001).
[309] Cf. Ewenz II (2002/2007), pp.270/300.
[310] Ewenz I (2002/2007), pp.673/682.
[311] Ibid., pp.686/695: letter to G.F. Hartlaub, 26 February 1944.
[312] Ibid., pp.691/700: letter to Irene Lessing and Klaus Gysi, 25 March 1944.
[313] Hartl, *Ursula von Kardorff: Berliner Aufzeichnungen*, p.151.

metropolitans who fanatically hang on in the bombed-out cellars of their Berlin *Heimat* rather than choose evacuation and safety.[314]

Hartlaub ponders longer the spatial and psychological disjunctures: the city, personified, has grown accustomed to its ruins, and the city districts, cut off from knowledge of one another's fates following heavy attacks, call to mind for him the shrinking of the West-Roman Empire in the late antique into separated and practically independent territories:

> Hier auch in Berl., das sich, scheint mir, völlig an seine Ruinen gewöhnt hat, [...] Schon die einzelnen Stadtteile wissen nach einem schweren Angriff so wenig voneinander, [...] diese dauernde Schrumpfung des Horizonts, diese Verengung aufs Territoriale ist schon sehr merkwürdig, es fällt schwer, nicht an den Reichszerfall der Spätantike zu denken.[315]

Hartlaub had felt his own connection to reality to have been long distorted. The inner monologue of the war-diarist in 'Im Dickicht des Südostens' – Hartlaub is credited with writing much of the War Diary chronicle of the South-East theatre[316] – reveals a mind struggling to order a torrent of events; the speaker feels the want of real experience, even if it be that of shots fired in anger and of bombs:

> ...der Mensch altert eben nur an den Erlebnissen, und die fehlen hier völlig, hier ist noch kein scharfer Schuss, noch keine einzige Bombe gefallen, diese seltsame Ausgespartheit hier, manchmal kommt sie einem etwas unheimlich vor.[317]

Hartlaub speaks already in January 1942 of the home-comer psychosis, of an eerie revenant feeling, "schaurigen Revenantgefühlen."[318] He seems to have intuited a caesura in experience that would prevent him from ever writing *Trümmerliteratur*:

> ...zwischen einer Bombe und einer Wohnung fehlt irgendwie das Zwischenglied. In einer Wohnung kann man sich einen Mord vorstellen, eine individuelle Feuersbrunst und dergl., [...] Na, und so weiter und so fort... Im Übrigen handelt es sich ja leider nur um Plagiate.[319]

He does, however, offer a calculated assessment of the housing problem in the rubble, the problem that would be solved in the East by the *Plattenbauten*:

---

[314] Ibid., pp.122-123.
[315] Ibid., pp.735/744: letter to parents, 15 December 1944.
[316] Cf. Wilke, *Die letzten Aufzeichnungen*, bibliography, pp.165-66.
[317] Ewenz I (2002/2007), pp.200/202.
[318] Ibid., pp.509/517: letter to parents, 22 January 1942.
[319] Ibid., pp.586/594: letter to Melita Laenebach, 7 March 1943.

> Man muss bedenken, dass das Wohnungsproblem in Deutschland schon bei Beginn des Krieges eigentlich überhaupt nicht mehr zu lösen war, dass 3 Millionen Menschen, glaube ich, keine eigene Wohnung hatten. [...] Das Privileg des Steinhauses wird anderen vorbehalten bleiben.[320]

The reference to the privilege of a "Steinhaus" reveals a social consciousness and is an implicit criticism of a regime that wilfully brought about so much waste of resources. The rubble world itself, as it stood, was intellectually intriguing to Hartlaub. The mind could not digest the actual emptiness behind the still-intact facades. The ruins had to be seen soon after, so that they might become reality in the inner *Seelenschrein*, the 'soul-reliquary':

> Man muss wohl richtig mit den Trümmern »zusammenleben«. [...] sie zu verschiedenen Tageszeiten und vor allem bei ihrer Entstehung oder kurz danach sehen, damit sie Wirklichkeit werden im inneren Seelenschrein. Die eigentliche Leere hinter den stehengebliebenen Fassaden hat sich noch nicht ins Bewusstsein gefressen.[321]

The scrupulous street-care adds to illusion of undisturbed continuity. The incomprehensible is swept, like the rubble, to one side and a conviction takes hold that what is lost is not finally so:

> ... fast alles zwischen Tiergarten und Wittenbergplatz, der »alte Westen« [...] ist entschieden das Unheimlichere, weil die äusseren Umrisse meist noch irgendwie stimmen und man angesichts der wieder ausschlagenden Bäume und spiegelsauberen Strassen das Gefühl hat, dass es dort noch irgendwie weiter leben muss und nicht endgültig verloren ist.[322]

Life in the ruins even had a certain attraction and *frisson*. Böll would recall this later in flatly simple terms:

> Aber das Leben in einer zertsörten Stadt, einer total zerstörten Stadt, hatte natürlich nicht nur schwierigkeiten, sondern auch Reize. Es war sehr still, es war wunderbar ruhig.[323]

Hartlaub, with the urbanity of the *flâneur*, formulates a European distillation of the bizarre continuity:

---

[320] Ewenz I (2002/2007), pp.636/645: letter to G.F. Hartlaub, 13 September 1943.

[321] Ibid. (2002/2007), pp.682/691: letter to Irene Lessing and Klaus Gysi, 20 February 1944.

[322] Ibid., pp.718/727: letter to G.F. Hartlaub, 23 August 1944.

[323] Böll, *Eine deutsche Erinnerung* (Munich: DTV, 1981) p.139.

> Dass das Leben im übrigen weitergeht und sogar nicht ohne eine gewisse sommerliche Eleganz und mit allerlei neuen Nuancen steht nicht nur in den Zeitungen, sondern stimmt auch wirklich. [...] In Gegenden, von denen kaum noch die Strassennamensschilder stehen, weht einen die Atmosphäre der Pariser Banlieue, der italienischen Piazza, des ukrainischen Dorfplatzes an [...] es ist schon alles sehr merkwürdig und ich würde es gerne näher festzuhalten versuchen, wenn ich wirklich in diesem Leben drin wäre.[324]

If only he were part of it, "wenn ich wirklich in diesem Leben *drin* wäre". Hartlaub's estrangement from civil life resulted not from the trauma of front-line service, but from his long isolation in an ordered calm that did not correspond to any reality, military or civil, without. He realised that the connection to any reality was maintained by a web of unseen links and that one was surprised to discover these links to have atrophied:

> ...die grosse Unruhe, die die plötzliche Rezivilisierung mit sich bringt. Man möchte an möglichst vielen Stellen einsetzen, wiederanknüpfen und entdeckt, dass man überall weit im Hintertreffen ist.[325]

Hartlaub's assignment to *OKW* war diary work did not bring with it any special leave concessions. By Christmas 1942 he saw leave as in itself a cruelty:

> Wenn diese sog. Urlaube nur nicht immer so scheusslich kurz bemessen wären! Sie genügen immer gerade, um einem zu demonstrieren, wie unvertraut mit menschlichen Dingen man geworden ist.[326]

By 1944, his fictional alter ego even welcomes the prohibition on leave, preferring not to be made aware of the artificiality of his life under the bell jar of the *FHQ*:

> In gewisser Weise hat es sein Gutes, dass es keinen Urlaub mehr gibt, sie würden es einem draussen gleich anmerken, dass man gewissermassen unter der Glasglocke lebt.[327]

At the end, he wishes for a restoration of the personal connection to reality and pronounces himself thankful to be sharing in the fate of Berlin. Geno Hartlaub's autobiographical sketch of the last phone call with her brother conveys his concern for her safety: he counsels her to remain in Oslo, on no account to risk posting elsewhere; advice founded on his

---

[324] Ewenz I (2002/2007), pp.718/727-28: letter to G.F. Hartlaub, 23 August 1944.

[325] Ibid., pp.505/513: letter to parents, 11 December 1941.

[326] Ibid., pp.555/563-564: letter to Melita Laenebach, 23 December 1942.

[327] Ibid., pp.200/202.

estimation of the coming lottery of death in Berlin.[328] The wording here is, however, far from heroic; his admiration for the unbroken spirit of the Berliners seems to evoke a shamed courage in him, and he speaks of a bashful, *schüchtern*, reconnection of his own severance from the "reality of these days":

> Nett sind die Leute im Luftschutzkeller, lauter noch völlig ungebrochene Urberliner, mit weitgehend gelöster Zunge, von erstaunlich frischem Aktionsgeist, der sich aber ganz auf den privaten Sektor, d.h. auf den Kampf um die Lebensmittel u.s.w. beschränkt. [...] Ich selbst bin alles in allem natürlich sehr dankbar dafür, das ich aus einiger Nähe an dem Schicksal dieser Stadt teilnehm[e] und den gänzlich verlorengegangen Anschluss an die Realität dieser Tage wieder schüchtern anknüpfen kann.[329]

It is for Hartlaub an untypical declaration of solidarity and, even rarer for him, of participation; it is clearly also a deeply felt expression of loyalty, not to regime or country, but to the country of the self-effacing *flâneur*, as in Paris, so in Berlin: to the city.

---

[328] See Geno Hartlaub, 'Wird noch Gesprochen', *Merkur. Deutsche Zeitschrift für europäisches Denken*, Heft 7, Jahrg. 28, July 1974 (Stuttgart: Klett), pp.936-940.

[329] Ewenz I (2002/2007), pp.745/755.

6. Conclusion

6.1. Fortunes of war

Handwritten notebooks and furtively typed drafts on box-squared service notepaper bear all of Harlaub's wartime creative literary work. The appearance of literary research, some of it genuine, deflected suspicion. Erhart Kästner was fortunate in having an assignment for the duration which allowed of literary pursuit without need for concealment. Gerhard Nebel, indiscrete in his utterances, was fortunate to escape with banishment to the Channel Islands. Fortune, chance and circumstance determined how well or how far a writer might succeed, preserve his moral integrity, and physically (or not) survive. Fortune and modest family and collegiate connections preserved, but also trapped Hartlaub. He bore an undue share of the burden of the war-diary work. P.E. Schramm, Hartlaub's superior, acknowledged that he, Schramm, put his private work before his war-diary duty, and on his own admission returned from his war-diary service with the MS material for two of his subsequently published books.[1] It must be granted, against this, that it was Hartlaub's very indispensability to Schramm (and Schramm's pleading of this to General Jodl) which spared him from front line duty until almost the end. Counter-insurgency warfare almost cost Kästner his life while on Crete: he recounts in *Kreta* how on one occasion, but for the Cretan law of hospitality, he himself would have perished.[2] In the end, Hartlaub, Raschke and Rexroth did perish (as did Guido Brand, in unclear circumstances, very shortly before the war's end, while recuperating from injury received while on fire fighting duty); Walter Bauer, Göpel, Kästner, Nebel and Lange survived – Lange wounded, with the loss of the sight of one eye. Walter Henkels too survived; after war-reporter service on the Caucasus front he was posted to the Arctic in October 1942, and for two years flew as (gunnery trained) reporter on weather and reconnaissance sea-patrols from northern Finnland and Norway. Thirty five years later the prominent political journalist and author of many books of political portraiture and humour published a memoir of his Arctic service, *Eismeer Patrouille* (1978). The account is un-heroic; Henkels insists that the word *hero* did not need to be stricken from his original sketches – it was nowhere there used. Some nuances, '*Zwischentönen*', had since, Henkels admits, been excised. Everything written then was made to serve one purpose: propaganda, and

---

[1] See Schramm, *Kriegstagebuch des Oberkommandos der Wehrmacht*, vol. IV/8, pp.1810,1812.

[2] Cf. Erhart Kästner, *Kreta* (1946), p.233; *Kreta* (1975), pp.204,254-59.

the dead and the deaths he commemorates could not at the time have been mentioned.[3]

The authors here studied were subject, besides censorship, to military discipline (Kästner's illustrator was vindictively assigned to a punishment battalion on the Eastern front). Kästner's survival stratagem was to relegate military service itself, and hence the murderous realities of anti-partisan warfare, to a given, understood backdrop to a foregrounded aura of classical Greece – which formula found a ready acceptance. Possibly through his common Dresden connection, with Kästner, to Hans Posse, the art historian Göpel found himself centrally involved in one of the Nazi art acquisition/seizure programs. Some of the authors, because of their writing assignments attached to propaganda companies (Raschke, Rexroth), or as reporters attached directly to military units (Lange), wrote in the full knowledge that they might not survive: Raschke died of a gunshot wound to the stomach on the Eastern front in November 1943; Rexroth survived the East only to die of gunshot wounds in northern Italy in September 1944, a second volume of *Der Wermutstrauch* unfinished.[4] Hartlaub knew that sooner or later he, like other colleagues before him, would be culled and dispatched to active service, as indeed he was, with a fatal pointlessness in his case.

The surviving authors all continued to pursue careers in writing, in Kästner's case resuming a prewar career also, securing appointment as head of the prestigious Wölfenbüttel library. Kästner and Göpel, friends of Raschke, retained their mutual regard and remained in contact; Heinrich Wiegand Petzet, a colleague of Hartlaub's in the war-diary unit, later published the correspondence of Erhart Kästner and Martin Heidegger. Percy Ernst Schramm edited the postwar edition of the *OKW* war diary. Kurt Lothar Tank of the *Pariser Tagebuch* collaborated with Paul Raabe, Kästner's successor at the Wölfenbüttel library, on an illustrated biography of Kästner's literary idol, Gerhart Hauptmann. Ehrengard Schramm-von Thadden, the wife of Percy Ernst Schramm and sister of the denounced and executed Elisabeth von Thadden, published a memoir of her postwar engagement on behalf of the surviving victims of the German anti-partisan reprisals in Greece. Ursula von Kardorff, instrumental in Kästner's first appearances in print in the *Deutsche Allgemeine Zeitung*,[5] and whose Berlin diary is insightful into the personalities and backgrounds of the German resistance plotters, remained Kästner's literary confidante in the immediate

3 Henkels, *Eismeer Patrouille* (Düsseldorf: Heyne, 1978), here cited from 4th edition (1988), pp.12,15,22-3,24,151.

4 Cf. Horst Denkler, *Werkruinen, Lebenstrümmer: literarische Spüren des 'verlorenen Generation' des Dritten Reiches* (Tübingen: Niemeyer, 2006), pp.205,206.

5 Cf. Hiller von Gaertringen (1994), p.92.

postwar years.[6] These overlapping connections, though coincidental, are suggestive of a relatively small cohort of engaged intellectuals in the humanist cause, even if the writings here considered may be considered to be a general outcome, direct or indirect, of the 'third humanism' influence in German *Gymnasium* education.

The writings may be seen as falling into two groups: the titles *Die Bretagne*, *Die Normandie*, *Frankreich*, *Hellas* and *Der Peloponnes*, since being in the scheme of their ultimate publishers presumptive of a German pre-eminence in European cultural determination, are generically similar and therefore form one group. The Paris writings of Hartlaub, private and subversive, though in whimsical disguise, and Kästner's *Griechenland* and *Kreta* which concede very little at all to the appropriative propaganda on Greece, form a second group. In this second group, in which may be included the between-the-lines content of Göpel's *Bretagne* and *Normandie*, humanism championed by Kästner combines with Hartlaub's sardonic parodies and elegiacally coded studies of occupied Paris to project past the action of the war to the war's absorption into the continuum of European history, thus to its *Bewältigung*. Eastern Front writings are a quite separate case: Germany's war was deemed to be have been concluded with regard to France and Greece as states; the issue in the East would never be settled, even temporarily, to that degree, and therefore writing there still continued to address an enemy, or rather, two enemies: the rival ideology, and the vastness of the land which outstripped both German military capacity and the capacity for literary comprehension.

While they lived and endured, psychological survival was for all of them a prerequisite for creative output. On the example of Hartlaub this was difficult, even behind the lines. He had found some release from stress while at Winniza: "Bei uns war es ja im Sommer, in der Ukraine, sehr gemütlich;"[7] but, by December, the memory was itself re-introducing stress: "Die Monate in der Ukraine gehen noch mächtig in mir um und haben ein ziemliches Schwergewicht angesetzt."[8] These remarks are the more poignant in view of the happy photographs in the Ukraine notebook, of a wedding party and of an open air country dance at a kolkhoz, and of the flower garlanded Anja and Tanja in their rowing skiff.[9] Snapshots record the riverside encounter on the banks of the Bug between Hartlaub and colleagues Walter Dietz and Fritz Puhl and the Ukranian girls who had come boating by.[10] Anja, a trainee

---

[6] Cf. ibid., pp.298,316,323,405.

[7] Ewenz I (2002/2007), pp.553/561: letter to Michael Hartlaub, 10 December 1942.

[8] Ibid., pp.552/560-61.

[9] Walter Dietz typescript, *DLA* 95.76.3, p. 11, also photographs by Walter Dietz in the Ukraine notebook of Felix Hartlaub, *DLA* 93.17.17.

[10] Marose, 'Das Eigentliche ist unsichtbar', p. 127, illustrations pp.40-42.

teacher, could speak German, and Hartlaub and his colleagues were guests at her house on the following Sunday in the company of her friends Tanja and Katja,[11] which three Dietz photographed in their demure Sunday frocks playfully seeking to detain Hartlaub, "ein schöner Jüngling in den festen Händen der drei Charittinnen oder Grazien, die nach der griechischen Sage Dienerinnen Aphroditons sind, Agleia, Euphrosyne und Thalia."[12] The Arcadian images are at odds with the well documented horrors of the *Barbarossa* invasion and with the subsequent systematic expropriation of food supplies from the Ukrainian population, particularly that of the cities.

In the Ukraine it was the inability to communicate that oppressed most: "Der Mutismus mangels Beherrschung der Landessprache ist natürlich ein unmöglicher und unerträglicher Zustand."[13] The state of being mute, *mutismus*, strikes a forlorn note. Human contact at an intellectual level with non-military people leading non-military lives was something Hartlaub craved. The sketches from the three-month Ukraine interval include *Landser* dialogue in parodies of the crude *Landser* viewpoint, but because of the language barrier, the voices of the people of the occupied territory are unheard.

Only once in the sketches does Hartlaub's observer encounter lethal atrocity, in the sketch sequence from the Winniza headquarters. Conflating real events in the vicinity, the first sketch alludes to the general fate of the Jews.[14] The sequence opens with the phrase "der forstwirtschaftlich mustergültige Kiefernwald" (the headquarters at Winniza was located in a small pine plantation). The model order of the sheltering pine trees is ironic symbol of the organised disorder emanating from their midst. The callous indifference of the anonymous narrator who recounts the construction of the headquarters by forced labour and the subsequent fate of those workers evident from the mass grave nearby, is indicated by a dismissive brevity and by a disjunctive switch to an account of the prohibition by camp-order of the keeping of fowl in living quarters and the slaughter to which this prohibition led. The description of chicken cadavers and severed parts appears to stand metaphorically for the slaughtered construction workers. In the occurrence of the words *Gefangene* and *Geflügel* in such proximity Marose (2000) sees an intentional associative metaphor.[15] Typically for Hartlaub, the distasteful truth of the war is neither concealed nor explained, but simply noted, by an amoral observer and in an offhand manner. The pointedly callous and unfeeling tone of the narrating voice serves to underscore the

---

[11] Ibid.

[12] Walter Dietz typescript, *DLA* 95.76.3, p.21.

[13] Ewenz I (2002/2007), pp.543/552.

[14] Cf. Ewenz II (2002/2007), note 5, pp.67-69/80-82.

[15] Marose, 'Das Eigentliche ist unsichtbar', p.132.

gruesomeness of the events. In Conrad Wiedemann's elucidation: "H.s suggestive Stilkunst einer passiven Erlebnisweise unter Verzicht auf Wertung steht allein in der deutschen Literatur seiner Zeit."[16]

6.2. The modes of literary response: an evaluation

The premise, discursively examined in the preceding sections here, is that there is a case to be made for a literature, in German, of the occupation of Europe; that further there was such a literature that was aesthetically accomplished and original and that was unprepossessed though not dispassionate in its humanism (Kästner, on the aura of the antique in Greece, is eloquently passionate). Originality of literary form has been determined (e.g. Hartlaub's alternating *flâneur* narrator and anonymous *acteur*, "Er", the sender/receiver actant); equally so, Kästner's demonstration that the travel diary, indeed, the literary diary per se, was a *creative* form. An intensity of high aesthetic has been found to have had application (e.g. Kästner's lyric compounds on the imagined Aegean refraction of light in Greece; Hartlaub's coded atmospheric compounds of Paris). Intellectual integrity has been found to have stood the test: under censorship such integrity was sometimes only obliquely possible (e.g. Erhard Göpel), and even private, covert writing as in the case of Hartlaub was at risk of discovery. These primary examples are not mutually exclusive. From out of a propaganda campaign directed not at the enemy, but at projecting an image of a backward and barbarous, racially, culturally and politically threatening 'other', insightful observations on the East-West cultural gulf did emerge (e.g. Raschke), and bourgeois literary form was turned to good effect (Lange, Rexroth). Examples of essay work (*Frankreich*) have been shown to have been perceptive and sympathetic, if here and there tinged with, though not in the overall tainted by, conscious or subconscious patronising. Examples of archaeo-historical research have been shown in example of *Hellas* to be, apart from its introduction and just one other, partial, exception (Kirsten), professional and objectively enlightening. An implicit rhetoric of that publication may be read as one of the German presence being a liberation from British 'interference', and of Greece being now an intellectual protectorate, but that is not in general the presumption of the individual texts. Further, it is here argued that, in the example of *Der Peloponnes*, similar research with added geologic, agronomic and internal-colonisation aspects has been shown to be a remarkably instructive adaptation of military cartography.

---

[16] Wiedemann, in Kunisch, *Handbuch der deutschen Gegenwartsliteratur* (Munich: Nymphenburger, 1965), p.241.

Forms of market publishing may also be distinguished. Specifically commissioned Baedekers, as in the examples of *Die Normandie* and *Die Bretagne* in France, find no direct single-volume counterparts in Greece: there, *Der Peloponnes* corresponds to *Die Normandie* in geographic remit, but under its sub-title of *Landschaft, Geschichte, Kunststätten* are offered comprehensive surveys rather than guide-book checklists. Though *Frankreich* and *Hellas* were produced as large-format presentation volumes, the *Feuilleton*-style content of the former is wholly absent in the latter: *Hellas* is an academic *Festschrift* dedicated to ancient Greece. As commissioned works of cultural appreciation all these publications were implicitly political in intent, but *manifest* political intent, excepting the introduction to *Hellas* as already remarked on here, is absent from the writing of the contributors and sole authors. The publications on France and Greece thus range from the instructive or densely informative to the leisurely feuilletonistic, to the intensely impressionistic. At the other end of the market scale there was an undemanding product for consumption by the ordinary occupation soldier, as for example, from 1943, *Nacht unter Sternen*, sub-titled *Weihnachtsbuch für den deutschen Soldaten in Norwegen*.[17] Fronted by *Edda* epigrams, sentimental seasonal stories – from the Norwegian also – and including a 1939 'Norwegian Diary' piece from Walter Bauer, present an impression of a land and culture as though already peacefully absorbed into the Germanic *Völkergemeinschaft* of the new Europe – exactly as intended in the *Kulturpolitik* of Goebbels and Rosenberg.[18]

The literary sketchbook and diary genres pursued by Bauer, Böhmer, Henkels, Leitgeb, Raschke and Tank were by definition more personal in impressions and reflection, but even there, circumspection was a pre-condition of publication. Martin Raschke's journal sketches, 'Im Schatten der Front',[19] include an (anti-communist) *Antigone* story,[20] and his *Zwiegespräche im Osten*[21] is a pseudo-philosophical flyting, musing on questions of the war and its meaning for its (German) participants, but these latter, though literarily experimental, appear after censorship politically conformist.[22] Reductive censorship alone, however, may not necessarily account in over two chapters of *Zwiegespräche im Osten* for such utterances, set

---

[17] Ed. by Karl Rauch & Carl H. Erke (Oslo: *Wehrmachtpropagandagruppe*, 1943).

[18] Cf. Hildegard Brenner, *Die Kunstpolitik des Nationalsozialismus*, p.131; also Jacobsen, citing Gruchmann (1962), in Schramm, *Kriegstagesbuch des OKW*, vol.I/1, p.94E.

[19] For publication history, see Haefs & Schmitz, *Martin Raschke* (Dresden: Thelem, 2002), pp.263-64.

[20] Ibid., p.261.

[21] Martin Raschke, *Zwiegespräche im Osten* (Leipzig: Paul List, 1942).

[22] See Haefs & Schmitz, op. cit., p.264.

against the backdrop of a burning Russian village, as "Vorm Kriege ist alles gleich,"[23] or (invoking Philip of Macedon), "Er erkannte die blutige Münze, um die wir allein dem Schicksal ein wenig Größe abhandeln."[24]

The conventional fictional forms of the novel and the novella were applied, by H. G. Rexroth and Horst Lange respectively, with creditable effect in critical commentary on the war, *as war*, in the East. In the German philhellenic disposition Erhart Kästner found a cloak for allusion and metaphor. That Kästner was a brilliant stylist added a dazzle factor which deflected penetration by the censor. Only Felix Hartlaub, writing covertly, could pen sardonic parody, but that, too, is cloaked as idiosyncratic whimsy so as to pass for oblique nonsense, were it discovered. Since discovery was always a possibility and since eventual publication could not be envisaged beyond the prevailing system, resort was made for camouflage in the Paris sketches to ingenious codes of colour and mood. Hartlaub's last sketches, from the war-diary headquarters, where the mood was already cynical and decadent, eschewed allegorical camouflage and used instead a magic realism for satirical parody on the disconnection from reality prevalent in the seclusion of the dictator's theatrically named lairs. Discovery at this point could well have proved fatal: the first and longest of the last sketches set directly in the *Sperrkreis* surrounding the Hitler headquarters, 'Im Dickicht des Südostens', is in fact extraordinarily frank on the disarray on the Balkan front and on the climate of fear following the 20th of July plot and even includes, unthinkable in publication terms, an imagined denunciation.[25]

Kästner's *Griechenland* was not re-published in the original text, but precisely because of its metaphysical impressions and intimations of the aura of the antique in the Greek landscape, still reads as a call to the sublime. That such a call, in wartime, was an elitist and escapist resort is the substance of the ethical criticism on Kästner. Why Kästner's wartime oeuvre should not be judged against peer literature on classical appreciation is less clear – Walter Bauer's *Wanderer im Süden* (1938) offers a comparison. A sequence of five chapters deals with the perception of the Greek aura in southern Italy. Bauer begins with Goethe's voyage to Sicily in the *Italienische Reise*, noting that Goethe [like Kästner] was accompanied by the artist, Kniep, who provided the illustrations. As the focalising voice, Bauer paraphrases Goethe's own preoccupation with an Arcadian antique:

> ...das Meer der Griechen und Römer, das Meer Nausikaas und Iphigenies, und des irrenden Odysseus und das Meer von Salamis [...] Das Wasser [...] ist ein Teil des

---

[23] Raschke, *Zwiegespräche im Osten*, p.47.
[24] Ibid., p.53.
[25] See Ewenz I (2002, 2007), pp.183/185.

> Elementes, alt und jungfräulich, das Griechenland berührt. [...] ...das Mittlemeer, das griechische Wasser.[26]

Like Kästner, Bauer celebrates the light of the South: the landscape is *lichtüberschüttet*; the light is *von unsäglicher Klarheit* (p.95). The sea is *unirdisch blau – das Meer der alten Welt* (p.97). That the sea is *unearthly* is the distinction that Bauer makes. Goethe had wondered at the beautiful *Tenne*, barn floor, that the retreating tide had left in the lagoon of Venice: Bauer places him on the margin of "dieses ungeheuren, wogenden Silberfeldes" (p.82), another *land* metaphor. Goethe's ship had not simply put to sea, but had *sich endgültig vom Lande befreit* (p.87). At Paestum, Bauer perceives the inaudible: *das Unhörbare dieser Abendstunde: das tiefe, leidlose Weben der Erde* (p.115). The stillness of the Earth, *die Stille der Erde*, surrounds him (p.119); he listens to the heartbeat of the Earth: *ich lauschte dem Herzschlag der Erde* (p.120). Bauer dedicates a chapter to 'Das Licht von Agrigent', where the evening light clothes the temple columns *wie eine kostbare, rötliche Haut* (p.112), and stays to see *wie das Licht von der alten Erde fortging*; quoting Hölderlin, "O Geist der uns erzog, [...] und du, o Licht, und du, o Mutter Erde!", the Earth is the source of light (p.113). Light awakens longings in him, is the sentimental, the unobtainable: *die Farbe des Gewölbes [...] die Sehnsucht erweckenden grünlichen Blau* (p.115).

Bauer's metaphor of a pulsating Earth is predominantly aural, whereas Kästner's overarching metaphor is visual. What the American poet Richard Wilbur terms "the water's blue, which is the shade of thought" and "the sky's blue speech"[27] are almost in a literal sense such for Kästner. The land receives the spectrum of light which seems to issue from the prism of the sky, and which the sea returns; hence blue, the dominant colour in his working of language as series and clusters of word-picture cells, *Bild-Zelle*.[28] Kästner's theory of language as a system of communicated images is formulated in his last work, *Aufstand der Dinge*,[29] but is already and most uninhibitedly displayed in the wartime works. The animation of inanimate landscape features, as if these were still in a state of rapid tectonic formation, is a feature of the writing.[30] Light, however, is the supreme agent of a *self-aware* animation. In *Griechische Inseln*, the extended preliminaries to a Greek wedding are brought to order by the *Pappas*, who is described signally: "das weiße Haar [...] gewandet in leuchtendes Rot [...] bedeckt vom schwarzen

---

26 Walter Bauer, *Wanderer im Süden* (Recklingshausen: Bitter & Co., 1940), pp.83,89.

27 Richard Wilbur, *New and Collected Poems* (London: Faber and Faber, 1989), p.29, 'Trolling for Blues'; p.282, 'Conjuration'.

28 See Kästner, *Aufstand der Dinge* (Frankfurt am Main: Insel, 1973), p.292.

29 Ibid., pp.289-92.

30 See Hiller von Gaertringen (1994), p.217.

Rundhut [...] Kreuz aus Silber [...] Der Goldstrom des Abendlichts fiel auf ihm und blendete ihn [...] verehrenswerte Gestalt, vom Lichte umflossen".[31] This burst of colour and light is the first after ten pages of the account, and spotlights the high ceremonial moment of the wedding. The evening celebrations which follow are conducted under moonlight: "Der Mond überschmolz alles mit weißem, rinnendem Licht. [...] erweckte das Lied dieses südlichen Dorfs [...]. Es hob sich empor, dieses Lied, in die stumpfblaue Nacht, in den ewigen Vorrat von Blau, aus dem alles geschöpft ist."[32] Colour thus applied supplies not only image and mood, but a language register deriving directly from images and denoted in word coinages and metaphors of animation. The whole enterprise was that of offering a humanist counter-image to the wartime reality, which image however, as Hiller von Gaertringen explicates, was also availed of by the propaganda services.[33] That point is not contested here. What should be accorded due recognition is the literarily innovative construction of an alternative world view which, illuminated in cascading images of light, outshone the then overtly prevailing presumptions of the official view.

Felix Hartlaub's Paris sketches, not published in German as a self-contained work until April 2011,[34] still read as a literally atmospheric impressionist portrait of a city and as a tribute to that city's impregnability against alien *possession*, as distinct from mere *occupation*, a metaphysical notion well conveyed, again, by lines of Richard Wilbur:

> A gardener works before the heat of day
> [...]
> He and the cook alone
> Receive the morning on their old estate,
> Possessing what the owners can but own.
> (*A Summer Morning*) [35]

Durs Grünbein's afterword to the new edition of the Paris sketches is an expanded version of his 1996 essay, 'Einer wie Felix Hartlaub', and suggests that Hartlaub anticipated the experiments of Arno Schmidt and Walter Kempowski. Schmidt developed the notion of the 'etym', by which language operates at two levels: that of conscious direct communication, and through neologisms which emerge from a reservoir of language fragments in the subconscious. Kempowski adopted a technique of free association to

---

[31] Kästner, *Griechische Inseln*, p.130, 'Hochzeit'.
[32] Ibid., p.133.
[33] See Hiller Von Gaertringen (1994), pp.252,255,256.
[34] *Felix Hartlaub. Kriegsaufzeichnungen aus Paris* (Berlin: Suhrkamp, 2011).
[35] Wilbur, *New and Collected Poems*, p.188.

eliminate biased retrospective interpretation.[36] The Paris sketches are characterised in like mode by a Joycean parataxis, neologistic compounds, and an avoidance of interpretation.

Erhard Göpel's *Die Bretagne* and *Die Normandie* are the modestly aspiring works of an art historian who, as his friend Erhart Kästner said of him, was, exceptionally for a *Kunstschreiber*, one who avoided all show of erudition and who dared show warmth for objects, and with his unaffected style succeeded supremely at art concealing art.[37] Horst Lange's *Die Leuchtkugeln* remains an allusively compelling portrait of the artist, in this instance a composer, who courted popularity at the expense of his art and who seeks redemption in solitariness and self-sacrifice. Hermann Georg Rexroth's *Der Wermutstrauch*, 'the wormwood bush', carries in its title the bitter experience of war and in its text an imagist and psychologically insightful picture of a war whose scale and reach was beyond normative comprehension.

Writing became for Kästner, as Hiller von Gaertringen has noted, a psychotherapeutic survival strategy.[38] As Kästner himself reflected during his internment in the Egyptian desert; by writing, the writer fathomed himself, and the re-creation of experience, even when not improving on or sparing reality, was of itself a creative act:

> Wenn das Schreiben überhaupt einen Sinn hat, dann ist es der, daß man sich dabei selber ergründet; [...] Jede Erzählung von etwas Erlebtem verklärt, auch wenn sie nicht im banalen Sinne verschönt, nur durch die wiedererschaffende Kraft, die auch eine Schöpferkraft ist.[39]

The *Zeltbuch von Tumilad*, the title spelled by the author on purely euphonic grounds with the variant Tumilad instead of Tumilat,[40] may well be considered here a transition book, since it was written, literally, in the transition period from military service to release into postwar civilian life. It twice invokes an epigram which in context appears to express only the beginning of Kästner's preoccupation with a personal philosophy: "Was ist der Mensch? Ein Träger von Bildern, die nicht mitteilbar sind."[41] Language as system of communicated images afforded therefore not denotative syntagms, but only associative images, through which traumatic impressions could be transmitted; this for Kästner as for all the Occupation writers.

---

[36] See also Furness and Humble, *Twentieth Century German Literature*, pp.163,258.

[37] See Raabe, *Erhart Kästner. Briefe*: letter of June 1966 to the fatally ill Göpel, pp.190-92.

[38] See Hiller von Gaertringen (1994), p.261.

[39] Kästner, *Zeltbuch von Tumilad* (Wiesbaden: Insel, 1949), pp.257,258.

[40] See Raabe and others, *Erhart Kästner. Werkmanuskripte* (Wolfenbüttel: Herzog August Bibliothek, 1985), p.34.

[41] Kästner, *Zeltbuch von Tumilad*, pp.9,147.

Of the occupation quotidian: fear for livelihood, hunger, latent terror, there is little explicit in these works. Kästner in *Griechenland* does indicate the catastrophic scale of the Greek hunger, but must remain oblique as to its root causes. Kästner's perception is often suspended in light, or the light of the past, above the terrestrial. Hartlaub paints a picture of a subdued Paris, but substitutes the fabric of the city metonymically for its population. In the East, the land offers no cultural-intellectual point of contact, and its vastness of itself casts doubt on the possibility of its subjugation. Correspondingly, the Eastern writings are introspective studies of character under stress, in which the indigenous population is not encountered as a functioning societal whole. From all three theatres: from France, the contemporarily sophisticated West; from Greece, the imagined land of a Hellenist education; from the East, the threatening unknown, the writings, by the common fact of their inevitably creative re-creation of historical realities, are literary constructs. For their particular merits argued, the several works are each distinguished literary or scholarly achievements, and within the limited remit afforded some of the writers, signal attainments. There is work that is unsentimental, non-partisan, and humane. There is also skilled literary adaptation and innovation (Hartlaub, Kästner; Lange, Rexroth); elsewhere there is honest, journeyman talent, and elsewhere still, high academic professionalism.

In sum, this was a literary output that sought, with some success, to attest to civilised values despite the contradiction in its authors' situations. The reports of murderous methods which must on occasion have reached the authors' ears were among many other accounts of mass death and destruction. The full script of the exploitatively hegemonic and ruthlessly genocidal ultimate plan in which they were actors was not known to them. The writers, largely the products of the Wilhelmine education system, had found themselves catapulted into a second period of continental upheaval, the embarkation on which the German military leadership itself had sought to avoid.[42] An evaluation of the authors' work with historicist detachment requires recognition of these facts.

---

[42] Cf. Gedenkstätte Deutscher Widerstand Berlin (2001), *Beiträge zum Thema Widerstand*, No.7, ed. by Klaus-Jürgen Müller, 'Witzleben-Stülpnagel-Speidel: Offiziere im Widerstand.'

Bibliography

Original manuscripts and typescripts from the Felix Hartlaub papers at the *Deutsches Literatur Archiv*, Marbach, with the following folder references:

93.17.6	typescript of Hartlaub's 'Berliner Tagebuchblätter' (33 pages);
93.17.7	typescript, 'Beschäftigung mit griechischer Mythologie', 9 pages;
93.17.32	'Das Unglück des begabten Kindes', fragment;
93.17.34	'Die wahre Bedeutung des Rheins' (1931), 25-page manuscript and 37-page typescript;
93.17.59	notebook diary of Hartlaub's Italian journey, 1931, with pen and pencil sketches;
93.17.40	fragments in 28-leaf ms. notebook and in typescripts;
93.17.6	typescript of Hartlaub's 'Berliner Tagebuchblätter' (33 pages);
93.17.17	manuscript of 'Jan' (circa 1939-1940), 6 A5 pages, double-sided;
93.17.17	Hartlaub notebook from the Ukraine, 1942;
93.17.26	Hartlaub notebook from Paris, 1940-1941;
93.17.36	Hartlaub notebook from Wilhelmshaven, Kiel, Odermünde, 1939-1940;
93.17.38	Hartlaub notebook from Paris, Romania, 1940-1941;
93.17.106	letter dated 23 October 1940 to Hartlaub from Wilhelm Scheidt of war-diary section, *OKW*;
93.17.105	letter dated 14 May 1941 to Hartlaub from Achive Commission;
95.76.3	Walter Dietz typescript monograph on Felix Hartlaub (28 pages).

Anz, Thomas, and Baasner, Rainer, eds., *Literaturkritik* (Munich: Beck, 2004), pp. 209-207.

Bargatzky,Walter, *Hotel Majestic. Ein Deutscher im besetzten Frankreich* (Freiburg: Herder, 1987).

Bauer, Walter,

Wanderer im Süden (Recklingshausen: Bitter & Co., 1938).

Tagebuchblätter aus Frankreich (Dessau: Karl Rauch, 1941).

Tagebuchblätter aus dem Osten (Dessau: Karl Rauch, 1944).

'Walter Bauer – Zeittafel seines Lebens', Walter Bauer archive, Stadtbibliothek Merseburg: http://www.fh-merseburg.de/index.php?id=1353, accessed 31 January 2012.

de Beauvoir, Simone, *In den besten Jahren* [*La force de l'âge*], German translation by Rolf Soellner (Reinbek bei Hamburg: Rowohlt, 1969, 1985).

de Beauvoir, Sylvie le Bon, ed., *Simone de Beauvoir, Kriegstagebuch September 1939-Januar 1941*, German translation by Judith Klein (Reinbek bei Hamburg: Rowohlt,1994).

Behler, Ernst, 'Das Fragment', in *Prosakunst ohne Erzählen*, ed. by Klaus Weissenberger (Tübingen: Max Niemeyer, 1985), pp. 125-143.

Behrenbeck, Sabine, 'Heldenkult oder Friedensmahnung? Krigerdenkmale nach beiden Weltkriegen', in Gottfried Niedhart and Dieter Riesenberger, *Lernen aus dem Krieg*, eds., (Munich: Beck, 1992), pp. 344-364.

Benz, Wolfgang, Otto, Gerhard, and Weismann, Anabella, eds., *Kultur-Propaganda-Öffentlichkeit. Intentionen deutscher Besatzungspolitik und Reaktionen auf die Okkupation* (Berlin: Metropol, 1998).

Blume, Eugen, *Erhard Göpel. Rede anläßlich des 100. Geburtstages* (Munich: Max Beckmann Gesellschaft, 2006).

Böhmer, Günter, *Pan am Fenster* (Berlin: Suhrkamp, 1943).

Böll, Heinrich,

Heinrich Böll. Briefe aus dem Krieg 1939-1945, (Cologne: Kiepenheuer & Witsch, 2001), 2 vols.

Eine deutsche Erinnerung. Interview mit René Wintzen (Munich: Deutscher Taschenbuch Verlag, 1981).

Das Vermächtnis (Bornheim-Merten: Lamuv, 1982).

Das Vermächtnis (Cologne: Kiepenheuer & Witsch, 1990), commentaries, afterword, pp. 101-144.

Heinrich Böll. Werke, Kölner Ausgabe vol.1 (Cologne: Kiepenheuer & Witsch, 2004). pp. 461-464.

Heinrich Böll.Werke, Kölner Ausgabe vol.2 (Cologne: Kiepenheuer & Witsch, 2002), pp. 121-137, 'Gefangen in Paris'.

Heinrich Böll.Werke, Kölner Ausgabe vol.3 (Cologne: Kiepenheuer & Witsch, 2002), pp.115-129, 'Vive la France!', pp.459-466, 'Unsere gute, alte Renée'.

Brand, Guido K.,

Zwischen Domen und Bunkern. Westeindrücke eines OT-Kriegsberichters (Amsterdam: Volk und Reich, 1944).

Ein Winter ohne Gnade. Osteindrücke eines OT-Kriegsberichters (Prague: Volk und Reich, 1943).

Brenner, Hildegard, *Die Kunstpolitik des Nationalsozialismus* (Reinbeck bei Hamburg: Rowohlt, 1963).

Brenner, Peter,
Der Reisebericht in der deutschen Literatur. Ein Forschungsüberblick als Vorstudie zu einer Gattungsgeschichte (Tübigen: Max Niemeyer, 1990).
Reisekultur in Deutschland: von der Weimarer Republik zum »Dritten Reich« (Tübingen: Max Niemeyer, 1997).

Buchbender, Ortwin and Sterz, Reinhold, *Das andere Gesicht des Krieges. Deutsche Feldpostbriefe 1939-1945* (Munich: C.H. Beck, 1982).

Bullough, Edward, *Aesthetics* (London: Bowes & Bowes, 1957).

Collinson, Diané, *Fifty major philosophers, a reference guide* (London: Routledge, 1988).

Danilenko, Vladimir, 'German Occupation of Kiev in 1941-1943: Documents of the Nazi-controlled City Administration', at: http://www.eastview.com/docs/CM807408_rev.pdf, accessed 1 February 2012.

Delabar, Walter, Denkler, Horst, and Schütz, Erhard, eds., *Banalität mit Stil. Zur Widersprüchlichkeit der Literaturproduktion im Nationalsozialismus* (Bern: Peter Lang, 1999).

Denkler, Horst,
Werkruinen, Lebenstrümmer: literarische Spüren des 'verlorenen Generation' des Dritten Reiches (Tübingen: Niemeyer, 2006).
'Was war und was bleibt? Versuch einer Bestandsaufnahme der erzählenden Literatur aus dem ‚Dritten Reich', *Zeitschrift für Germanistik*, vol.IX.2 (1999), pp. 279-293.
'„So war der Krieg noch nie." Neues von der Ostfront', in *Literatur und Demokratie.Festschrift für Hartmut Steinecke zum 60.Geburtstag*, ed. by Alo Allkemper and Norbert O. Eke (Berlin:Erich Schmidt, 2000), pp.185-95.

Drost, Wolfgang and others, *Paris sous l'occupation. Paris unter Deutscher Besatzung*, (Heidelberg: C.Winter, 1995).

Droulia, Luka and Fleischer, Hagen, eds., *Von Lidice bis Kalavryta. Widerstand und Besatzungsterror. Studien zur Repressalienpraxis im Zweiten Weltkrieg* (Berlin: Metropol, 1999).

Eagleton, Terry, *Literary Theory. An Introduction* (Oxford: Blackwell, 1996).

Eckhardt, Heinz-Werner, *Die Frontzeitungen des deutschen Heeres 1939-1945* (Vienna·Stuttgart: Wilhelm Braumüller, Schriftenreihe des Instituts für Publizistik der Universität Wien, 1975).

Egyptien, Jürgen and Louis, Raffaele, '100 Kriegsromane und –Erzählungen des Zeitraums 1945 bis 1965', *Treibhaus. Jahrbuch für die Literatur der fünfziger Jahre*, 3 (2007), pp. 211-237.

Ewenz, Gabriele Lieselotte, ed., *Felix Hartlaub »In den eigenen Umriss gebannt«* (Frankfurt am Main: Suhrkamp, 2002; 2nd edn, 2007, rev. by A.Angrick, H.Lüst, R.Strotbek), 2 vols.

Feuersenger, Marianne, *Mein Kriegstagebuch: zwischen Führerhauptquartier und Berliner Wirklichkeit* (Freiburg im Breisgau: Herder, 1982).

Fleischer, Hagen,

Im Kreuzschatten der Mächte. Griechenland 1941-1944 (Frankfurt am Main: Peter Lang, 1986).

'Siegfried in Hellas. Das nationalsozialistische Griechenlandbild und die Behandlung der griechischen Zivilbevölkerung seitens der deutschen Besatzungsbehörden, 1941-1944', in Armin Kerker, ed., *Griechenland – Entfernungen in die Wirklichkeit. Ein Lesebuch* (Hamburg: Argument, 1988), pp. 26-48.

'Die „Viehmenschen" und das „Sauvolk". Feindbilder einer dreifachen Okkupation: der Fall Griechenland', in W. Benz, G. Otto and A. Weismann, eds, *Kultur-Propaganda-Öffentlichkeit. Intentionen deutscher Besatzungspolitik und Reaktionen auf die Okkupation* (Berlin, Metropol, 1998), pp. 135-169.

'Deutsche „Ordnung" in Griechenland 1941-1944', in L. Droulia and H. Fleischer, eds, *Von Lidice bis Kalavryta. Widerstand und Besatzungsterror* (Berlin: Metropol, 1999), pp. 151-212.

Flügge, Manfred, ed., *Letzte Heimkehr nach Paris. Franz Hessel und die Seinen im Exil* (Berlin: Arsenal,1989).

Hiller von Gaertringen, Julia, Freifrau,

"*Meine Liebe zu Griechenland stammt aus dem Krieg*". *Studien zum literarischen Werk Erhart Kästners* (Wiesbaden: Harrassowitz, 1994).

Perseus-Auge Hellblau. Erhart Kästner und Gerhart Hauptmann: Briefe, Texte, Notizen (Bielefeld: Aisthesis, 2004).

'Im Herzen Griechen und im Geiste Christen zu sein, das oder das Garnichts ist unsere Lage' Zum 100. Geburtstag Erhart Kästners', at http://www.llb-detmold.de/wir-ueber-uns/aus-unserer-arbeit/texte.html , (2004), accessed 27 January 2012.

'Antike und Christentum. Die Griechenlandbücher Erhart Kästners'. Vortrag zum 100. Geburtstag des Bibliothekars und Schriftstellers Erhärt Kästner, at http://www.llb-detmold.de/wir-ueber-uns/aus-unserer-arbeit/texte.html, (13 March 2004), accessed 27 January 2012.

'Leserbrief zu dem Artikel „Über dem Krieg schweben" von Wolfram Wette in der Badischen Zeitung vom 28. Juli 2006',

at http://www.llb-detmold.de/wir-ueber-uns/aus-unserer-arbeit/texte.html , accessed 27 January 2012.
'Erhart Kästner. Ein Annenser und unbeirrbarer Humanist'. Festvortrag zum Jahrestreffen des „Societas Annensis", at http://www.llb-detmold.de/wir-ueber-uns/aus-unserer-arbeit/texte.html , (Augsburg, 2006), accessed 27 January 2012.

Hiller von Gaertringen, Julia, Freifrau and Nitzschke, Karin, eds, *Was die Seele braucht. Erhart Kästner über Bücher und Autoren* (Frankfurt am Main: Insel, 1994).

Gedenkstätte Deutscher Widerstand Berlin (2001), *Beiträge zum Thema Widerstand*, No. 7, Klaus-Jürgen Müller, ed., 'Witzleben- Stülpnagel-Speidel: Offiziere im Widerstand.'

Göpel, Erhard,
Der Buchbinder Ignatz Wiemeler (Leipzig, Vienna: Brünn, 1938).
Die Bretagne: Volkstum · Geschichte · Kunst (Paris: army HQ, 1940).
Die Normandie (Paris: HQ, 1940-41, also Leipzig: Staackman, 1942).
Paul Gauguin (Munich-Vienna-Basel: Kurt Desch, 1954).
Deutsche Holzschnitte des XX. Jahrhunderts (Frankfurt am Main: Insel,1955).

Göpel, Erhard, ed., *Otto Julius Bierbaum. Eine empfindsame Reise im Automobil* (Munich: Langen-Müller, 1954; repr. 1979).

Gordon, Bertram M. '*Ist Gott Französisch?* Germans, tourism, and occupied France, 1940-1944', *Modern & Contemporary France*, vol.4, issue 3 (1996), pp. 287-298.

Grössel, Hanns, ed., *Jean-Paul Sartre: Paris unter der Besatzung. Artikel, Reportagen, Aufsätze 1944-1945* (Reinbek bei Hamburg: Rowohlt, 1980).

Grünbein, Durs,
'Einer wie Felix Hartlaub', in *Galilei vermißt Dantes Hölle und bleibt an den Maßen hängen. Aufsätze 1989-1995* (Frankfurt am Main: Suhrkamp, 1996), pp. 190-195.
'Der Verschollene', in *Felix Hartlaub. Kriegsaufzeichnungen aus Paris* (Berlin: Suhrkamp, 2011), pp. 147-163.

Günther-Hornig, Margot, *Kunstschutz in den von Deutschland besetzten Gebieten 1939-1945* (Tübingen: Institut für Besatzungsfragen Tübigen, 1958).

Haefs, W., Schmitz, W., eds., *Martin Raschke (1905-1943). Leben und Werk* (Dresden: Thelem, 2002).

Hammermeister, Kai, *The German Aesthetic Tradition* (Cambridge: Cambridge University Press, 2002).

Hartl, Peter, ed., *Ursula von Kardorff: Berliner Aufzeichnungen 1942 bis 1945* (Munich: DTV, 1994).

Hartlaub, Geno, ed.,
Von unten gesehen, pp. 5-15, foreword (Stuttgart: Koehler, 1950).
Das Gesamtwerk, pp. 5-9, foreword (Frankfurt am Main: Fischer, 1955).
Im Sperrkreis, pp. 5-10, foreword (Hamburg-Basel: Rowohlt, 1955).
Im Sperrkreis, pp. 211-218, afterword (Frankfurt am Main: Fischer, 1984).

Hartlaub, Geno,
'Der Mann im Sperrkreis', interview with Thilo Koch, Norddeutscher Rundfunk, Drittes Programm, 14 April 1957, 20.15-21.20 (transcript at *DLA* Marbach).
Introductory talk to 'Von Überleben der Literatur. Ein Versuch über Felix Hartlaub von Manfred Francke', Süddeutscher Rundfunk,10 Nov.1965, 23.00-24.00 (transcript at *DLA* Marbach).
'Wird noch gesprochen?', *Merkur. Deutsche Zeitschrift für europäisches Denken*, Heft 7, Jahrg. 28, July 1974 (Stuttgart: Klett), pp. 936-940.
'Antifaschistische Literatur im „Dritten Reich" ', in Uwe Naumann, ed., *Sammlung 5. Jahrbuch für antifaschistische Literatur und Kunst* (Frankfurt am Main: Röderberg, 1982), pp. 16-18.
Interview with Sigrid Weigel reproduced in *Der Mond hat Durst* (Frankfurt am Main: Zweitausendeins, 1986), pp. 125-159.
'Zum Geleit', foreword to *Felix Hartlaub. Die Zeichnungen*, Seemann, Hellmut, ed., (Frankfurt am Main: Verlag Schirn-Kunsthalle, 1993).

Hauptmann, Gerhart, *Griechischer Frühling* (Berlin: Propyläen, 1966).

Heller, Gerhard and Grand, Jean, *In einem besetzten Land. Leutnant Heller und die Zensur in Frankreich 1940-1944* (Bergisch Gladbach: Bastei-Lübbe, 1982).

Henkels, Walter,
Östliche Silhouetten (Berlin: Scherl, 1943).
Eismeer Patrouille (Heyne: Düsseldorf, 1978).

Hessel, Franz, *Ein Flaneur in Berlin* (Berlin: Arsenal, 1984).

von Heydebrand, Renate and Winko, Simone,
Einführung in die Wertung von Literatur (Paderborn: Schöningh, 1996).

Hirschfeld, Gerhard and Marsh, Patrick,
Collaboration in France. Politics and Culture during the Nazi Occupation 1940-1944 (Oxford/New York/Munich: Berg, 1989).

Hoffman, Dieter, ed., *Hinweis auf Martin Raschke* (Heidelberg: Lambert Schneider, 1963).

Hohoff, Curt,

'Junge deutsche Erzähler' *Hochland*, 41 (1948/49), 282-88 (p.287).

Hoven, Herbert, ed.,
Heinrich Böll. Die Hoffnung ist wie ein wildes Tier. Briefwechsel mit Ernst-Adolf Kunz, 1945-1953 (Munich: Deutscher Taschenbuch Verlag, 1997).

Humburg, Martin, *Das Gesicht des Krieges. Feldpostbriefe von Wehrmachtsoldaten aus der Sowjetunion 1941-1944.*
(Opladen/Wiesbaden: Westdeutscher Verlag, 1998).

Inwood, Michael, *Heidegger*
(Freiburg: Herder, 1999).

Iser, Wolfgang, 'The reading process: a phenomenological approach', *New Literary History*, vol.3 (Winter 1972), pp. 279-299, cited from Lodge (1988; here 10th impression, 1995), *Modern Criticism and Theory.*

Jäckel, Eberhard,
Frankreich in Hitlers Europa. Die deutsche Frankreichpolitik im Zweiten Weltkrieg (Stuttgart: Deutsche Verlags-Anstalt, 1966).
Hitlers Herrschaft (Stuttgart: Deutsche Verlags-Anstalt, 1986).

Jens, Walter, 'Felix Hartlaubs Notizen', in *Zueignungen*
(Munich, Piper, 1963), pp. 79-88.

Jünger, Ernst,
Strahlungen I. (Munich: DTV/Klett-Cotta, 1988).
Strahlungen II.(Munich: DTV/Klett-Cotta,1988).

Kafka, Franz, *Betrachtung*
(Leipzig: Rowolt, 1913; facsimile reprint, Frankfurt am Main: Fischer, 1994).

Kästner, Anita and Kästner, Reingart, *Erhart Kästner. Leben und Werk in Daten und Bildern* (Frankfurt am Main: Insel, 1980).

Kästner, Erhart,
Griechenland: ein Buch aus dem Kriege (Berlin: Gebr. Mann, 1943).
Kreta (Berlin: Gebr. Mann, 1946).
Zeltbuch von Tumilad (Wiesbaden: Insel, 1949).
'Der intellektuelle Gefreite',
Allgemeine Zeitung (Mainz) 16 April 1949.
'Wiedersehen mit Griechenland',
Schwäbische Landeszeitung (*SLZ*) 03 May 1952.
'Enttäuschte Liebe zu den Deutschen',
Schwäbische Landeszeitung (*SLZ*) 31 May 1952.
Ölberge, Weinberge: ein Griechenlandbuch (Wiesbaden: Insel, 1953).
Aristide Maillol. Hirtenleben (Frankfurt am Main: Insel, 1957).
'Martin Raschke 1905-1943', *Jahresring 56|58*
(Stuttgart: Deutsche Verlags-Anstalt, 1957), pp. 99-107.

Offener Brief an die Königin von Griechenland
(Frankfurt am Main: Suhrkamp, 1973).
Aufstand der Dinge. Byzantinische Aufzeichnungen
(Frankfurt am Main: Insel, 1973).
Kreta. Aufzeichnungen aus dem Jahre 1943
(Frankfurt am Main: Insel, 1975).
Griechische Inseln 1944 (Frankfurt am Main, Insel, 1975).

Erhart Kästner. Was die Seele braucht. Über Bücher und Autoren, ed. by J. Hiller von Gaertringen and K. Nitzschke (Frankfurt am Main: Insel, 1998).

Kilian, Katrin Anja, 'Das Feldpost als Gegenstand interdisziplinärer Forschung. Archivlage, Forschungsstand und Aufarbeitung der Quelle aus dem Zweitem Weltkrieg', [doctoral dissertation] (Technische Universität Berlin, 2001).

Knoch, Peter, ed., *Kriegsalltag. Die Rekonstruktion des Kriegsalltags als Aufgabe der historischen Forschung und der Friedenserziehung* (Stuttgart: Metzler, 1989).

Kraft, Thomas, ed., *Lexikon der deutschsprachigen Gegenwartsliteratur seit 1945*, vol.1, A-J (Munich: Nymphenburger, 2003), pp. 483-484.

Krauss, Erna and Hartlaub, G.F., eds, *Felix Hartlaub: in seinen Briefen* (Tübingen: Wunderlich, 1958).

Lange, Horst, *Die Leuchtkugeln. Drei Erzählungen* (Hamburg: H. Goverts, 1944).

Lehnert, Erik, *Gerhard Nebel. Wächter des Normativen* (Schnellroda: Antaios, 2004).

Leitgeb, Josef, *Am Rande des Krieges* (Berlin: Otto Müller, 1942).

Löhr, Hanns Christian, *Das Braune Haus der Kunst. Hitler und der »Sonderauftrag Linz«. Visionen, Verbrechen, Verluste.* (Berlin: Akademie Verlag, 2005).

Lorenz, Heinz, ed.,
Frankreich: ein Erlebnis des deutschen Soldaten (Paris: Ode, 1942).
Soldaten Fotografieren Frankreich (Paris: Wegleiter, 1943).

LXVIII Army Corps, *Der Peloponnes* (Athens: Christu, 1944).

MacNeice, Louis, *Collected Poems* (London: Faber and Faber, 1979).

McNeil, William and Feldman, Karen S., eds., *Continental Philosophy* (Oxford: Blackwell, 1998).

Marchand, Suzanne, *Down from Olympus* (Princeton: Princeton University Press, 2003).

Marko, Kurt, 'Felix Hartlaubs Zeugenschaft wider den Missbrauch der

Vergangenheit. Mehr als 40 Jahre danach', *Zeitschrift für Politik. Organ der Hochschule für Politik, München,* issue 34, year 3 (1987), pp. 280-291.

Marose, Monika,
'Das Eigentliche ist unsichtbar' [doctoral dissertation] Essen University, 2000.
Unter der Tarnkappe. Felix Hartlaub, e*ine Biographie* (Berlin: Transit, 2005).

Meyer, Werner, 'Felix Hartlaub in der éenwaldschule', *Die Sammlung. Zeitschrift für Kultur und Erziehung,* Herman Nohl (ed.), 13 Jahrgang (Göttingen: Vandenhoeck & Ruprecht, 1958), pp. 623-631.

Michels, Eckard, *Das Deutsche Institut in Paris 1940-1944* (Stuttgart: Steiner, 1993).

Müller, Frederike, 'Felix Hartlaub – Ein 'poeta minor' der Inneren Emigration. Problematisierung seiner literaturgeschichtlichen Stellung' [MA dissertation] (Saarbrücken: Universität des Saarlandes, 1997).

Müller, Wolfgang G., 'Der Brief', in: Weissenberger, Klaus, ed., *Prosakunst ohne Erzählen* (Tübingen: Niemeyer, 1985), pp. 67-87.

Nauhaus, Julia M., *Erhart Kästners Phantasiekabinett. Variationen über Kunst und Künstler* (Freiburg im Breisgau: Rombach, 2003).

Nebel, Gerhard, *Von den Elementen. Essays* (Wuppertal: Im Marées, 1947).

Neumeyer, Harald, *Der Flaneur. Konzeptionen der Moderne* (Würzburg: Königshausen & Neumann, 1999).

Oehler, Dolf, 'Autobiographische Paris-Literatur von Rilke und Kafka zu Weiß, Nixon und Handke', in Wiedemann, Conrad, ed., *Rom-Paris-London. Erfahrung und Selbsterfahrung deutscher Schriftsteller und Künstler in den fremden Metropolen; ein Symposion* (Stuttgart: J.B. Metzler, 1988).

Parker, Stephen and others, *The Modern Restoration. Re-thinking German Literary History 1930-1960* (Berlin, New York: Walter de Gruyter, 2004).

Peitsch, Helmut, '„Am Rande des Krieges"? Nichtnazistische Schriftsteller im Einsatz der Propagandakompanien gegen die Sowjetunion', *Kürbiskern* 3/84 (Munich: Damnitz, 1984).

Petzet, Heinrich W., *Martin Heidegger - Erhart Kästner. Briefwechsel 1953-1974* (Frankfurt am Main: Insel, 1986).

Plard, Henri, '»Tout Seul« La Conscience de la solitude chez Felix Hartlaub', *Etudes Germaniques,* Paris: April/June 1959, pp. 128-147.

Raabe, Paul, *Erhart Kästner. Briefe* (Frankfurt am Main, Insel, 1984).

Raabe, Paul, and others, *Erhart Kästner. Werkmanuskripte*

(Wolfenbüttel: exhibition catalogue no. 43 of the Herzog August Bibliothek, 1984).
Raschke, Martin, *Zwiegespräche im Osten* (Leipzig: Paul List, 1942).
Rauch, Karl and Erke, Karl H., eds., *Nacht unter Sternen. Weihnachtsbuch für den deutschen Soldaten in Norwegen* (Wehrmacht Propaganda Group: Oslo, 1943).
Rexroth, H.G., *Der Wermutstrauch* (Hamburg: H.Goverts, 1944).
Ehrke-Rotermund, Heidrun and Rotermund, Erwin, *Zwischenreiche und Gegenwelten. Texte und Vorstudien zur ‚Verdeckten Schreibweise' im „Dritten Reich"* (Munich: Fink, 1999).
Sagarra, Eda and Skrine, Peter, *A Companion to German Literature* (Oxford: Blackwell, 1999).
Schäfer, Hans Dieter, *Das gespaltene Bewußtsein. Deutsche Kultur und Lebenswirklichkeit 1933-1945* (Frankfurt am Main: Ullstein, 1981,84).
Scherpe, Klaus R., *Stadt. Krieg. Fremde. Literatur und Kultur nach den Katastrophen* (Tübingen, Basel: Francke, 2002).
Schiller, Friedrich,
Kallias oder über die Schönheit; Über Anmut und Würde (Stuttgart: Reclam, 1993).
Über die ästhetische Erziehung des Menschen (Stuttgart: Reclam, 1993).
Schimmang, Jochen, 'Wo warst du, Felix?', *Berliner Morgenpost*, 12 May 2002.
Schnell, Ralf, *Literarische innere Emigration 1933-1945* (Stuttgart: Metzler, 1976).
von Schoenebeck, Hans, and Kraiker, Wilhelm, eds., *Hellas. Bilder zur Kultur des Griechentums* (Burg bei Magdeburg: August Hopfer, 1943).
Schonauer, Franz, *Deutsche Literatur im Dritten Reich. Versuch einer Darstellung in polemisch-didaktischer Absicht* (Olten und Freiburg-im-Breisgau: Walter, 1961).
Schramm, Ehrengard, *Ein Hilfswerk für Griechenland* (Göttingen: Vandenhoeck & Ruprecht, 2003).
Schramm, Percy Ernst, *Kriegstagebuch des Oberkommandos der Wehrmacht*, student edition, 8 vols, vols I/1, IV/8 (Frankfurt am Main: Bernard&Graefe, 1961-1965; student edition, 1982).
Schwab-Felisch, Hans, 'Die Literatur der Obergefreiten' *Der Monat*, year 4, vol.42 (March 1952), pp. 644-651.
Schweiger, Werner J., ed., *Peter Altenberg. Extrakte des Lebens. Gesammelte*

Skizzen 1898-1919 (Vienna and Frankfurt: Löcker/S.Fischer, 1987).

Sebald, W.G., *Luftkrieg und Literatur* (Frankfurt am Main: Fischer, 2001).

Seemann, Hellmut, ed., *Felix Hartlaub, Die Aufzeichnungen* (Frankfurt am Main: exhibition catalogue of Schirn- Kunstalle Frankfurt, 1993).

Seibert, Peter, 'Deutsche Ansichten der besetzten Stadt', in Drost, Wolfgang, and others, *Paris sous l'occupation. Paris unter deutscher Besatzung* (Heidelberg: C.Winter, 1995), pp. 58-73.

Seibt, Gustav, 'Im Sperrkreis des Dilettantismus', *Süddeutsche Zeitung*, 6 February 2003, p. 16.

Severin, Rudiger, *Spuren des Flaneurs in deutschsprachiger Prosa* (Frankfurt am Main: Peter Lang, 1988).

Stollmann, Rainer, *Ästhetsierung der Politik. Literaturstudien zum subjektiven Faschismus* (Stuttgart: Metzler, 1978).

Tank, Kurt Lothar, *Pariser Tagebuch 1938-1939-1940* (Berlin: S.Fischer, 1941).

Tewes, Ludger, *Frankreich in der Besatzungszeit 1940-1943. Die Sicht deutscher Augenzeugen* (Bonn: Bouvier, 1998).

Tiedemann, Rolf, ed., *Walter Benjamin: Gesammelte Schriften*, 7 vols, vol.5.2 (Frankfurt am Main: Suhrkamp, 1982).

Treue, Wilhelm, 'Zum nationalsozialistischen Kunstraub in Frankreich. Der „Bargatzky Bericht"', *Viertelsjahrshefte für Zeitgeschichte* no.13, vol.3 (Munich: Oldenburg, 1965), pp. 285-337.

Vogelgesang, Claus, 'Das Tagebuch', in Weissenberger, Klaus, ed., *Prosakunst ohne Erzählen* (Tübingen: Niemeyer, 1985), p.199, citing Horst (1965) in Kunisch, ed., *Handbuch der deutschen Gegenwartsliteratur*, p. 734 ff.

Vollmer, Hartmut, and Witte, Bernd, eds., *Franz Hessel, Sämtliche Werke in fünf Bänden*, vol.II (Oldenburg: Igel, 1999).

Wallrath-Janssen, Anne M., *Der Verlag H.Goverts im Dritten Reich* (Munich: K.G. Saur, 2007).

Warlimont, Walter, *Im Hauptquartier der deutschen Wehrmacht 1939 bis 1945* (Augsburg: Weltbild, 1990, 2 vols.).

von Wedel, Hasso, *Die Propagandatruppen der Deutschen Wehrmacht* (Neckargemünd: Kurt Vowinckel Verlag, 1962).

Weyrauch, Wolfgang, ed., *Tausend Gramm. Ein deutsches Bekenntnis in dreißig Geschichten aus dem Jahr 1949* (Reinbek bei Hamburg: Rowohlt, 1989).

Widmer, Urs, 'Über Robert Walser', in Keel, Daniel, ed., *Robert Walser. Der Spaziergang. Ausgewählte Geschichten* (Zurich: Diogenes, 1973), pp. 145-166.

Wiedemann, Conrad, ed.,
Rom-Paris-London. Erfahrung und Selbsterfahrung deutscher Schriftsteller und Künstler in den fremden Metropolen; ein Symposion (Stuttgart: J.B.Metzler,1988).
'Felix Hartlaub', in Kunisch, ed., *Handbuch der deutschen Gegenwartsliteratur* (Munich: Nymphenburger, 1965), p. 241.

Wilbur, Richard, *New and Collected Poems* (London: Faber and Faber, 1989).

Wilke, Christian-Hartwig,
Die letzten Aufzeichnungen Felix Hartlaubs (Bad Homburg: Gehlen, 1967).
'Die Jugendarbeiten Felix Hartlaubs. Ein Vergleich der veröffentlichten Fassungen mit den Originalen', *Literaturwissenschaftliches Jahrbuch der Görres Gesellschaft*, Munich 1966, pp. 262-301.
'Felix Hartlaub', in Arnold, Heinz Ludwig, ed., *Kritisches Lexikon zur deutschsprachigen Gegenwartsliteratur* (Munich: 1983), pp. 1-6.

Wittrock, Christine, 'Das Frauenbild in faschistischen Texten und seine Vorläufer in der bürgerlichen Frauenbewegung der zwanziger Jahre' [dissertation], Johann Wolfgang von Goethe Universität, Frankfurt am Main (1981); also as *Weiblichkeitsmythen* (Frankfurt am Main: Vervuert, 1988).

Worthmann, Friederike, *Literarische Wertungen. Vorschläge für ein deskriptives Modell* (Wiesbaden: Deutscher Universitäts- Verlag, 2004).

von Xylander, Marlen, *Die deutsche Besatzungsherrschaft auf Kreta 1941-1945* (Freiburg im Breisgau: Rombach, 1989).

Zeller, Bernhard, ed., *Das 20 Jahrhundert. Von Nietzsche bis zur Gruppe 47*, catalogue of permanent exhibition at the Schiller National Museum and German Literature Archive at Marbach am Neckar (Munich: Kösel, 1980), p. 276.

Illustrations

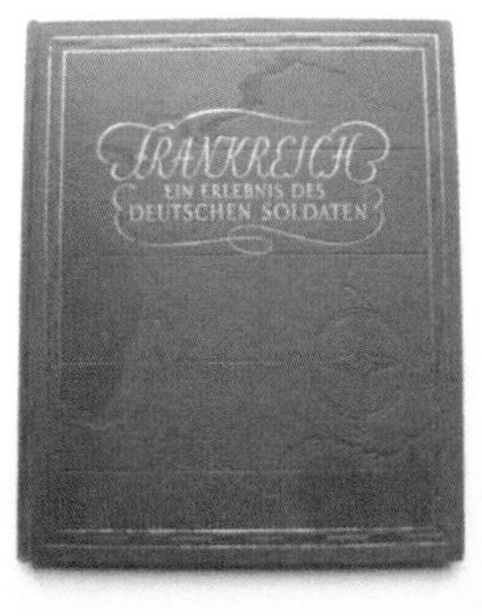

Frankreich (1942)

view of Beauvais (K. Fisch) oriel turret, Burgundy (K. Schöllkopf)

Soldaten Fotografieren Frankreich (1943)

Die Normandie (1940, 1942)

pull-out map: *Die Normandie*

Die Bretagne (1940)

Walter Bauer,
Tagebuchblätter aus Frankreich (1941)
Tagebuchblätter aus dem Osten (1944)

Kurt Lothar Tank,
Pariser Tagebuch (1941)

Erhart Kästner
Kreta ([1944]1946)

Griechenland (1943)
illustrations by H.Kaulbach †1942

view from Cape Sounion

refugee quarter, Piraeus

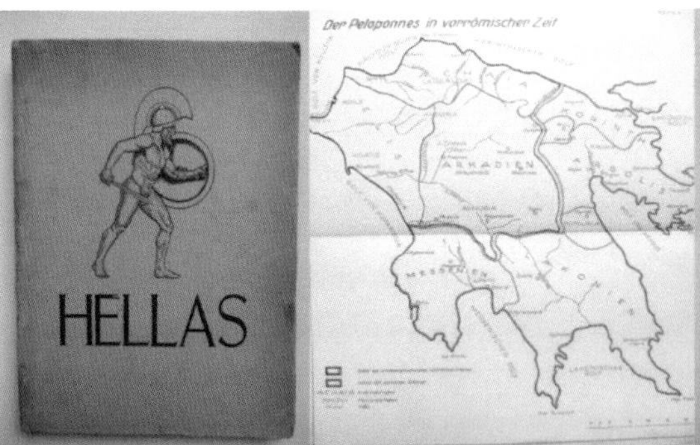

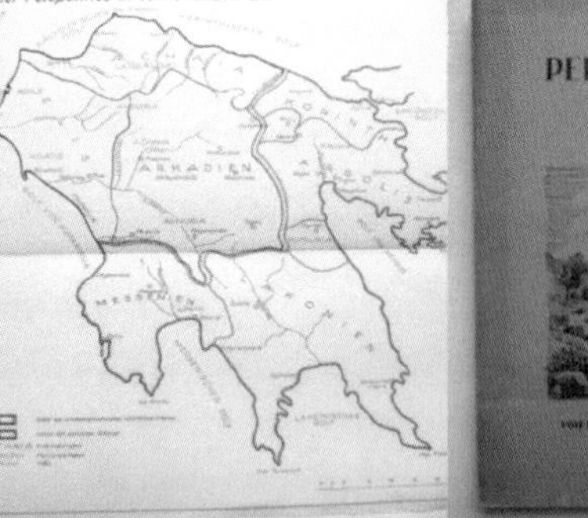

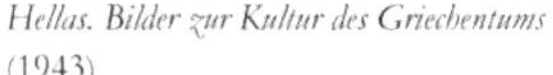

Hellas. Bilder zur Kultur des Griechentums (1943)

pull-out map: *Der Peloponnes*

Der Peloponnes: Landschaft, Geschichte, Kunststätten (1944)

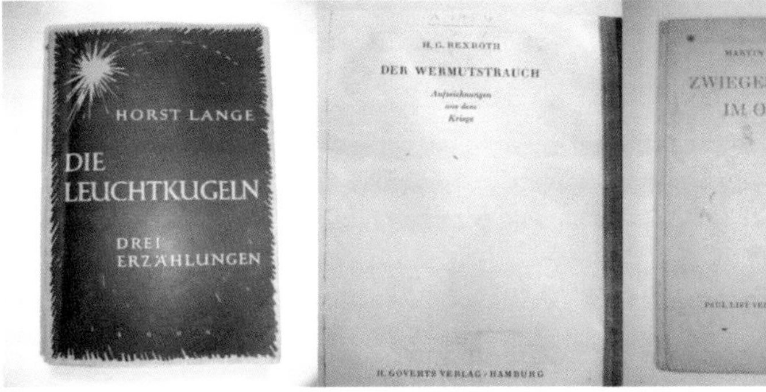

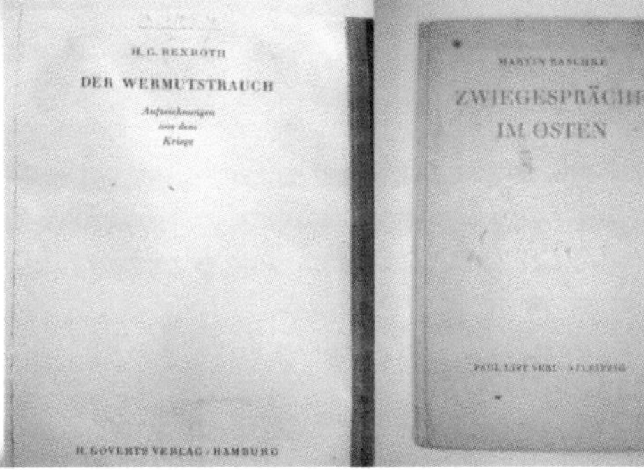

Die Leuchtkugeln (1944/5) *Der Wermutstrauch* (1945) *Zwiegespräche im Osten* (1942)

Zwischen Domen und Bunkern (1944) *Ein Winter ohne Gnade* (1943) *Östliche Silhouetten* (1943)

Nacht unter Sternen (1943)

The provenance of the book images depicted here above, in order of appearance, is as follows:

Frankreich
appeared under the imprint of Ode publishers, Paris (1942)
Soldated fotografieren Frankreich
appeared under the imprint of the German army publisher, Wegleiter (1943)
Die Normandie
is a direct publication of a Germany army command (1940, 1942)
Die Bretagne
is a direct publication of a Germany army command (1940)
Tagebuchblätter aus Frankreich
is a publication of Karl Rauch publishers, Dessau (1941)
Tagebuchblätter aus dem Osten
is a publication of Karl Rauch publishers, Dessau (1944)
Pariser Tagebuch
is a publication of S. Fischer publishers, Berlin (1941)
Kreta
is a publication of Gebrüder Mann publishers, Berlin (1946)
Griechenland [1]
is a publication of Gebrüder Mann publishers, Berlin (1943)
Hellas
is a publication of August Hopfer publishers, Burg bei Magdeburg (1943)
Der Peloponnes
is a direct publication of a German army command, Athens (1944)
Die Leuchtkugeln
is a publication of H. Goverts publishers, Hamburg (1944/45)
Der Wermutstrauch
is a publication of H. Goverts publishers, Hamburg (1944/45)
Zwiegespräche im Osten
is a publication of Paul List publishers, Leipzig (1942)
Zwischen Domen und Bunkern
was published by Volk und Reich publishers, Amsterdam (1944)
Ein Winter ohne Gnade
was published by Volk und Reich publishers, Prague (1943)
Östliche Silhouttten
appeared under the imprint of August Scherl publishers, Berlin (1943)
Nacht unter Sternen
is a direct publication of the Wehrmachtpropagandagruppe, Norway (1943)

[1] the illustrations from *Griechenland* (1943) are reproduced by kind permission of Dietrich Reimer Verlag GmbH.